THE GEORGE GUND FOUNDATION
IMPRINT IN AFRICAN AMERICAN STUDIES

The George Gund Foundation has endowed
this imprint to advance understanding of
the history, culture, and current issues
of African Americans.

Resurrecting the Black Body

The publisher and the University of California Press Foundation gratefully acknowledge the generous support of the George Gund Foundation Imprint in African American Studies.

Resurrecting the Black Body

RACE AND THE DIGITAL AFTERLIFE

Tonia Sutherland

UNIVERSITY OF CALIFORNIA PRESS

University of California Press
Oakland, California

© 2023 by Tonia Sutherland

Library of Congress Cataloging-in-Publication Data

Names: Sutherland, Tonia, 1976– author.
Title: Resurrecting the black body : race and the digital afterlife / Tonia Sutherland.
Other titles: Race and the digital afterlife
Description: Oakland, California : University of California Press, [2023] | Includes bibliographical references and index.
Identifiers: LCCN 2023002887 (print) | LCCN 2023002888 (ebook) | ISBN 9780520383869 (cloth ; alk. paper) | ISBN 9780520383876 (pbk. ; alk. paper) | ISBN 9780520383883 (ebook)
Subjects: LCSH: African Americans—Social aspects—United States. | Memorialization.
Classification: LCC E184.7 .S88 2023 (print) | LCC E184.7 (ebook) | DDC 305.896/073—dc23/eng/20230315
LC record available at https://lccn.loc.gov/2023002887
LC ebook record available at https://lccn.loc.gov/2023002888

Manufactured in the United States of America

32 31 30 29 28 27 26 25 24 23
10 9 8 7 6 5 4 3 2 1

for Asa

Contents

	Author's Note	ix
	Acknowledgments	xi
	Introduction: Trouble These Waters	1
PART I	RECORDS	
1.	Recording Trauma	17
2.	Recording Hate	38
PART II	RESURRECTION	
3.	The Resurrection of Henrietta Lacks	59
4.	The Resurrection of Tupac Shakur	83
PART III	RIGHTS	
5.	The Right to Be Forgotten	105
6.	The Right to Be Remembered	127

Conclusion: Homegoing   147

Notes   161
Bibliography   185
Index   201

Author's Note

I ask that readers please be aware that this book explores themes that include racial violence against Black people and Black people's bodies. There are, in various places throughout the book, careful and candid descriptions of images that depict such violence, but you will not find these images reproduced in the following pages. I have made a very intentional decision to not provide pictures or illustrations of Gordon ("Whipped Peter"), Renty and Delia Taylor, Jesse Washington, George Floyd, Henrietta Lacks, Tupac Shakur, and others whose stories are discussed in this book because to do so would further sustain the intended visceral response to and emotional agency of those images. To reproduce such images would also further contribute to the ongoing commodification of Black people and their bodies: replicating images (particularly violent or disparaging images) of people who are not alive to grant their permission effectively perpetuates the very harms to which I draw attention in this book. Doing this work with integrity demands that I honor and respect what permissions have been granted—*and not granted*—both directly and indirectly.

Acknowledgments

This book would not have been possible without the support of many people, whom I'd like to publicly acknowledge and thank.

I am extraordinarily thankful to Michelle Lipinski, my editor at the University of California Press, for seeing the potential in my vision for *Resurrecting the Black Body* and for guiding the project with steady hands and a steadfast heart. I am unremittingly grateful to her for believing in this book—and for believing in me. Michelle is a brilliant thinker as well as a beautiful human; her careful editorial eye was enormously helpful in tightening the manuscript and making this book eminently more readable than it otherwise might have been. (Please know, as I do, that as she reads this, she is drawing mental delete marks and may even be sighing audibly at my insistence on excessive adverbing.) Thank you, Michelle—I am forever in your debt.

The best arguments in this book have been tempered and sharpened by Shilo R. McGiff, my developmental editor and yearslong sisterfriend, who has been by my side every day as this book came into being. Shilo has, at every turn, been fully present in this process. I am grateful not only for her mastery of craft but also for her—without fail—holding space, making time, and showing up with love and light. Like me, Shilo made the crafting of this book her breath of life for the better part of two years. Without Shilo's keen instinct for the rhythm of the text, her emphasis on precision of language, and her unyielding devotion to the iterative process of writing as an artform, this book would not have the deep resonances that it does. Shilo, I could never thank you enough for sharing your spirit and your smarts with me. You are truly loved.

I am eternally grateful for the support I received from the editorial, design, and production teams at UC Press without whom this book would (literally) not exist. I will never be able to express how much I appreciate their patience and professionalism but even more so, their humanity and good humor. I am also grateful to the many people who offered feedback on early drafts of the manuscript and who took the time to share thoughts after academic conferences. In particular, I extend my gratitude to LeKeisha Hughes at UC Press and to Vanessa Irvin at East Carolina University, both of whom offered support and substantive feedback on this work.

I would like to acknowledge the extraordinary debt I owe to my intellectual community. The people named here are more than colleagues, more than friends: they are the brightest threads in the tapestry with which I have chosen to cover myself in life. As fantasy writer Guy Gavriel Kay might say, if this book is brightly woven, it is because I have been blessed to walk in the path of their light. Thank you so very much Zakiya Collier, Miriam Sweeney, Michelle Caswell, Saifya Noble, Stacy Wood, André Brock, T. L. Cowan, Jas Rault, Kelly Bergstrom, Sarah T. Roberts, Lisa Nakamura, Amelia Gibson, Marika Cifor, Patricia Garcia, Anna Lauren Hoffmann, Catherine Knight-Steele, Megan Finn, Nilofaur Salehi, Anita Say Chan, Charlton McIlwain, Meredith D. Clark, Rachel Kuo, Matthew Bui, Mario Ramirez, Sarah J. Jackson, Sarah Park Dahlen, Renate Chancellor, Daniel Greene, Britt Paris, Megan Threats, Beth Patin,

Chris Gilliard, Aymar Jean Christian, Erique Zhang, Todd Freeborn, Jennifer Wemigwans, Richard Hydomako, Jarrett Drake, Bergis Jules, Ricky Punzalan, Roderic Crooks, Marisa Parham, Akiemi Glenn, Isabel Espinal, Kafi Kumasi, Alondra Nelson, and Ruha Benjamin.

I am long indebted to the scholars from the Archival Education and Research Initiative (my AERI family) who have offered patient, thoughtful, careful, and iterative feedback over more than a decade of summer Institutes. I would especially like to thank Jamie A. Lee, Jennifer Douglas, Ego Ahaiwe Sowinski, Itza Carbahal, Sumayya Ahmed, Adam Kriesberg, Edward Benoit III, Robert Riter, Heather Soyka, Janet Céja, Joel Blanco, James Lowry, Jamila Ghaddar, Rebecka Sheffield, Gracen Brilmyer, Mali Collins, Sony Prosper, Ellen LeClere, Rebecca Frank, Joanne Evans, and Andrew Flynn.

The writing in this book benefited tremendously from the collective wisdom of the beautiful souls in the Black Memory Workers Group. These pages reflect years of thinking about Blackness and anti-Blackness in archival spaces, Black community memory, and documenting violence against Black people around the globe. None of that would have been possible without the incredible privilege of being invited to work and love in community with this tremendous group of people.

The strength of the arguments in this book are due in part to the support of my collaborators at the Center for Critical Race and Digital Studies, AfterLab, the Feminist Data Workshop, the Center for Critical Internet Inquiry (C2i2), the McLuhan Center at the University of Toronto, and the UCLA Community Archives Lab. I would also like to share my deep gratitude for my colleagues and students at UCLA, the University of Hawaiʻi at Mānoa, and the University of Alabama. I would particularly like to acknowledge the support I received from Cheri Ebisu, Sarah Bryant, Robert Montoya, Natacha Cesar-Davis, Tina Christie, Todd Franke, Greg Leazer, Jonathan Furner, Thuy Vo Dang, Miriam Posner, Meera Garud, Andrew Wertheimer, Noriko Asato, Steven Yates, John Burgess,

Jamie Campbell Naidoo, Anna Embree, Mandi Hull, Violet Harada, and Jenifer Sunrise Winter.

Many people invited me to speak about this book as I was writing it, offering tremendous opportunities for discussion and thoughtful critique. I am particularly grateful to the Data, Archives, and Information Seminar at the University of Michigan iSchool; the iSchool at the University of Washington; DigiPres; the Massachusetts Digital Commonwealth Annual Conference; the Research Data Access & Preservation Association; and the Irish Museum of Modern Art in collaboration with the Intersections: Feminism, Technology, and Digital Humanities group (IFTe).

I have been forever changed by more than a decade of mentorship and friendship from Geof Bowker, Joyce Berkman, Len Berkman, and Linden Lewis, all of whom have modeled for me, in their own unique ways, how to be a better person and a more generous scholar. I am forever indebted to my mentors in archival studies and archival theory and practice over the past two decades, including Richard J. Cox, Anne Gilliland, Elizabeth Yakel, Jeannette Bastian, Paul Conway, Danielle Kovacs, the late and much beloved Robert S. Cox, and finally, my very dear friend Alison Langmead.

I am thankful to the following members of my chosen family—Gailyn Bopp, Ilana Turner (who graciously took the photograph of me that appears on the book jacket), Jennifer Houtz, Tucker G. Perry, RBR, Kristina Larsen, Anna Larsen, Karla Zarate-Ramirez, Kevin Ramirez, Mo McFeely, Daniel Krechmer, Keegan Bakos, Rich Gazan, and Leah Gazan—for reminding me to sleep and eat, for asking if I have made it into the pool or the ocean lately, and for making themselves available for anything—anytime. Thank you for loving me exactly the way I need to be loved.

Sometimes people aren't even aware of how much they have influenced your life and helped create the space for your work to exist. I want to draw attention to some of those people in my life, to acknowledge them by name, and to express my gratitude for their presence and the love and grace they have shown me. I am so lucky to have been embraced in love and friendship by Zakia and Ian Spalter, Amelia Acker, Nora Mattern, Brian Halley, Majeeda Al-Amin, Aisha Blanchard Collins, and Allana Coffee.

I am grateful to my ancestors, without whose grace and guidance this work would not be possible, especially my grandmothers Germaine Reid and Amy Sutherland. I am grateful to the angels who lift me up each and every day, those whose spirits I have felt with me in my moments of greatest accomplishment—and also my moments of greatest despair—as I wrote this book. I count among them Sara Sutherland, Senami Lewis, Whitney Baker, Bonnie Swofford, Susan Leigh Starr, and Bernadette Callery.

I would be remiss in not acknowledging the unceasing love and support that I receive from my family in Trinidad and Tobago, Saint Vincent and the Grenadines, and Saint Lucia, as well as my family in New York, New Jersey, and Pennsylvania. I am especially beholden to the Sutherland, Reid, Hazelwood, Laurence, Alvarez, and Diaz families. I am grateful for the support of my Swofford family, especially Mark Swofford, Eric and Heather Swofford, Susan and John Sapier, and Lauri Weatherly, who have each in turn made a home for me in their hearts. I am deeply appreciative for the unconditional love of my nieces, Emily Sapier, Caroline Sapier, Olivia Sapier, and Lydia Swofford; my nephew, Isaac Swofford; and my goddaughters, Alexis Houser and Kathryn Snyder. Each of you has displayed tremendous love for and patience with me over the years. I love you all beyond measure.

I am bound by love and light to my parents, Olson and Sandra Sutherland; my brothers, Omar Sutherland and Erik Sutherland; and my sister-in-law, Maleana Kepler. Your unconditional love allows me to exist in this world every day. I am because we are.

Few words are sufficient to express my gratitude to my beloved son, Xavier Swofford, who is truly a mother's dream—quick to comfort, quick to laugh, slow to anger, never cruel. Thank you for being my sun and moon. Thank you for allowing me to love you so fiercely. And thank you for saying nice things to your friends about your mama's book. Finally, I offer my deepest appreciation to my partner in life and love, the inimitable Kevin Swofford. Thank you for sustaining me. Thank you for believing in me, unwaveringly. Thank you for being a constant protector, defender, and friend. Thank you for a quarter century of unexpected (and often irreverent) laughter. Thank you for a quarter century of unconditional love.

Introduction

TROUBLE THESE WATERS

Remember to imagine and craft the worlds you cannot live without, just as you dismantle the ones you cannot live within.

Ruha Benjamin

In the late summer of 2005, I was enrolled as a graduate student at the University of Pittsburgh. Busy and distracted, I was raising a toddler, working part-time at a local public library, and wrapping up an advanced archives course I had been taking one evening a week. As the summer heat cooled and preparations for the fall semester occupied my attention in Pennsylvania, I had little awareness of how much the world was about to change—and how much I would be changed by coming events. In late August I watched, horrified, as Hurricane Katrina slammed into the city of New Orleans and other parts of the US Gulf Coast. Having grown up in the Northeast, I had experienced hazardous weather conditions such as snow and blizzards. But as the first-generation child of Caribbean immigrants, I knew how devastating the Atlantic hurricane season could be. I had watched and worried many times with my parents as storms made their way toward the tiny islands that my family still called home.

When Katrina hit, it was a recognizable kind of pain, a familiar deep worry. The next day, I watched as the news media talked about flooding, about the waters that had broken through levees that had been installed twenty years earlier under the supervision of the US Army Corps of Engineers. As the city flooded, I watched. Along with so many others, I was devastated. I watched as people became trapped inside their homes, *knowing* I was witnessing—that we were collectively bearing witness to—a significant loss-of-life event. As the disaster progressed and it became clear the federal government's response would be pallid at best, my feelings shifted from overwhelming despair and profound sadness to an ever-increasing sense of anger. I was incensed. Each day there was a new encounter with television and internet footage—a daily barrage of images. Rooftops damaged beyond repair. Houses in parts of the city deemed unsalvageable. Dead bodies floating in the overflowing waters of Lake Pontchartrain.

Those images stayed with me. They haunted me. They haunt me still, today. Months after the hurricane, still reeling, I wrote my final paper as part of my master's degree in library and information science. In it I recounted in painstaking detail the loss of cultural heritage in New York City and Washington, DC, during the September 11th attacks. Although I now know I wasn't ready, I also wrote about Katrina. It was my first attempt—somehow reckoning with the sheer volume of material loss—at coming to terms with the scale of the hurricane. It was also my first attempt to reckon with the cruel disregard for human life that I had seen from both the US government *and* that I had observed via internet and television media. As I wrote that paper, I grew even more troubled. I was concerned about my own approach to the work at hand, which by its very focus seemed to deem the loss of cultural property more important than the loss of life. I was concerned about the very act of doing that work against the backdrop of the ongoing Katrina coverage.

What kept sticking for me was the inescapable fact that as the media talked about the scope of Katrina's destruction and rebuilding the city of New Orleans, the images that accompanied their coverage weren't just damaged buildings or debris-strewn streets. Rather, the scale and scope of the city's damage was demonstrated by showing the American public dead bodies—and the dead bodies were addressed (if at all) as an afterthought to the property. Animating an even deeper sense of horror and distress was the inescapable, visual, and visceral fact that the images of dead bodies on television and on the internet were almost *exclusively* Black people's bodies. I was sickened by the truth of it: Black people's bodies were being callously displayed on TV as part and parcel of signifying the scope of the hurricane's *property* damage.[1]

Years after Katrina, in another August and while I pursued another degree from the same university, Michael Brown was killed in Ferguson, Missouri. Brown, who was only eighteen, was killed by police officer Darren Wilson. He was shot in the back, and when his lifeless body hit the ground, law enforcement left him there in the hot August sun in the middle of the street for four hours. While Brown's body lay uncovered in the streets of Ferguson, he was photographed, and those photographs were quickly published to and widely circulated on the internet. I was yanked back to the feelings that the media coverage of Katrina had evoked. Black people's bodies—under duress, in the throes of a trauma event, without the light of life—were still a sociocultural commodity almost a century and a half after the institution of slavery had been abolished in the United States. I learned then that to monetize the white savior complex, American society must valorize Black suffering. I also learned that to diminish the perceived impact of white suffering, white Americans must see and believe that Black people are suffering *more*.

Performance studies scholar Harvey Young has argued that in the United States societal ideas around "the Black Body" (defined as an imagined yet inescapable *myth* of Blackness) are too often projected onto the actual material bodies of Black people.[2] Ideas about the Black Body that mythologize Blackness also frequently render Black people targets of abuse. Thinking with Young, I argue that the devaluing of the Black Body, when viewed alongside its simultaneous commodification, is not a phenomenon that is particular to individual Black people. Rather, the Black Body is seen as a collective, its pain "shared among the majority of recognizably 'Black' bodies... who live an objectified existence within the Western world."[3] I agree with this notion of the Black Body collective. But also, the misrecognition of individuated bodies as a monolithic "Black Body" recreates a functional dynamic that views Black people as a commodifiable aggregate. Societal ideas of the "Black Body" flatten individual Black experiences onto a blank palate upon which narratives can be projected and around which harmful mythologies can be formed, such as the myth of the strong and/or angry Black woman or the violent, dangerous Black brute.

These multiple understandings of the Black Body are a central theme in this book. I argue that the separation of the "Black Body" imaginary from the lived experiences of Black people is dangerous because it creates the conditions necessary for the severing of idea from corpus. Too often, we have seen that the *idea* of the Black Body is easily separated from the actual life of a Black human being; it was exactly this severing that motivated Mamie Till Mobley to demand that America visually confront the brutal reality of her son's 1955 lynching. In choosing an open casket for her son, Emmett Till, Mobley was firm in her assertion that the world should see what America's racist hatred had wrought under cover of darkness—not the suppression of some societal idea of a dangerous Black brute but rather the cold-blooded murder of a living, breathing, laughing, playful, beloved fourteen-year-old boy.

This separation of the "Black Body" imaginary from the lived experiences of Black people manifests in even more pronounced ways in digital spaces, particularly when pain, trauma, joy, and other embodied experiences fail to connect—or, stated differently, when there is a failure to translate the virtual image to the experience of the physical flesh. Too often when a person sees visual pain on a screen, even if that screen is a handled technology, there is a failure to connect that pain to actual human suffering. I assert again and again what Zellie Imani articulated in June 2020 after the murder of

George Floyd: "You shouldn't have to see footage of murdered Black people to be convinced of their humanity."[4]

This book was birthed in the pain of the aftermath of Hurricane Katrina in 2005, forged in the collective grief of Michael Brown's death in 2014, and is offered with the hope of a new way forward. Tracing the commodification of the deaths of Black people in the United States from the analog era through the digital era and, using cases that represent both historical archival and contemporary data practices, this book addresses the ways that our cultural understandings of death have been changed by the affordances of digital technologies. I seek to articulate the intensity of the brutal disposability and precarity of Black life, while also celebrating the spirit and sensibilities of Black lived experiences. I take up questions about what happens to Black people's bodies postmortem using the critical and analytical frameworks of archival studies, performance studies, and digital culture studies. I began this work as a Black feminist archival scholar by asking questions such as: What does it mean for someone who thinks about Black people as "the Other" to create, maintain, use, and share records of deceased Black people? How have these archival and digital practices normalized the deaths of Black people? What narratives—and *counternarratives*—emerge from the historical record, and how might these counter/narratives contribute to our understandings of issues around Black death in the present? I began this work in the service of critical resistance. I began this work because it was, for me, a matter of life and death.

Resurrecting the Black Body represents the cohesion of more than fifteen years of thinking about what happens to the digital documentation and (re)presentation of Black people after they die, about who gets a say in how Black bodies are treated, and about who benefits from enduring practices around the "Black Body" as digital archival record. Taking as its foundation questions and concerns about records, representation, embodiment, ritual, memorialization, and oblivion in digital technologies and in digital spaces, this book pays particular attention to the ways Black people's bodies are used as records and as evidence in the interplay between the permanence of the digital sphere and the concept of the *right to be forgotten*. It is now (and has long been) my contention that in the United States, even after their deaths Black people's lives are extended, prolonged, and ultimately changed in the present, future, and in history through new circulations, repetitions, and recontextualizations to various publics. For Black Americans these changes and extensions tend to not include the ability to construct our own agency, realities, and representations.[5]

I use the term *digital culture* to define this work because it simultaneously references an array of digital technologies and related practices that span a host of fields and disciplines. This term distinguishes my engagement with these interdisciplinary sites of inquiry from earlier turns in both cultural studies and media studies. Methodologically, this book engages critical race theory, performance studies, archival studies, and digital culture studies, asking how existing technologies (analog and digital) reflect the wider social world offline, how they create new cultural interactions, and how those new interactions in turn reshape our understandings of the world. It has been my goal to articulate some contemporary conceptions of what it means to be Black and dead in digital culture without reverting to simplistic or socioculturally invested notions of the coherent, bounded, and stable body. Instead, I draw from Harvey Young's theorizations about the Black Body and Katherine Dunham's ideas around Black embodied culture. I think alongside Saidiya Hartman and others, such as Christina Sharpe and Temi Odumosu.[6] I conceive of Black memory work as a process that combines and multiplies possibilities rather than Western archival notions that might replace the materiality of bodies and people. Importantly, I reject the tendency to associate virtual experiences and digital technologies with an escape from the body, challenging the notion that the digital sphere is any less "real" than our analog lives. Threaded throughout this book are stories that center Black lives as both individually and collectively lived and valued, and I have intentionally sought out Black thinkers, scholars, and memory workers in the crafting of these narratives and arguments.

I was asked many times as I crafted this manuscript why I am so concerned about Black digital afterlives. The answer—while complex enough to fill a book—is, I think, easily conveyed. When we die, we leave behind our bodies and belongings as our ancestors have for millennia, but unlike our ancestors, today we also leave behind unique footprints and a trail of digital litter scattered across our online environments. Such material—digital and digitized photos, our social media posts, our gaming worlds, our email, our text and chat exchanges—all of this detritus, from full digital records to the most miniscule of digital traces, can be thought of as our digital remains. These digital remains are not only what we create but also what is created about and for us. As each of us generates gigabytes of data daily, our online movements are increasingly tracked for machine learning and data analytics; at the same time, our analog traces are increasingly moved to digital environments—such as documentation about our health, education, work, and travel. Although the concept of digital remains as a potential problem space has only existed throughout the relatively short history of the internet, as we age in the era of big data, what to do with a person's digital remains after they die—*the digital afterlife*—has increasingly become a significant social, cultural, and economic issue.

While in theory we may—as wealthy, white performers like Carrie Fisher did—stipulate how and if our digital afterlives are crafted, in the case of Michael Brown, neither he nor his loved ones ever had agency over the posthumous photographs that were taken on August 9, 2014. Neither did the family of George Floyd have agency over the 2020 video documenting his violent murder in real time. This lack of personal agency regarding the digital evidence that documents both Black life and Black death—the lack of *agency* over our digital remains—is one of the central concerns of this book. These pages offer examples of what evidence I have found and some of the concerns I have identified in interrogating this intersection where race, records, and the digital afterlife converge. I track the historical social interactions between humans and their data alongside the development of data technologies, offering critical interventions about the scale and speed of personal data creation, capture, collection, and reuse, drawing on a wide range of disciplinary perspectives as well as theoretical and empirical research. At its heart, *Resurrecting the Black Body* challenges the narrative that Black people's lives are disposable.

The chapters in *Resurrecting the Black Body* call our attention to several concomitant and interrelated concerns: the relationships between the digital public display of visual memory objects and the emotional agency of images; the ways that Black people's bodies are commodified and weaponized through widespread circulation of documentary evidence from cell phones, dashcams, bodycams, and media outlets that depicts the violent deaths of Black men, women, and children; the impulses, consequences, and ethics that accompany acts of digitally raising the dead; the digital engagements that constitute culturally significant acts of ritual remembering and memorialization; the rights and desires of humans to be forgotten in a time when the internet is understood to be an expression of "forever"; and the unique ways that Black cultures have fought against the silence and erasure of oblivion.[7] Paying particular attention to the relationships between and among documentary practices around the violent deaths of Black Americans from slavery through the present, these pages also explore marked tensions and liminal spaces. I deepen my study of the spaces between memorialization and commodification and between digital permanence and historical oblivion, building and shaping my arguments from a deep exploration and examination of Black digital afterlives.

Arranged in three parts (Records, Resurrection, and Rights), this book first considers the question of records, asking how the archival record has been (re)animated in digital environments and what the implications of this digital afterlife are for records that represent Black bodies specifically. Particular attention is paid to visual records and the emotional agency of images, especially where visual representations that conjure emotional trauma and hate are involved. In the second part I take up two digital resurrection case studies, challenging notions of the desirability of a digital afterlife and examining the role race—and to a lesser extent gender—plays in digital resurrection practices. The third part addresses rights, considering both the right to be forgotten and the right to be remembered, teasing out arguments for and against each and searching for a balance between the two that allows Black life to be honored and celebrated—while also being respected and valued.[8] Finally, the book concludes with a celebration of Black memory work, honoring the Black funerary tradition known as *homegoing*.

Challenging both the implied simplicity of digitization and problematizing how records created during the era of chattel slavery in the United States have moved to online environments, chapter 1 explores the digital afterlives of the archives of Atlantic slavery. This chapter speaks to slavery's afterlife and how it is documented in the historical archival record. I argue that the digitization of slavery-era archives deeply complicates present-day experiences of historical Black trauma. Because the affordances of digital technologies allow us to elide the temporal gap between the violence of past and the visual (and visceral) experience of the present, records created during the era of expansive colonial power and chattel slavery circulate and appear in different contexts. This simultaneously decontextualizes and removes the immediacy of trauma and gives archives of trauma new afterlife. Whether the environment is analog or digital, archives as sites of racialized exploitation and capital accumulation are both ongoing and mutually reinforcing. Complicating the lens through which we view these records, the chapter also addresses legacies of commodification and other economies of Atlantic slavery's enduring afterlife. Deep engagement with the records created during this era allows us to examine how our uses and understandings of these records have shifted to and in online environments. This chapter poses a set of critical questions about the archives of Atlantic slavery, the histories they represent, and our affective relationship to the memories they evoke.

Chapter 2 uses the history of lynching postcards in America as a backdrop to explore the relationships between lynching records and present-day digital records of the violent deaths of Black people in the United States. Dead Black bodies have taken on the archival permanence of digital records, and race and racism—the forces that contribute to Black death—endure online, making and remaking, starring and restaging Black death. Visual media such as Darnella Frazier's video documenting the murder of George Floyd has been mobilized—to galvanize a white public, to convince white Americans that Black lives have value, and in the broader service of justice. Such media has also been put to more deleterious uses: maintained as a commodity in the service of white America's sociopolitical and economic interests and animated as a means of social power and control. The social apparatus of visual media that documents anti-Black violence in the United States is—and has always been—impelled by racism, enabled by technology, and motivated by profit. The historical seeds of this social apparatus, as well as its modern-day functions (such as the role of visual media in documenting extrajudicial violence and anti-Black hatred in the United States), were sown and anchored during the era of racial terror lynching in America.

Chapter 3 is a retelling of the story of Henrietta Lacks, a Black woman from Virginia who died of cervical cancer at Johns Hopkins Hospital in 1951. The purpose is not simply to recast the Lacks narrative—as made knowable through a succession of problematic projects that (in)famously decenter Lacks in her own story (Rebecca Skloot's 2010 book, *The Immortal Life of Henrietta Lacks*, is just one example)—but rather to draw specific attention to how digital resurrection technologies have been and are being deployed in ways that are neither race- nor gender-neutral. Importantly, I approach this chapter on the resurrection of Henrietta Lacks through a Black feminist lens because I understand the story to be—at its heart—a Black woman's story. More broadly, the Lacks case offers us an opportunity to think through the Black Body as record; allows for a discussion of how a simple cell can represent an entire Black Body; and creates space for a conversation about how a single cell, as an embodied record, can also be manipulated and disarticulated from the humanity of the Black Body from which it came. In what is now a widely discussed case of medical and racial ethics, Lacks's cells were used, without permission or informed consent, to create an immortal cell line (HeLa cells), the commercial use of which continues today in contemporary biomedical research. In March 2013, for instance, German researchers mapped Lacks's DNA genome and published the code online. Lacks's family argued that the published genome was a violation of their privacy and laid bare their most intimate health information, making family health information digitally available to the public and denying them the opportunity to craft their own narratives about their bodies, their heritage, their health, and their future selves.

This chapter considers the case of Lacks's digital afterlife from the perspective of human bodies as records and data, arguing that being reduced to data makes Black people even more vulnerable to potential abuse, even posthumously. While many versions of the HeLa origin narrative exist, the enduring element is that of Lacks herself, the woman whose cells live, even though she does not. In the minds of many, the HeLa cells stand for Lacks and she for them, creating a paradox. Lacks's (im)mortality in death is necessary to elevate her cells from life to immortal life. This chapter explores (and necessarily lingers in) this space between her death and her immortality, complicating the records, technologies, and erasures that constitute the resurrection of Henrietta Lacks.

Chapter 4 examines the implications of holography and other 3D technologies, as well as 2D illusions such as Pepper's Ghost, that have been used to create lifelike reproductions of deceased performers and political figures—reproductions capable of addressing the audience, moving around stage, and interacting with others using prescripted effects. Employing a complex mix of digital technologies including creative sound editing, motion-capture techniques, CGI, and holographic technologies, it is now possible to see a reanimated virtual facsimile of the dead. In May 2014, for example, a Pepper's Ghost reproduction of Michael Jackson (1958–2009) performed Jackson's 1991 song "Slave to the Rhythm" at the Billboard Music Awards. The practice of resurrecting performers and public figures who have died has become popular with audiences around the world. The use of technology to reanimate the dead comes with a complex set of social, cultural, technical, and ethical concerns—including questions of race, representation, embodiment, commodification, memorialization, and spectacle. Entering the digital afterlife conversation at the intersection of archival studies, performance studies, and critical race and digital media studies, this chapter aims to investigate and stimulate discussion around some of the cultural, social, and technological tensions created by increasingly common digital resurrection practices.

Chapter 5 examines how social media sites and commercial search engines such as Facebook and Google have amended their algorithms to accommodate a digital afterlife as more people have become concerned about what happens to their digital assets when they die. At present, for example, there is no consensus among social media companies about how to handle deceased user accounts, raising a set of ongoing concerns that are further muddied by legal issues of ownership and privacy. This chapter's provocations are propelled by the argument that nascent digital immortality practices (while ostensibly created for purposes of memorialization) have already begun to recapitulate the white supremacist compulsion to own and commodify Black bodies. As new AI tools and technologies have made it possible to create digital facsimiles of the dead (facsimiles that text, instant message, and post on social media) and as digital immortality and other digital afterlife practices have been shaped and informed by the social, cultural, and economic forces of white supremacy, deeper critical analyses and interventions have become imperative.

The chapter further argues that Blackness (or its overlay, as seen in instances of digital blackface) often undergirds white social and commercial revenue in digital environments. These same tendencies toward appropriation likewise impede Black people's rights and privileges related to privacy, self-expression, self-determination, and sovereignty. By mobilizing Black feminist epistemologies such as Ruha Benjamin's "informed refusal," I propose conditions of possibility under which Black people might refuse to be documented, represented, and remembered in digital settings. This chapter compels us to ask: Rather than trying to fit into systems that embrace Blackness but not Black people, what would it mean for Black subjects to articulate and practice rights of refusal? What does it look like to assert a prerogative of Black digital sovereignty? What would shift if Black people collectively affirmed a digital right to be forgotten?

Chapter 6 explores the promise and potential of liberatory Black memory technologies as an alternative to Western digital afterlife practices. In societies where written culture has favored documentary history, memory has become institutionalized and crystalized in museums, archives, and other documentation centers. In a digital era, however, with content being appropriated and reproduced by users across the world, questions about access to cultural memory become even more urgent. Of all this vast cultural production, what should be seen, by whom, and when? This chapter challenges Western archivy as it participates in these structures and reflects on antidotes to the limitations of Western archivy. In crafting her unique style of culturally informed movement, anthropologist, dancer, and choreographer Katherine Dunham manifested and externalized a Black memory technology: the Dunham Technique. As this chapter endeavors to see the promise in a different way forward, I use Dunham's work and the Dunham Technique as sites of inquiry to define Black memory technologies and to explore how they might help us remember old (and imagine new) ways of remembering Black lives. In the spirit of Afrofuturism, I read Dunham Technique as a framework through which to better understand Black memory work and to theorize modes of transmission that are grounded in Black liberation. How might we define Black memory technologies? What do these technologies look like in defiance of and in opposition to enduring slavery, racism, and anti-Blackness? How might Black memory technologies help us create the sacred space necessary to hold Black memory in ways that make more robust Black life possible?

The conclusion is a celebration of Black memory work and Black memory workers. These closing words are offered in gratitude and in hope—that together we might make a new way forward, a collective crafting of what Ruha Benjamin reminds us to do: to imagine and craft the worlds we cannot live without, just as we dismantle the ones we cannot live within. Throughout the book I reckon with the ways the troubled waters of post-Katrina New Orleans changed and shifted how I think about the deaths of Black people in the United States and the afterlives of archival records, particularly in digital environments. The narrative arc interweaves the past and the present, examining both our present moment and the histories that have informed it. These questions and provocations are at the same time intimate and academic, professional and deeply personal.

What I have taken from the lessons in these pages, the spirits that live on through these words, is a profound respect for Black memory work and the alternate epistemologies that emerge from uniquely and distinctly Black practices. Articulating the ways that Western and white supremacist ideals shape and reshape the ways Black lives are lived and Black death are repurposed for entertainment, financial gain, and maintaining the status quo is a vitally important aspect of this project. The heart of this book, however, is my hopeful attempt at repair, at making Black lives visible in a way that celebrates our joys and honors our pains but does not make us vulnerable to further harm. I invite each reader to join me in this ongoing reparative project.

PART I Records

1 Recording Trauma

> No man can put a chain about the ankle of his fellow man without at last finding the other end fastened about his own neck.
>
> Frederick Douglass

The Liljenquist Family Collection of Civil War Photographs at the Library of Congress comprise more than three thousand ambrotype and tintype special portraits and cartes de visite that document both the Union and the Confederacy during the American Civil War (1861–1865).[1] Among the cartes de visite is an 1863 image depicting a shirtless man, seated sideways in his chair, with his back to the camera. His face is in profile, his left hand resting on his hip with his elbow out to the side, accentuating the shape of his muscular back. His back, meant to be the focal point of the image, is covered in a spidery network of thick, knotted, keloid scars.

Printed on the verso are the words: "FROM LIFE, Taken at Baton Rouge, La., April 2d, 1863." Also on the verso is a hand-scrawled note to one Colonel L. B. Marsh from J. W. Mercer, assistant surgeon with the 47th Massachusetts Volunteers at Camp Parapet, Louisiana, that reads: "I have found a large number of the four hundred contrabands examined by me to be as badly lacerated as the specimen represented in the enclosed photograph." In November 2015 a nearly identical carte de visite, dated April 12, 1863, was sold by Boston-based auction house Skinner Auctioneers for $7,995.[2] On the verso, this card displays typescript text on a separate piece of paper affixed to the card's surface, and an ink stamp declares this albumen image to be the work of photographer A. I. Blauvelt of Port Hudson, Louisiana.[3] The typed text reads:

> Ten days from to-day I left the plantation. Overseer Artayou Carrier whipped me. I was two months in bed sore from the whipping. My master come after I was whipped; he discharged the overseer. My master was not present. I don't remember the whipping. I was two months in bed sore from the whipping and my sense began to come— I was sort of crazy. I tried to shoot everybody. They said so, I did not know. I did not know that I had attempted to shoot everyone; they told me so. I burned up all my clothes; but I don't remember that. I never was this way (crazy) before. I don't know what make me come that way (crazy). My master come after I was whipped; saw me in bed; he discharged the overseer. They told me I attempted to shoot my wife the first one; I did not shoot any one; I did not harm any one. My master's Capt. JOHN LYON, cotton planter, on Atchafalya, near Washington, Louisiana. Whipped two months before Christmas. // The very words of poor, PETER, taken as he sat for his picture.

This text is the documented written record of oral testimony given by Gordon, known also as Peter, as he was photographed during a medical examination conducted in April 1863 by a Union Army doctor with the XIX Corps along the banks of the Mississippi River near Baton Rouge, Louisiana.

Gordon, the man whose image appears on these two archival cartes de visite, was an enslaved man who self-emancipated in March 1863 from the 3,000-acre plantation of John and Bridget Lyons in Saint Landry Parish, Louisiana, after having barely survived the savage beating that produced the tendrilled scars that crisscrossed his back. Gordon reported the ten-day journey on foot from Saint Landry Parish to Baton Rouge to be a perilous one: he was barefoot, had been chased by John Lyons along with several neighbors and a pack of bloodhounds, and was in dire fear for his life. When he reached the Union Army encampment along the Mississippi River, his clothes were torn and covered with dirt and mud from his long and harrowing trek through Louisiana's swamps and bayous.[4] At the encampment, where Gordon was subsequently mustered into military service, the Union Army conducted a "surgical examination," at which time Gordon's scourged back was observed and photographed by two itinerant photographers, William D. McPherson and his partner, Mr. Oliver, of New Orleans.[5]

The photograph of Gordon, which has come to be known as "The Scourged Back" (sometimes also referred to as "Whipped Peter") was reproduced as a popular carte de visite in the American North and widely circulated as evidence of both slavery's cruelty and America's racism—particularly as experienced in the American South. On Saturday, July 4, 1863, the "scourged back" portrait and two others of Gordon appeared as wood engravings as a special Independence Day feature in *Harper's Weekly*, paired with a brief narrative about Gordon as well as an excerpt from a letter that had been published in the *New York Times* recounting the treatment of enslaved people on an estate situated on Louisiana's Black River. McPherson and Oliver's portrait of Gordon—presented alongside Gordon's narrative—was well-received, and photography studios throughout the American North began to duplicate and sell prints of "The Scourged Back." Within months the carte de visite of Gordon had become an early example of what would eventually become the wide dissemination and circulation—particularly among white Americans in the North—of ideologically abolitionist photographs depicting what they argued were the social ills of human enslavement.

Among Black abolitionists, including Frederick Douglass who had also self-emancipated, a different narrative emerged. Black abolitionists like Douglass argued that while photographs and other images might serve to demonstrate the fundamental humanity of enslaved Black people and subvert anti-Black racism, the seductive technology of photography should not be a means of documenting the brutality of one's previously enslaved condition; rather, photography might be better employed as a means of making politically minded abolitionist points about the individual humanity of Black people.[6] Although Douglass insisted that those who were enslaved be seen as people, this demand for a fundamentally human gaze was never fully realized—even among Northern white abolitionists who were ostensibly using such photographs toward noble and moral ends.

The visceral image of Gordon's scarred back was quickly appropriated by white abolitionists who, in circulating the photograph, described Gordon using phraseology such as "[displaying] *unusual* intelligence and energy"—and, as demonstrated by the carte de visite in the Liljenquist Family Collection at the Library of Congress, terminology such as "contraband" and "specimen"—in their ever-virtuous attempts to reconcile the willful violence in the image with declarations about Gordon's apparently surprising humanity.[7] And although the photograph of Gordon is itself a powerful visual testimony to the brutality of American slavery, as is evidenced by the inclusion of Gordon's oral testimony on the Skinner carte de visite, emancipated people who had been enslaved were perfectly capable of testifying on their own behalf. Instead, however, it was the white gaze, a position of privilege characterized by power and authority (often acquired through brute force), that determined which of these testimonies was to be imbued with enduring sociocultural value.

Thus the same power relations Gordon was subjected to under the conditions of enslavement were subsequently embedded in the visual display of his tortured Black body. The "scourged back" image of Gordon, like all visual depictions of Black people in pejorative poses (particularly when viewed through the white gaze), is one that is simultaneously objectifying and disconnected from the realities of Gordon's actual personhood and identity. As a result, Gordon himself disappears in this trauma narrative, becoming dehumanized and disarticulated—conferred to the annals of history as little more than a tortured "Black Body."[8] That white abolitionists perceived a need to use individual portrayals of Black trauma as propaganda to make other white people appreciate the expansive brutalities of human enslavement is offense enough on its face, but that this white-gaze project was ultimately a political—rather than a humanistic or even *humanizing*—agenda is even more so.

Northern abolitionists were not the only ones using this new visual technology for political purposes. In the South, enslavers also commissioned studio portraits of enslaved people (most frequently individual portraits and interracial pairings of enslaved women holding white children). As proslavery rhetoric, these images suggested that bondage was benevolent and attempted to erase the violence against—and commodification of—the Black human bodies that were central to the Southern socioeconomic system.[9] One example of these alternate uses of slavery-era photography can be found in two images long stored away in an attic at Harvard University. The images are two daguerreotypes, commissioned by Louis Agassiz, a Swiss-born zoologist and Harvard professor who is sometimes referred to as the father of American natural science. The images were part of his quest to "'prove' Black people's inherent biological inferiority and thereby justify their subjugation, exploitation, and segregation."[10]

Made in 1850 by J. T. Zealy in a studio in Columbia, South Carolina, the daguerreotypes feature individual portraits of a man and his daughter, Renty and Delia Taylor, who were among seven enslaved people whose images were captured in fifteen photographs that Zealy produced at the time.[11] The images are haunting and experiencing them feels akin to voyeurism. Photographed nude from the waist up, clothing gathered around their hips, Renty and Delia's images were captured in profile and front-facing portraits. Delia's dress is visible in the lower portion of the picture and appears to have been unbuttoned and peeled from her skin with the express purpose of exposing her breasts.[12] Both Renty and Delia stare at the camera with detached expressions. Author Ta-Nehisi Coates, quoted in the *New York Times* in 2019, has said of the image of Renty: "That photograph is like a hostage photograph. This is an enslaved Black man with no choice being forced to participate in white supremacist propaganda—that's what that photograph was taken for."[13]

These simultaneously disparate and dissonant uses of photographs and photographic technologies during the period of Atlantic slavery underscore not only the racial tensions of the era but also provide important context for images from that era that comprise today's historical record. This context is neither meaningless nor insignificant. Many of the images, text, and even audio recordings that endure from this period are the creations of slaveholders: rather than being faithful representations of those who were enslaved, the archives of American slavery represent a deeply complex, fraught, and often problematic set of historical records that inform our understandings of the past in the present. In the case of Renty and Delia, in 1976 Harvard realized they held the daguerreotypes in campus storage, recognized their incalculable value as the earliest known photographs of enslaved Black Americans, and proceeded to "[commence] a decades-long campaign to sanitize the history of the images and exploit them for prestige and profit."[14] To this day, Harvard insists that anyone seeking to view the photographs sign a contract, and anyone wishing to reproduce the images, even for educational purposes, pay a hefty fee to the university. In other words, Harvard—one of the wealthiest universities in the world—has seen fit to further enrich itself from images that exist only because a Harvard professor forced enslaved men and women to participate in their creation without consent, dignity, or compensation. Harvard's ongoing assertion of exclusive legal rights to possess, restrict access to, and profit from Renty and Delia Taylor recalls slavery's enterprise and extends dangerous and exploitive past practices around Black bodily autonomy into the present.

American slavery was, first and foremost, a capitalist enterprise. It was also, without doubt, a racialized enterprise.[15] For the better part of the sixteenth century, Italian and Portuguese endeavors dominated the European slave trade with the Atlantic coast of the African continent, supplying enslaved African labor for their colonial plantations, including those in the West Indies and the mines of New Spain and Peru. As the colonies grew, so did their appetites for their *piezas de Indias* (pieces of the Indies), the enslaved Africans they regarded as captives of a just war.[16] Belgian historian and anthropologist Jan Vansina estimates that as early as 1530, the nation of Angola alone was exporting between four thousand and five thousand enslaved people each year; if there were no more, Vansina argues, this "was only due to the lack of ships to carry them."[17] As early as 1530, the Atlantic slave trade was already exceeding the boundaries of its commercial origins and of its technological capabilities.[18]

As a capitalist enterprise, the role of Black labor in the expansion and preservation of American slavery cannot and should not be understated; indeed, historians estimate that nearly thirteen million Africans were conscripted into slavery and shipped across the Atlantic Ocean in the service of trade markets and other capitalist endeavors. The history of the capitalist enterprise of slavery—and the concomitant legacy of commodifying Black human bodies—is long, and it is global. As I argue throughout this chapter, and as evidenced both by Harvard's current revenue from the Renty and Delia Taylor daguerreotypes and by the 2015 sale of Gordon's carte de visite for nearly $8,000, this legacy of capitalist commodification is also enduring. This chapter addresses this legacy of commodification—and other economies of Atlantic slavery's enduring afterlife—as documented in the historical archival record. Problematizing the records created during this era of expansive colonial power and examining how our uses and understandings of these records have shifted to and in online environments, the chapter asks a set of critical questions about the archives of Atlantic slavery, the histories they represent, and our affective relationship to the memories they evoke, while taking up the central argument that—whether the environment is analog or digital—sites of racialized exploitation and capital accumulation with regard to these archives are both ongoing and mutually reinforcing.

Arguably coequal to the economic justifications for slavery, the concept of race—and its correspondent, racial supremacy—was also used to justify the conscription of African people into human bondage. Racial supremacy—*white supremacy*—was used to defend the treatment of the enslaved as chattel: individually owned commodities that could be bought, sold, and traded. At the forefront of this racial supremacist analysis was the question of whether African people were to be classified as human or less than human—a question that was often answered through the lens of eugenics and race-based science.[19] The intentionally dehumanizing enterprise of human enslavement in the United States—with the violence and generational trauma of hereditary slavery—is not only documented extensively in the historical record but has borne new fruit in the (now digital) archives of the twenty-first century. Although slavery was abolished by law in the United States in 1865, Black lives in America are continuously imperiled and devalued by the sociocultural, economic, and aesthetic (representational) inheritances of slavery that endure. Such injustice is largely a result of what African American studies scholar Saidiya Hartman identifies as a "racial calculus and a political arithmetic" that was entrenched centuries ago. "This," Hartman asserts, "is the afterlife of slavery."[20] And slavery's afterlife is sustained, fed, and nurtured by the archives of Atlantic slavery.

As is the case with most other professions, archivists employ their own professional vocabulary. Archivy has its own set of words and phrases that evoke meaning and invoke action in the field; this lingua franca helps archivists structure and define the work that they do. Much of this lexicon is recognizable to those outside the profession, but the particular meaning and significance of some terms are different for those within the field. Archives, as memory and cultural heritage institutions, are tasked with the long-term care and preservation of *records*, which in the field of archival studies are generally defined as "persistent representations of activities, created by participants or observers of those activities or by their authorized proxies."[21] The act of creation is where archives begin, and creating records means different things to different cultures and societies at different times. In archival theory and practice, records are assigned meaning not only by their creators but also by subsequent custodians, researchers, and scholars.

As a result, records are imbued with cultural significance. The repositories in which they are held are located in our society's collective consciousness as sites of memory, legacy, and in some cases even survival. For archivists the act of creating a record implies a desire to also create a documentary history and imbue artifacts with cultural meaning; the creation of *archives*, however, implies a desire to systematize and support the preservation of cultural evidence and societal memory. Archival records are kept and maintained because they are deemed to have continuing value for their creators and the potential for future use. As the documentary evidence of the past, records are more than fragments of data or pieces of information: they represent the substance and the underpinnings of the facts that are used to interpret and understand history. For archivists, determining the institutional, cultural, and historical value of records based on their evidentiary, documentary, and informational value is a central part of the professional endeavor. This determination is significant to the processes that render records archival.

Another such process is known as *representation* (arranging and describing archival records), in which archival classification and descriptive practices are used as means of access and discovery. Description, in its most effective form, works to increase access to archival materials by revealing the structure and content of archival collections while highlighting materials within collections that may be of particular interest to researchers. In *Describing Archives: A Content Standard*, the Society of American Archivists foregrounds the idea that "the nature of archival materials, their distribution across many institutions, and the physical requirements of archival repositories necessitate the creation of... descriptive surrogates, which can then be consulted in lieu of directly browsing through quantities of original documents."[22] In this way, description simplifies and streamlines discovery; and for this reason, archival tools such as finding aids—which result from professional descriptive practices and therefore also become part of the historical record—are often a researcher's first encounter with a repository's collections and other archival materials.

Archival descriptive practice is often fraught with violence and Othering. Scholars Marisa Duarte and Miranda Belarde-Lewis describe descriptive standardization as a violent process that inherently valorizes some perspectives while simultaneously silencing others.[23] Archival description is a highly political act. The terms that are used to describe archival materials help to define the records themselves, and description, as an access tool, plays a role in determining how archival records are used and by whom. In this vein, descriptive practices, like any other tool, can be (and have been) weaponized as a means through which colonial and anti-colonial power structures are reaffirmed and reinforced. The archives of Atlantic slavery—inclusive of records such as Gordon's cartes de visite at the Library of Congress and the daguerreotypes of Renty and Delia Taylor held by Harvard University—are profoundly problematic. These records represent a constellation of concerns that converge at the intersection of race, descriptive practices, and ideas about *archival permanence*, which defines both the inherent stability of archival materials that allows them to resist degradation over time and the long-term preservation that is connected to archives' long history of acting as agencies of accountability. That archival accountability is connected to notions of trust, transparency, and responsibility, however, betrays the true nature of the archives of Atlantic slavery.

Rooted in European documentary traditions and created by enslavers and colonizers, these records challenge ideas about trust, transparency, and responsibility. Rather than being the enduring voice of the enslaved or colonized, they speak instead to how archives hold, produce, and reproduce agency, privilege, and power. Until the mid-twentieth century, preserving the master narratives of society was the archivist's primary concern and sufficiently satisfied archival mandates. This meant that those whose voices appear in the historical archival record represent the privileged and powerful, those whose voices were deemed most noteworthy at the time. It is not, for example, Gordon's own oral testimony to which modern-day researchers look for historical evidence of him and the revulsions of human enslavement. Instead, the interpretation of his lived experience is explicated and commodified via the image of his scourged back. Is this image—created not by Gordon but about him—how Gordon himself would have preferred to enter the historical record? Remembered not for who he was, but instead by what was done to him? And while one might read this image as evidence of Gordon's perseverance, might he not have sooner had the two other images of himself that appeared in *Harper's Weekly* be the enduring records upon which those in the present would look back and remember his humanity?

Given the nature of slavery-era archives, and the problematics of the history of archival production, we will likely never know. It is not enough to recall the history of slavery as one derived solely from the capitalist production of human labor. We must also locate and center the actual human beings behind that labor. Enslaved Africans deposited on the shores of the Caribbean and the Americas brought an amalgamation of cultures with them: languages; cosmologies and folklore; Indigenous African medicinal knowledge; and traditional practices, including rituals, thoughts, and beliefs around death and dying. As scholar Cedric Robinson so eloquently asserts: "African labor brought the past with it, a past that had produced it and settled on it the first elements of consciousness and comprehension."[24] These were the terms of their humanity.

This poses a set of critical questions about the archives of Atlantic slavery, the history they represent, and our affective relationship to the memories they evoke. For example, how can descendants of enslaved people use these records to pin their discursive locations in history? How have formerly enslaved people become enduring and constitutive figures in the archival corpus? How does resurrecting images and ideas from the era of Atlantic slavery fashion modern-day individual and collective identities and ideologies? What is the relationship between the symbolic capacity of images of enslaved people and the truth of their personhood, which includes, but of course is not limited to, the facts of their lives? And, central to this chapter, how do the answers to these questions shift or change when these records are rendered digital?

For archives and for those who use them, digitization is often presented as a panacea for problems of archival preservation and access. The laudable aim of such digitization projects is to make archival material, historically only available for in person viewing because of their uniqueness (and therefore irreplaceability) as well as their fragility, accessible to the general public via the internet. For example, physical access to the carte de visite of Gordon in the Library of Congress (LoC) is restricted by the Library; one may view the original image by appointment only. Instead, digital access to the image is provided via the Library's Prints and Photographs Online Catalog where, per the LoC, the image is easier to see than in the original carte de visite and viewers can manipulate the digital image, zooming in and out for detail and perspective. The Library also notes that the digital images are used in preference to the original carte de visite as an archival preservation measure; the original item is, as one might expect, quite fragile, and repeated handling puts it at risk for irreparable damage.

Providing broad access to digitized artifacts (and even their preservation)—especially in the longer term—is oftentimes problematic. These problems, when they arise, are not only technological; they are also economic, political, legal, and moral. As art historian Temi Odumosu argues, now digitized artifacts and documents have "come to represent their own forms of remembrance and are in general positively viewed as the means through which access to out-of-reach and/or decaying collections can be brokered."[25] However, digital technologies and the new artifacts they produce can themselves also be seen as a form of cultural imperialism that supports racialized hegemony and often results in distinct expressions of anti-Blackness. In her 2020 article "The Crying Child," Odumosu uses a single photograph of a crying Afro-Caribbean child from Saint Croix that was digitized by the Royal Danish Library to demonstrate the unresolved ethical matters that retrospective attempts to understand human enslavement in the digital era present. Like the image of Gordon, Odumosu correctly asserts that this photograph "suspends in time a Black body... [clearly] in visible distress, with a running nose and copious tears rolling down its face."[26] She further argues that

> [b]ecause all the natural and affecting sounds of a child's cry are muted via the photographic lens onto paper, and further still in the digital image, the pregnant silence one experiences in encounters with this photograph across media is particularly arresting. The initial camera silenced the cry. Thus, it is what we cannot hear that marks the violations taking place in and around this image; and we need to perform a "bone deep listening, a sensing of the unbridgeable chasm" to fully access this "seen cry unheard."[27]

While digitization has undeniably provided a range of new innovations for viewing and experiencing historical records—including 3D scanning, 360-degree photography, and optical character recognition (OCR)—the digitization and datafication of the archives of Atlantic slavery has also contributed to a distancing of the lived experiences of enslaved people from what might be described as slavery's historical imaginary. When slavery-era records are digitized, records appear and circulate in different contexts, further exacerbating the already significant temporal gap between the violence of the past and the visual experience of the present. The visual experiences of Gordon's scourged back, Renty and Delia's subjugation, or Odumoso's crying child, isolated in Google image search results are far removed from the contexts of their lived experiences: a harrowing, painful, and life-threatening journey during which Gordon carried himself on foot toward self-emancipation, the efforts to use Renty and Delia as proof of Black inferiority, the tears of a frightened child. This decontextualization removes the immediacy of trauma and gives archival documents that record that trauma new digital afterlives as these visual records are read and experienced in the present, entirely dislocated from the human suffering that produced them.

This extension of analog records into the digital—and the subsequent removal of historical context—exacerbates the inability of the historical subjects of the archives of Atlantic slavery to construct their own agency, realities, or representations in the present. Although digital archives have the potential to create what have been called "third spaces" in which descendants of enslaved people might have more control over their ancestral materials and records, working with these records in the present ought to compel us to stop and consider, for example, the ways that privacy is racialized and only afforded as a condition of whiteness, and at the same time force us to reckon with disparate—and often conflicting—cultural positions on notions of archival sovereignty, ownership, and access. For example, Tamara Lanier, who through deep genealogical research has identified Renty and Delia Taylor as family ancestors, has filed a lawsuit for the repatriation of their daguerreotypes from Harvard University's Peabody Museum. Although Lanier's success would mark the first time the descendant of an enslaved person in the United States would be granted return of property rights, the daguerreotypes are highly contested records.

After a long period during which they were believed to have been lost, Harvard has since used the daguerreotypes, the wary and weary faces of Renty and Delia, as commercial enterprise—in keeping with the long-entangled histories of racial capitalism and human enslavement.[28] Renty and Delia have appeared on book covers, on event banners, and other forms of advertising and merchandise. Renty's image currently appears on the cover of a Harvard anthropology publication that the university sells for forty dollars. As Lanier's lawsuit alleges, by denying her superior claim to the daguerreotypes, Harvard is "perpetuating the systematic subversion of Black property rights that began during slavery and continued for a century thereafter."[29] Harvard's claim to ownership of the daguerreotypes recalls for many Black people in the United States the claims to human ownership made by Renty and Delia's enslavers: slavery was abolished over 150 years ago, but "Renty and Delia remain enslaved in Cambridge, Massachusetts. Their images, like their bodies before, remain subject to control and appropriation by the powerful, and their familial identities are denied to them."[30] The further commodification of Renty and Delia's Black bodies is also a considerable worry as the daguerreotypes have moved to digital platforms, where death and trauma are continuously reinscribed and reexperienced, visually and perhaps eternally.[31]

Closely associated with the daguerreotypes are written inventories of enslaved people that have also been published online in the time since Lanier's case came to national attention. Used in part to verify Lanier's ancestral claims to the daguerreotypes, these inventories—which account for human "property"—are replete with all the problems previously noted about archival classification and descriptive practices. The inventories are a stark reminder that it is not only images from the era of Atlantic slavery that are problematic in the archives and even more problematic when those archives are digitized. Images carry significant emotional agency; at the same time, inventories of enslaved people and advertisements in search of the self-emancipated also carry descriptive agency—and text-based description in digital archives can be (and is being) mined and quantified as technology advances and societies move to more data-centered approaches to historical research and analysis. While it is true that trends within this data can be more easily found using computational, big data approaches to archival records—this is, for example, a growing trend in digital humanities research—too often, little thought is given to the human lives rendered invisible in those trends. Olivia Carlisle, writing commentary for the North Carolina Digital Library about the NC Runaway Slave Advertisements Database, notes that "certain descriptions are more commonly found than others. Skin color, for example, ranges in description from 'black' to 'mulatto' or 'yellow skinned.' Physical descriptions usually included a veritable inventory of scars, either from diseases like smallpox, property markings (i.e. branding) or as a result of labor-related accidents (e.g. cotton gins, 'cut of an axe,' etc.) Accounts of other physical traits include limps, deformities, birthmarks, and missing limbs."[32]

Carlisle's description recalls the work of such scholars as Simone Browne, Jessica Marie Johnson, and Jacqueline Wernimont, who have each argued that data is deeply embedded in the colonial histories of quantification that have a defining moment in the accounting and marking of enslaved bodies.[33] As Johnson cautions in her work, if left unaddressed, the violence of these archival processes can "reproduce themselves in digital architecture."[34] In keeping with long unchallenged archival praxis, digital archives frequently mirror descriptive practices and the organization of information as they already exist, rather than taking up goals such as redescription or rearrangement. In the now-digitized archives of Atlantic slavery, this means archivists have uncritically adopted and reproduced the descriptive practices and structures of knowledge organization that were used by slave traders, slaveholders, and colonial officers.

As Johnson argues, and as is evidenced in Carlisle's description of the NC Runaway Slave Advertisements Database, these newly created databases of artificially collocated archival records also often reinscribe the biometric measures used to describe enslaved people by carrying the racial nomenclature of the time period (e.g., mulatto, octaroon) into the present and "encode skin color, hair texture, height, weight, age, and gender in new digital forms, replicating the surveilling actions of slave owners and slave traders."[35] Taken alongside the societal and professional archival values of permanence and fixity, the social structures embedded in the archives of Atlantic slavery remain the same even as technology changes: colonial modes of knowledge organization, now built into the database, are often amplified by tools and features that offer users new modes of mining the archives—for instance, the zooming lens or the thumbnail image—which can result in modes of access that further commodify and abstract the "Black Body."

It is vital to remember, as we encounter and engage the archives of Atlantic slavery, that technological development and change, then and now, are not—and cannot inherently be—linked to social justice. Instead, as these digitization projects increasingly foster a drive for data and as researchers are increasingly encouraged to data- and text-mine these archives, the digital archives of Atlantic slavery have led to what Hartman calls a "second order of violence," whereby the Black bodies already numbered in the archives are requantified, becoming a new form of raw material from which new values can be extracted.[36]

In March 2017 the Danish National Archives launched The Danish West-Indies: Sources of History site, providing open online access to all its recently digitized records from the time when Denmark was a colonial slaveholding power in the West Indies, claiming ownership of what are now known as the United States Virgin Islands (USVI): Saint Thomas, Saint John, and Saint Croix. The digitization project targeted a broad audience: beyond the actual records the Archives aimed to communicate the history of the Danish colonies through articles and digital timelines. The digitization project, which started in 2013, was intended to mark and celebrate the 2017 centennial of the sale of the three colonized islands to the United States. During the three years prior to the project's launch, the Archives worked to digitize a vast quantity of historical records from the colonial era that had been physically divided among Denmark, the United States, and the USVI after the sale of the islands to the United States.

Archivists digitally scanned the equivalent of more than a kilometer of shelf space of colonial-era records, amounting to more than five million digital images. More than 150 volunteers from Denmark, the USVI, and other countries spent thousands of hours electronically transcribing the records to provide broad and open access to the materials. As Danish scholar Daniela Agostinho reminds us: "[When the bulk of the] records [were removed] from the islands, Virgin Islanders were left without approximately 250 years of written history. The digitization project thus offered the promise of greater access to these historical records, particularly for the descendants of the documented communities."[37] The project is problematic, however, in archival terms as well as humanistic concerns, especially because—as with the case of Renty and Delia—issues of ownership and access involve complicated claims.

The Danish National Archives project demonstrates that while digitization projects centered on the archives of Atlantic slavery hold the potential for powerful new humanistic narratives about Black resilience and redress to emerge, projects that take a more data-centric approach to the lived experiences of enslaved people have proven to be fraught and often problematic research sites. As Agostinho notes, "the privilege to grant access...is historically premised on a privileged subjecthood derived from the archives of colonial modernity," and thus the newly digitized archive might be seen as "a tool of raciality."[38] Agostinho further argues that it is in the archives that the universal subject position whose "right to access" or "right to information" is recognized. Yet this "right to access" is conceived and granted "at the expense of the racialized and gendered subjects that become accessed and newly available for inspection, legibility and consumption *as commodities*."[39]

The increasing number of digital archives, databases, and other digitization projects focused on the slavery era are effectively transforming the study of the history of human enslavement as colonial histories of quantification that have been allowed to structure contemporary technological encounters with the archives. On one hand, the mass digitization of slavery-era records holds both the promise of new historical knowledge and of genealogical reconstruction for descendants of enslaved peoples. On the other hand, this trend belies a growing tendency to datafy and quantify the dead, reinscribe racist ideologies, codify damaging ideas about knowledge organization, codify harmful descriptive practices, and uncritically circulate records rooted in generational trauma, hatred, and death.

Another example is Freedom on the Move, a "database of fugitives from North American slavery," with data sourced from individuals as well as previously curated collections such as the aforementioned North Carolina Runaway Slave Advertisements Database. A joint effort funded in part by the National Endowment for the Humanities and the National Historical Publications and Records Commission, the Freedom on the Move database is the product of collaborative work across several institutions including Cornell University, the University of Alabama, the University of New Orleans, the University of Kentucky, and the Ohio State University. The (mostly white) scholars behind Freedom on the Move assert that the database was "created to control the movement of enslaved people, the [runaway slave] ads ultimately preserved the details of individual lives—their personality, appearance, and life story. Taken collectively, the ads constitute a detailed, concise, and rare source of information about the experiences of enslaved people."[40]

It is clear from the database's design, however, that the racial nomenclature of the Atlantic slavery era has been encoded into this digital archival resource. Search within the Freedom on the Move database can be conducted under four primary categories: advertisement, runaway, enslaver, and runaway event. Under the "runaway" category, search may be further limited to produce more accurate results by entering additional known descriptors such as physical description (gender, age, height, weight, racial category, ethnic description, injuries/scars, possessions, self-presentation); skills (literacy, known and unknown languages, including English, Spanish, and French); location; and reward (amount, currency, criteria). However, the category of "enslaver" simply offers name, gender, type (current, former, deceased, alleged, estate), and location as potential search modifiers. Under the "racial category" classification, the database was designed for search terms such as "mulatto"—a term used by enslavers and colonial masters and long deemed offensive when the database was created in 2017. That one might search for ancestral trauma by identifying injuries and scars recalls Gordon and the dehumanizing centrality of his scourged back as well as the traumas endured by Renty, Delia, and Odumosu's crying child.

Although these repositories and databases might offer important information about enslaved people, they raise questions about whiteness, power, spectacle, commodification, and eventually about how more quantitative approaches, and a turn to data more generally through digitization, may transform how we understand the archives of Atlantic slavery. For those represented in these digital records, the narrative and liberatory potential of archives has been curtailed by the racial and sociocultural essentialism of colonial white supremacist power—as well as by conceptualizations of archival permanence and the indelibility of the digital. These records serve as symbolic objects, forever linked to a lived human life, with both the record and the human defined and confined by white supremacy's need to possess and control what is imaginable—and therefore attainable—for those whom it oppresses.

Can we reconstruct a disarticulated archival skeleton and make a person whole? Are modern-day slavery researchers trying to find the whole person in the archives of Atlantic slavery? The current scholarly trend is *not* in fact to do this repair work. Instead, it is to quantify, to allow the broken components to remain broken while the ordinary (and extraordinary) Black lives in the archives of Atlantic slavery—how they lived, how they died, how they are remembered, how their digital afterlives are constituted, and what happens to those afterlives—are forever intimately linked to systemic and structural practices of anti-Black (and often state-sponsored) violence. This violence is too frequently reinscribed and reified in—and also justified by—the archival record.

Trauma theorist Lucia Lorenzi once asked the Trinidadian-Canadian poet Dionne Brand how one might contend with the violence and pain of encounters with Black history archives.[41] Brand replied: "Look for the red ribbon." The red ribbon, a detail Brand had encountered in a historical newspaper advertisement for a "runaway slave" and of which she had taken note, referred to a description of an enslaved girl who had fled in an act of self-emancipation and was last seen—in flight, on her way to freedom—with a red ribbon in her hair. To "look for the red ribbon" is to seek fugitive hope, to see in the archival record a "struggle for the transformation from enslavement to freedom that is not within actual reach but sought after as/in flight."[42] The red ribbon is elusive: like freedom from the enduring bonds of Atlantic slavery, it is forever sought and forever just out of reach as the domain of the historical record is defined over and against the "Black Body," through the heinous violences of kidnapping, the Middle Passage, and slavery.

Most important, however, the red ribbon represents an act of refusal; it resists the trauma narratives that often emerge from the Atlantic slavery archives. The red ribbon can be seen as a refusal to be recorded as trauma, as nothing more than the conditions of one's enslavement. It can be read as a refusal to be defined by documentary spaces where, for Black people, survival was never guaranteed—or even necessarily desired. Brand's careful and poetic counsel to Lorenzi—to approach the archives of Black history with an eye toward liberation—evokes refusal and resilience, while at the same time acknowledging the very real affective trauma that often results from encounters at the intersection of the lived experience of Blackness and the digital afterlives of Atlantic slavery archives. Scholars who study the history of slavery in the United States are often tasked with looking for the red ribbon. And so, in hope and in solidarity with this struggle, it is here that this chapter closes. It is no small grace that the girl with the red ribbon in her hair is nowhere to be found in Freedom on the Move. Nor can she be located in the other archives discussed in this chapter. As we know she was once seen running toward freedom, we can only hope that she is, perhaps, free—at last.

2 Recording Hate

It wasn't right.

Darnella Frazier

On Monday May 25, 2020, at around seven o'clock in the evening, seventeen-year-old Darnella Frazier, a high-school student at Augsburg Fairview Academy in Minneapolis, Minnesota, was walking to a neighborhood convenience store called Cup Foods with her nine-year-old cousin. As they neared the entrance to Cup Foods, Frazier noticed a man on the ground. She quickly walked her cousin to the store's front door and ushered her inside before turning around to return to the man. It wasn't just that the man was on the ground; what had caught Frazier's attention was that the man was restrained—unable to move more than his head. Moreover, a police officer appeared to be kneeling on the man's neck while two other officers held him down.

Something didn't seem right: Frazier could see that the man was visibly scared, terrified. He was suffering and in pain, begging for his life. She heard him say, "I can't breathe" and then, "Please." And when the next thing the man did was cry out for his mother, Frazier, the only bystander witness on the scene, pulled out her cell phone and began recording. For ten minutes and nine seconds she filmed, until the officers and the man on the ground all left the scene; the former on foot, the latter on a stretcher. Frazier, a young Black woman who was raised in the North Star of America's heartland, knew one thing for certain about what she had witnessed: *It wasn't right.*[1]

The digital documentary record that Frazier created would shake the world to its core. Amid a deadly and global Covid-19 pandemic, with fears and tensions high, and with many people forced into isolation in their homes, Frazier's cell phone video went viral online. By Monday evening, it began circulating on social media: Frazier had posted the video as public on her Facebook page lamenting, "They killed him right in front of cup foods over south on 38th and Chicago!! No type of sympathy 💔💔 #POLICEBRUTALITY."[2] Frazier's post was shared by other accounts on Facebook and then screenshotted and cross-posted to accounts on Twitter and Instagram, where the video was also retweeted and reposted. Links to the Facebook video and local video downloads circulated through text messaging, direct messaging (DMs), and WhatsApp as well as on various blogs and through countless forums, including Reddit.

Unsurprisingly, it wasn't long before the news media had also picked up the story of a forty-six-year-old Black father of five named George Perry Floyd Jr. who was murdered in Minneapolis, Minnesota, by a white police officer who had detained him for allegedly using a counterfeit twenty-dollar note at the Cup Foods neighborhood convenience store. In no time at all, people around the world had seen police officer Derek Chauvin kneel on Floyd's neck for more than nine minutes during which time Floyd begged for his life, cried out for his mother, lost control of his bladder, and died—all of which had been captured in graphic and heartbreaking detail by Frazier, a seventeen-year-old bystander witness holding a cellphone camera.

The visual record of Floyd's death that Frazier created on Monday, May 25, 2020, was met with a mix of shock, outrage, praise, and criticism. It was quickly mobilized both as evidence and as a call to action. As evidence, the visual record laid bare a long national history of anti-Black police violence and originated a nationwide call for restorative justice. As a call to action, the Floyd video served to galvanize a country—one long steeped in racialized violence and hatred—to demand change. By the following day, Frazier's video, recordings made by others who arrived after Frazier on the scene at Cup Foods, and nearby surveillance footage of the roughly ten minutes leading up to Floyd's death had been broadcast by national and international news and entertainment media outlets on their television and streaming platforms. The footage was published online across news organizations' social media accounts, further contributing to its viral dissemination. In response to the killing of Floyd and the viral circulation of the video that captured his last breaths, protests against police brutality and police anti-Black racism erupted—first across the nation and then across the globe.[3] Within a matter of days, George Floyd had posthumously become the newest public face of a centuries-old American phenomenon: the viral and violent spectacle of hate-based Black death.

The day after Floyd's death, with video of the incident circulating and protests brewing in Minneapolis, the Minneapolis Police Department fired four officers—including Derek Chauvin—for their involvement in Floyd's demise. That night, the first of what would come to be called the George Floyd Protests took place in the Minneapolis–Saint Paul metropolitan area. Three days later, on May 29, 2020, the Hennepin County Attorney announced that the county had filed third-degree murder and second-degree manslaughter charges against Chauvin. In early June the complaint was amended to include a charge of second-degree murder, with prosecutors noting that Chauvin had "[perpetrated] an act eminently dangerous to others and [evinced] a depraved mind, without regard for human life" and that "the defendant and the other two officers stayed in their positions" even after Floyd could be heard saying: *I'm about to die.*[4]

Although it took media outlets less than a week to officially announce their intentions to televise the Chauvin trail, it took nearly a year for Chauvin's trial to begin. On Monday, March 29, 2021, in courtroom C-1856 at the Hennepin County Government Center, opening statements began in the case of *Minnesota v. Derek Chauvin*. Minutes into his opening statement, prosecutor Jerry Blackwell spoke about the widely circulated video captured by Frazier. Blackwell told the jury that the number to remember was nine-two-nine. Nine minutes, twenty-nine seconds—the amount of time Chauvin had Floyd pinned to the pavement with his knee. And then Blackwell played Frazier's ten-minute video in open court, providing incontrovertible documentary evidence of what had happened in front of Cup Foods on the day Floyd was murdered. Several additional bystander videos were played during the trial, demonstrating Floyd's murder from slightly different angles.

Footage from police body cameras was also introduced and played at length: roughly twenty minutes from when officers arrived and confronted Floyd to the moment his body was loaded into the ambulance. There was surveillance video from inside the Cup Foods store where Floyd was accused of passing the counterfeit bill, as well as street-level surveillance video outside the store from two different cameras—one from in front of Cup Foods and the other from a restaurant across the street. But it was seventeen-year-old Frazier's cell phone video that was most compelling: one juror reported that seeing Frazier's video, excerpts of which Blackwell played throughout the trial, was as if "every day was a funeral...like watching somebody die on a daily basis."[5] Three weeks later, during the trial's closing arguments, prosecutors urged jurors to "believe your eyes" as they replayed Frazier's video of George Floyd's death beneath the knee of Derek Chauvin.

It took the jury just over ten hours to convict Chauvin on all three charges. The nation reacted with relief: "It was a murder in the full light of day and it ripped the blinders off for the whole world to see the systemic racism," President Joe Biden said in televised remarks. "This can be a giant step forward in the march toward justice in

America," he noted. And Frazier's video, a digital record created by a horrified teenager that had first galvanized a global protest movement, was now credited with helping to right the long-standing racial wrongs of America—it was, ostensibly, not a record of *hate* but a record of *justice*. Many high-profile social media users and public figures praised Frazier for taking the video, which they credited with disproving the police narrative and facilitating the trial's historic outcome: "She is a stellar example of how everyday people can be powerful in documenting injustice and creating momentum for accountability," tweeted Virginia Senator Tim Kaine.[6]

While visual media such as Frazier's video documenting Floyd's murder has indeed long been mobilized in altruistic ways—to animate a white public, to convince white Americans that Black lives have value, and in the broader service of justice—it has also been employed more nefariously as a commodity in the service of white America's sociopolitical and economic interests and as a means of social power and control. This chapter demonstrates how the social apparatus of visual media that document anti-Black violence in the United States is—and has always been—impelled by racism, enabled by technology, and motivated by profit. I argue that the historical seeds of this social apparatus, as well as its modern-day functions (including the essential role visual media play in documenting extrajudicial violence and anti-Black hatred in the United States), were sown and anchored during the era of racial terror lynching in America.[7]

One hundred years before Darnella Frazier, Elizabeth Freeman was also called upon to bear witness when a Black man was murdered. A white woman and a suffragist, Freeman arrived in Waco, Texas, on May 16, 1916, one day after Jesse Washington, a disabled seventeen-year-old Black child, was lynched. Washington, who was employed as a farmhand, had been convicted of raping and murdering Lucy Fryer, the wife of his white employer, in Robinson, Texas. Washington had confessed to the crime, ostensibly because he had been promised protection and a fair trial; the next day, however, word of his confession was published in the Waco newspapers. A grand jury was assembled on May 11. They quickly returned an indictment against Washington and the trial was scheduled for four days later, May 15, 1916. On the morning of May 15, Waco's courthouse quickly filled to capacity in anticipation of the trial. Observers filled the sidewalks around the courthouse, making it difficult for jurors to enter (it is estimated that more than two thousand spectators were present). Washington's trial lasted only one hour before the jury began deliberations. After only four minutes of deliberation, the jury pronounced a guilty verdict—and a sentence of death.

According to Freeman's report to the National Association for Advancement of Colored People (NAACP), after his trial Washington was chained by his neck and dragged by a group of white spectators "between a quarter and a half a mile from the courthouse to the bridge" and then paraded several more blocks to City Hall, during which time he was stripped, stabbed, and repeatedly beaten.[8] When the men arrived at the bridge—where they were planning to throw Washington over the side and into the waters below—a member of the crowd informed them that a fire was already burning at City Hall, where indeed a small boy (at the time Texas law forbade arresting small children) had been tasked with lighting a fire in which to burn Jesse Washington alive. Washington, semiconscious and covered in blood, was doused with coal oil, hanged from a tree by the chain around his neck, and lowered to the ground where members of the lynch mob cut off his fingers, toes, and genitalia. Washington was repeatedly raised and lowered into the flames for two hours until he burned to death in front of an estimated fifteen thousand to twenty thousand spectators. When the fire was extinguished, those same spectators—whose appetites were merely whetted by witnessing a Black man's murder—gathered bits of bone and the remnants of the chain from Washington's neck, which, along with his fingers, toes, and genitals, were intended to be kept as souvenirs.

Jesse Washington's remains were not the day's only souvenirs, however; the archival holdings at the Library of Congress also comprise souvenirs from that day. While Washington was being dragged through the streets of Waco, photographer Fred "Gildy" Gildersleeve was setting up his camera. A white man and well-liked in the Waco community, Gildersleeve would eventually become known as a pioneer in aerial photography. He would also become known for the historic images he captured on May 15, 1916. Gildersleeve's photographs, captured using both high-angle shots and medium shots, depict two striking perspectives on Washington's lynching. The high-angle photograph—typically used to make the subject of the image seem vulnerable, powerless, and weak—was shot as Washington was burned alive, hanging from the tree at City Hall. The hanging tree is the focal point of the image; it is positioned dead center, with the mob of spectators, numbering in the thousands and dressed in suits, hats, and dresses—their Sunday best—surrounding Washington's still-burning body.

The other Gildersleeve images are of Jesse Washington's remains. Captured using a series of medium shots—which are often employed to convey intimate perspectives and to disarm the viewer—and taken over a period of time, each of these pictures details a different stage of Washington's suffering. There is one of Washington's charred corpse, parts of his extremities visibly burned away. There is one of Washington's head, burned black and partly buried in large chunks of ashen detritus, the chain-link around him visible as it runs parallel to the tree from which he was hanged. Finally, there is a photograph that speaks the unspeakable: a pile of ashen human remains framed by white spectators. Visible only from the waist down in the background, the spectators in the image are slightly blurred and their backs are facing the camera; while Washington's charred remains are still smoking in the foreground, the white spectators have already turned away and moved on with their day.

Today Gildersleeve's images are housed in the Library of Congress's Prints and Photographs Division among its collection of visual materials from the NAACP Records. They were circulated as a means toward two disparate ends. Gildersleeve, who had been personally invited to photograph the lynching by Waco's mayor, used the images to capitalize on Washington's murder. Throughout the early part of the twentieth century, lynching in the United States was a lucrative photographic endeavor: lynching photography was a subculture within the broader lynching culture, one that delighted in trading lynching postcards (as trading cards). It was common for white Americans to send their loved ones picture postcards of lynchings they had witnessed and photographs of themselves posed with hanging corpses, widely disseminating images of the disfigured (and often dismembered) victim. As historian Linda Kim argues, "photography was not an accidental byproduct of lynching, but was critical to the practice and its spectacular address."[9] Gildersleeve's photos of Washington's murder sold for ten cents each—about $2.50 in modern currency; today Gildersleeve is remembered not only for taking the photographs documenting Washington's murder but also for profiting from their circulation.

While Gildersleeve would circulate the Washington pictures for profit, selling postcards and prints of images captured for enthusiastic racists to a worldwide audience, Black scholar and civil rights activist W.E.B. Du Bois, in his role as founder and editor of the NAACP's monthly magazine *The Crisis*, circulated them as documentary evidence in the NAACP's anti-lynching campaign. The July 1916 issue of *The Crisis* included an eight-page supplement on the lynching of Jesse Washington that comprised portions of Elizabeth Freeman's report; testimony from members of the lynch mob; and six of Gildersleeve's gruesome images. It was the first time a journalistic source had published lynching photos, and Du Bois did so unapologetically.[10] Fifty-three years before Washington's lynching, Americans had seen the images of Gordon's scourged back, which for many made the violence of slavery undeniable; the publication of Gildersleeve's images in *The Crisis* was similarly convincing. As scholar Megan Ming Francis explains in her book *Civil Rights and the Making of the Modern American State*,

> Du Bois skillfully used photos to create a different frame from which to interpret lynchings: whereas lynching photos had been used to celebrate the carrying out of justice, *The Crisis* used photographs to expose that myth and convey the sheer injustice of lynching. The juxtaposition of text and horrific photographs made the logic of lynching harder to navigate in the white mind; it was one thing to read stories of African American innocence and another to see the consequences of white vigilante violence meted out on a mutilated African American body.[11]

For Du Bois it was imperative to show not only the horror of what had been done to Jesse Washington but also to demonstrate the casual cruelty of the thousands of white spectators who celebrated Washington's brutal murder. Like Frederick Douglass (one of the first critical theorists of photography), Du Bois believed photography could be employed as a means of making politically-minded points about the humanity of Black people. Despite concerns raised by the NAACP's Board of Directors about publishing the violence and trauma testified to in Gildersleeve's photos, it was Du Bois's contention that because this cruelty was a daily reality for Black people in America, the images—which depicted a hate crime witnessed by an estimated fifteen thousand people who did nothing to stop it— should not be censored.[12] Du Bois's assessment was not wrong: an October 1916 article in the *New Republic* noted with revulsion that Gildersleeve's photographs revealed a "typical straw-hatted summer crowd gazing gleefully at the hideous crisp of what was once a Negro youth."[13] Arranged chronologically, Gildersleeve's photos in *The Crisis* were evidence of racism's viciousness and of the banality of evil in America—presented in stark black and white.

Du Bois's and Gildersleeve's photographic campaigns reached vastly different audiences. *The Crisis*, established as America's leading publication focused on the state of Black Americans, was unable to use the same distribution channels as white publications.[14] Popular primarily among upper-class Black Americans living in northern cities, *The Crisis*'s circulation alone would not have reached Du Bois's intended audience. As a result, in their effort to circulate Freeman's report and the Gildersleeve images to a broader audience, the NAACP mailed the report, reformatted as a pamphlet, to 700 white newspapers. The pamphlet was also distributed to 500 wealthy men in New York, 670 members of the New York City Club, 600 members of the Indian Rights NAACP, 900 members of the Intercollegiate Socialist Society, 1,800 New York churches, and every sitting member of the United States Congress.[15] Du Bois and the NAACP were intentional in their use of Gildersleeve's images: they aimed the arrow of documented hate at the heart of justice.

The intent and precision of the NAACP's campaign to circulate Gildersleeve's photographs were, however, mediated by the countervailing factors of both American racism and early twentieth-century technologies. Many lynchings were announced in newspapers and on the radio, and when they were, photographers like Gildersleeve would arrive early on the scene, jockey for good positions for their cameras, and quickly mass-produce prints—sometimes from portable printing presses brought to the lynching site—of their photographs as mementos for the crowds. These photographic souvenirs were frequently made into postcards, in which form they worked to extend the visual rhetoric of lynching and its claims about white supremacy. They also worked to legitimize the violation of Black people's bodies beyond the crowds present at the lynching event to the far-off friends and family who received these graphic images via the United States Postal Service.

As scholars Dora Apel and Shawn Michelle Smith observed in their book *Lynching Photographs*, "when they circulated," these photographic postcards of lynching "effectively increased the size of the mob and spread its reign of terror to a wider network of witnesses."[16] Therefore lynching was arguably further culturally enabled and normalized by the circulation of records (lynching postcards, newspapers) through communities and through the mail; and this circulation was made possible by the technologies of the time—the telegraph and railroad, and according to some texts, the phonograph.[17]

Lynching itself thus became part of a new technological age. As historian Grace Elizabeth Hale explains: "Lynchers drove cars, spectators used cameras, out-of-town visitors arrived on specially chartered excursion trains, and the towns and counties in which these horrifying events happened had newspapers, telegraph offices, and even radio stations that announced times and locations of these upcoming violent spectacles."[18] It was arguably the explicit intersections of racism and technology that set the conditions of possibility for lynching to be used as a means of social control; to act as a powerful reminder for Black people in America that one must be ever-vigilant and ever in fear for one's life. And just as racism and the technologies of the early twentieth century made it possible to circulate the threat, trauma, and hatred that undergird lynching photographs, so too are race and technology among the modern actors that stage and restage racial hatred. These same actors enable records that document anti-Black violence to circulate in modern-day digital environments in ways that do not serve the Black community's demands for racial justice and accountability.

On the night of February 26, 2012, nearly *one hundred years* after the murder of Jesse Washington, seventeen-year-old Trayvon Martin, a Black teenager, was walking home from a convenience store when he was fatally shot by George Zimmerman, a white-Hispanic man who claimed to be acting in his role as "neighborhood watch coordinator" for the gated community in which he lived in Sanford, Florida. As a result of then rapidly growing digital culture trends—including digital documentary practices, emerging modes of online content-creation, for-profit photography, Instagram, and citizen journalism—photographs snapped of Martin's deceased body at the scene of his murder were quickly made available online, where they circulated throughout the nation and the globe.

Like Gildersleeve's photographs of Jesse Washington, the images of Martin's body set in motion a national epiphanic moment: white Americans were shocked that a Black child could be killed with impunity by a white man in the United States simply for buying Skittles and Pepsi at the corner store. Following Martin's death, rallies, marches, and protests ensued across the nation. An online petition was launched calling for a full investigation and prosecution of Zimmerman and the media coverage superseded that of the 2012 presidential race. It wasn't long, however, before Martin himself became the subject of online analysis as his brief life was reduced to the digital footprint he left behind. Every aspect of his digital life was scrutinized, but particularly his Twitter presence: tweets about Black urban life; YouTube excerpts from movies he enjoyed that also depicted Black life; tweets about and lyrics by his favorite rappers such as Tupac Shakur; and, importantly, pictures depicting Martin's tattoos, an empty marijuana bag, and gold grills on Martin's teeth.

Trayvon Martin's Twitter presence reflected his experience as a Black teenager growing up in the same country that had lynched Jesse Washington—and his critics used it to justify what scholar Safiya Noble has called "the legal right to fear Blackness."[19] Trayvon's digital presentation of self represented a Blackness to be feared, particularly in a country that created a racial, social, and economic underclass through centuries of chattel slavery, racial terror, and Black code laws. Blackness, in America, *is* a crime. As scholar Khalil Gibran Muhammad argues in his 2010 book *The Condemnation of Blackness: Race, Crime, and the Making of Modern Urban America*, there is a history in the United States of linking Blackness and criminality.[20] This manufactured link between race and crime is as enduring and influential in the twenty-first century as it has been in the past. Because rates of violent crime in the nation's urban centers are generally understood as a reflection of the presence and behavior of the Black men, women, and children who live there, Martin's digital body was criminalized, even as his physical body was the victim of an anti-Black hate crime.[21]

Even though a person's online persona may not reflect a true image of who they are, Martin's Twitter, like Gildersleeve's postcards, again exposed the racialized underbelly of two Americas. One that, like Du Bois, would encounter visual media depicting Martin's dead body and in turn launch a global campaign against extrajudicial violence and anti-Black hatred (in this case, the movement now known as Black Lives Matter). And another that would be served by what scholar André Brock calls "the white Western libidinal economy of anti-Blackness" of this new, digital version of the American social apparatus of visual hatred in much the same way it was served by Gildersleeve's postcard souvenirs.[22] When Zimmerman was tried for the second-degree murder of Martin, both the defense and prosecuting attorneys agreed that social media would play an unprecedented role in the case. They were right: using Martin's enduring social media footprint, the defense painted the murdered teen as a dangerous, urban, Black male criminal. The white police chief testified that Zimmerman had a right to defend himself against such danger with lethal force, and Zimmerman was acquitted.

That the creation and circulation of images of Trayvon Martin's deceased Black body recall the historical traditions of American lynching is not accidental. As I argued in chapter 1, for those in positions of power, there are political, social, and economic gains to be made by reinscribing images of Black death: these visual records serve as a means of power and control. Similar, too, is the role of technology—it was, after all, high-speed printing presses, telephones, radio, and the telegraph that exposed the violences of lynching that were happening in isolated communities to an entire nation. There is a critical difference between the ways that visual media of Trayvon Martin's physical remains and images of the charred remains of Jesse Washington were wielded as a social apparatus. By the time

Martin was murdered in 2012, technology had changed: the world was immersed in a digital environment, social media platforms had changed the way people communicate, Apple's iPhone had been on the market for five years.

Even though photographs, postcards, trains, and the telegraph—the technologies of the time—made it easier to circulate images of lynched Black men, women, and children, there was no social media on which to repost, replay, or autoplay this death, no surprise encounters with or repetition of moving images to reinstill trauma and reinscribe hate. There is a relationship between contemporary digital culture in the United States, the shifting nature of public display for visual memory objects such as photographs and moving images, and the emotional agency of images: Martin's dead body was cast, recast, and broadcast on small screens, handheld technologies—technologies that other humans literally wear on their own bodies. In this way, digital culture created an epistemic shift. Martin's death contributed to a shift in the landscape of public mourning practices on digital platforms, where hate can be continuously reinscribed and reexperienced using technologies that not only make possible, *but make profitable*, chance encounters with racialized terror, violence, and hate.

In lieu of watching lynched bodies on display in the night, Americans have moved the spectacle of Black death to the internet, to social media, and to comment sections, where dead Black people's bodies take on the archival permanence of digital records. In the years following Martin's death, Google Images—a search service owned by Google LLC that allows users to search the web specifically for still and captured image content—classified subsets of photographs of Trayvon Martin as "Body in Casket" and "Body on the Ground." Making matters worse, research on commercial search engines has revealed that both the popularity of terms and the linking of web results to advertising is a site of profit for companies like Google. In other words, for Google, like Gildersleeve, there are profits to be made from circulating images of a murdered Black child.

As Noble asserts, "[searches] on Trayvon Martin's name are

telling about the enduring ways in which he was criminalized and put on trial in the court of public opinion online, and reveal quite a different story about the nature of the narratives that are both constructed and circulated with great popularity on the Web. Web results and their popularity are also linked to websites that are profitable for Google, meaning there is a complex relationship between search results and advertising models created by Google's search algorithms."[23] Now, nearly a decade after his death, a search for "Trayvon Martin" on Facebook—a site driven by advertising sales—yields memorial pages, images of white people in blackface and "Trayvon Martin" costumes, several results for Trayvon Martin pages that are not hosted or populated by Martin's surviving family, and pages for activism on the part of Facebook community members inspired by the case. Martin is listed as a "public figure"—as is Emmett Till, whose death by lynching in 1955 long predates the existence of Facebook.

Because social media platforms and search engines such as Google are advertising-driven, their financial and earnings models depend on clicks and other evidence of consumer engagement. Social media platforms, like Facebook and Twitter, generate the majority of their revenue through selling advertising that can be hyper-targeted to users based on algorithmically mining those users' online (inter)actions. And because frequently the *sole* value proposition of social media companies is providing unfettered third-party access to their users, it is vital that those users continue to engage on the platform if the company is to maintain—and even increase—its revenue and profit margins. Facebook, for example, has more than 2.5 billion monthly active users worldwide. The company estimated that in the first quarter of 2021, their worldwide average revenue per user (ARPU) was $9.27—or roughly $23 billion. Although selling advertising is hardly a new model or concept—the adage remains true that if you aren't paying for the product, you *are* the product—for social media companies like Facebook and Twitter, the number of viewers whose eyes remain glued to their computer or smartphone screens is vital for their fiscal success. And so, when Darnella Frazier posted her video to Facebook, her Du Boisean motives in sharing what she had witnessed in front of Cup Foods—"My video went worldwide for everyone to see and know," she posted on Facebook after George Floyd died—combined with Facebook's profit model and boosted the visibility of the video to create a perfect storm.

By June 10, 2020, thousands of universities, scientific institutions, professional bodies, and publishing houses around the world had made public announcements that they were closing up shop and taking a moment to give researchers time to reflect and act upon anti-Black racism in the wake of George Floyd's murder. At the same time, several corporate entities began to run Black Lives Matter–themed advertising campaigns, including the National Basketball Association, Papa John's Pizza, Nike, Disney, Verizon, and the Coca-Cola Company. In the following days, hundreds of companies, sports teams, and celebrities followed suit with posts of their own, many of them nearly identical. By June 30, brands had spent a total of $1.6 million on racial justice TV advertising.[24] As brand managers worked quickly to create sensitive, aesthetically pleasing responses to Floyd's death and the resulting protests, moving further away from a once apolitical approach to marketing and advertising, it became clear that despite what their new ad campaigns said, companies were interested in profits not progress. As Amanda Mull wrote in *The Atlantic* just days after Floyd's murder:

> This template that brands use to respond to a national crisis has become standard in recent years, as people experience collective trauma on the internet in real time. Images of police violence, school shootings, or racist attacks appear on the same social-media platforms where companies sell mascaras or sneakers or delivery services, often side by side. Contemporary marketing theory implores brands to show up where people naturally congregate online and engage with the topics they care about. That means riding the wave of memes and random topics that sustain social-media chatter, posting in the same formats as everyone else, often acting more like a friend than a company—even in times of tragedy.[25]

Mull's observation about posting support for Black communities side-by-side with advertisements aimed at boosting sneaker sales, as well as her remarks concerning the commercial need to sustain social media chatter, reinforce the argument that profit remains the motivating factor behind corporate Black Lives Matter campaigns.

For corporations, speaking out on social issues is often a calculated decision; it is a form of values- and identity-driven targeted marketing. By aligning corporate values with what customers care about, companies are hoping to build a sense of loyalty and a deeper sense of personal connection. Because brands themselves hold global influence on multiple levels, from consumer to customer to employees and other parties, if brands choose to be silent in the wake of a major social or political moment, it could in fact be *harmful* to their bottom lines. Corporations take a stand during "epiphanic" moments like the murder of George Floyd not because they care about Black lives but because they understand—and are invested in—their own long-term economic enterprise.

Further strengthening this argument is the knowledge that many of the companies that released solidarity statements on social media in the wake of Floyd's death have long reaped the spoils of American racism. To provide just one of many examples, Reddit, which has unapologetically provided a safe space for both racist organizing and coordinating targeted online harassment of Black people, posted a long letter from its CEO, Steve Huffman, encouraging listening to and empathy for the Black community. His heart, Huffman said, was heavy. Just two years earlier in 2018, however, Huffman had made it explicit that white supremacists were welcome to share their beliefs on the Reddit platform, which like Facebook and Twitter, makes money by promoting what is popular—even if what is popular is anti-Black racism.

Given the nature of how Frazier's video and Gildersleeve's photographs were used and circulated—fueled by the competing motivations of (Black) justice and (white) profit—we must also ask *for whom* visual records such as these are created and maintained. For archivists, those charged with stewarding such records and providing for long-term access and use, two concomitant concerns arise. The first is borne of a deep understanding of how records function in a modern digital society: archivists appreciate that nothing—even death—has an expiration date online. Although the maxim "the internet is forever" may seem trite, it is nonetheless true. Everything that is uploaded, tweeted, blogged and reblogged, favorited, and liked contributes to what can be thought of as an endless and enduring record. Second, in the case of Frazier and Gildersleeve, the records that remain are predicated on harm. These records, which document violence against Black men, separate their lived experiences from what performance studies scholar Harvey Young calls the societal idea of *"the Black body."*[26]

The Black body, an imagined and inescapable myth of Blackness, creates the conditions necessary for severing the *idea* of "Blackness" from actual human beings who inhabit Black bodies. As scholar Jennifer C. Nash argues in *The Black Body in Ecstasy*: "The Black Body captured in the visual field is always called on to 'do something,' to produce a set of affective, cultural, and political 'results'... Exceptional images of singular Black Bodies become the vehicles through which Black Bodies in general are known, and what is often made knowable through those bodies is a narrative of racial progress."[27] This narrative of racial progress, however, as made knowable through the spectacle of the lynched or violated "Black Body," is one of terror as social control. The societal idea of the Black body is one upon which convenient narratives can be projected and around which racialized mythologies can be formed.

This makes the separation of the Black body imaginary from the lived experiences of Black people dangerous: *ideas about* Blackness are too frequently projected across the actual physical bodies of Black people, often rendering us targets of abuse. This separation is even more pronounced in digital spaces, particularly when pain and other embodied experiences fail to connect the virtual image to the physical flesh. At the intersection of these concerns—digital permanence and the myth of the Black body—is the knowledge that without intervention, records that document the violent deaths of Black people will continue to circulate on the internet in undead memes and as commodified data streams—in perpetuity. The work, then, is to resist the authority of archives that legitimate structures built on racial subjugation and spectacles of terror. For Black people there is little need to witness these violent spectacles; understandings about violence against Black bodies are deeply imbedded in the Black American cultural consciousness. Instead, for Black people, these records often serve as a painful and traumatic reminders that the argument Black Lives Matter must still be made.

PART II Resurrection

3 The Resurrection of Henrietta Lacks

Now, you're alive or you're dead. You can't be both.

Day Lacks

In April 1951, Dr. George Otto Gey, a cell biologist working at the Johns Hopkins Hospital, appeared in a special edition of the television program *The Johns Hopkins Science Review*. Titled "Cancer Will Be Conquered," the episode was devoted to Gey's career-long ambition: to rid the world of cancer.[1] Gey was convinced that the secrets to accomplishing this feat lay inside the human cell; indeed, for twenty years, Gey had been trying to grow human cells in test tubes. As he discussed his theories with the television audience, Gey drew comparisons between *normal* and *cancerous* cells, highlighting and demonstrating the chemical differences between them. He believed that studying cancer cells would lead to the development of viruses and other organisms that would be able to kill cancer cells without harming normal cells. On the evening of October 4, 1951, Gey again appeared on the television program. Broadcasting live, he was beaming. "Now let me show you a bottle in which we have grown massive quantities of cancer cells," he said. "We will show you some actual pictures of colonies in a test tube of cancer cells, such as those

I just showed you. It is quite possible, that from fundamental studies such as these, that we will be able to learn a way by which cancer can be completely wiped out!"

It was hoped, in the 1950s, that a virus would be revealed as the major cause of cancer, and that a vaccine could be developed for that virus to eradicate cancer. On that night in October 1951, Gey was excited because he had acquired a new specimen of cancerous cells that he believed held the secrets to what cancer was, and how it could be killed. He had assigned the cells a code name—*HeLa*—and told everyone they came from a woman called Helen Lane. The cells were not, in fact, from a woman named Helen Lane. They originated from a woman named Henrietta Lacks. And the day that Gey made his announcement was the day Lacks herself died—from the very cancer Gey claimed to be able to cure.

The complex—and often messy—story of Henrietta Lacks, long known to academic researchers and scientists, resurfaced in the popular consciousness in 2011 with the publication of Rebecca Skloot's book *The Immortal Life of Henrietta Lacks*. Skloot's book, which became a *New York Times* bestseller and eventually an HBO movie starring Oprah Winfrey and Rose Byrne, formed the basis of a Henrietta Lacks zeitgeist, one that sensationalized the story of Lacks and decentered her in her own narrative. The story of Henrietta Lacks—or more accurately, the *biological matter* of Henrietta Lacks—is one that has been told and retold; and while many versions of the HeLa origin narrative exist, an enduring part of that narrative is that of Lacks herself, the woman whose cells live, even though she does not. In the minds of many, the HeLa cells stand for Lacks, and she for them, creating a paradox. As scholar Hannah Landecker has observed: "That one party in this relation should be alive and the other dead creates a dramatic tension ... [and] the resolution of the paradox in these narratives is always the same: [the] woman and the cells are immortal—the woman through the cells' life and the cells through the woman's death."[2] Lacks's (im)mortality in death is necessary to elevate her cells from life to immortal life. This chapter explores—and necessarily lingers in—this space between her death and her immortality, complicating the records, technologies, and erasures that constitute the resurrection of Henrietta Lacks.

Although it was not uncommon for human cells to be used in scientific research in 1951, Gey's internationally televised announcement was noteworthy: he was claiming to have *grown* "massive quantities of cancer cells." Prior to this moment, cells used in medical and other scientific studies were generally procured from culture collections that provided standardized specimens to research laboratories around the world. These culture collections had been developed intentionally, with buy-in from across the scientific community. Gey's announcement therefore came as a shock. How had he *grown* a human cell line?

In December 1899 bacteriologists from across the United States convened in New Haven, Connecticut, to inaugurate the Society of American Bacteriologists (now the American Society for Microbiology). The Society's charter members shared an interest in taxonomy and nomenclature and had long felt the need for a central distribution agency for standardized bacterial cultures that would allow scientists to have a common reference point for comparing experimental data.[3] In 1911 the Bacteriological Collection and Bureau for the Distribution of Bacterial Cultures was established at the Museum of Natural History in New York with the following announcement: "The Department of Public Health at the Museum of Natural History has equipped a laboratory to serve as a central bureau for the preservation and distribution of bacterial cultures of both pathogenic and non-pathogenic organisms.... It is hoped that...those engaged in biochemical work of all sorts will furnish the museum with cultures at present in their possession.... The laboratory is ready to receive and care for such cultures."[4]

Cultures began arriving from all over the United States and Canada, and soon the famous Král Collection in Vienna had arranged to exchange cultures with the new bacteriological collection. By 1912 the collection included nearly 600 strains, representing approximately 375 different named species. During the first two years the collection distributed cultures to more than one hundred colleges and research laboratories, free of charge. By the mid-1920s the collection had been formalized as the American Type Culture Collection (ATCC). Officially established in 1925 as a national repository for microorganism cultures, the stated goal of the ATCC was to carefully select and maintain living cultures while providing adequate description and preservation measures. In 1925, providing adequate description for living culture would generally have entailed building a corpus of descriptive and documentary information about the microorganism cultures held by the ATCC to provide contextual information about (and facilitate access to) the repository's collections.

Descriptive practices in museums and archives have historically been sites of contention, however, as racial and other stereotypes are frequently reproduced in the architecture of institutional language and classification systems.[5] Preservation measures, though, would have been aimed at prolonging the usable life of the cultures in the collection. As is still the case today, preventive preservation techniques would have been necessary to reduce the risk of material damage and to slow the rate of deterioration in the cultures themselves. Typically accomplished by selecting strong cultures at the outset, providing suitable storage environments, and instituting safe handling procedures, the methods used by the ATCC—sometimes described as a biological "museum"—mirror historical (and contemporary) archival practices. The ATCC continues to collect, store, and distribute biological materials that are used for scientific research and development. Functioning in part as an archives for microorganisms, the ATCC aims to be the world's leading repository for biological materials—particularly standard reference cultures (i.e., organisms grown under controlled conditions to provide a baseline for testing in research laboratories) and the data associated with them.

As a biorepository, the ATCC provides for the long-term preservation of and access to biological materials for use across science, education, and industry in over 150 countries. With more than eighty thousand items cataloged and available for use by the scientific community, the ATCC is the largest biological culture collection in the world. During its first decade, the ATCC grew from an ephemeral idea into a physical space, one that could house more than two thousand biological specimens. By 1927 the ATCC was prepared to begin distributing specimens to research laboratories around the world; that year, they published their first catalog, with a second edition following just two years later. The ATCC's Catalogue of Cultures reflected the organization's focus on standardization, collection, and distribution: the Catalogues featured extensive cross-listings, emphasized quality control, and offered descriptive context for the biological materials in the Type Culture Collection. The ATCC continued to expand despite the financial exigencies of the Great Depression. Although the Rockefeller Foundation provided funding support in the early 1930s, the ATCC soon found they needed to charge researchers a nominal fee to help recover production and distribution costs. What had initially been an exercise in scientific generosity and the establishment of best practices had seeded the roots of what would become a major commercial enterprise.

Today ATCC's holdings include nearly four thousand cell cultures derived from plant, animal, and human sources.[6] Among these cultures is what is known as the HeLa CCL-2 epithelial cell line. With a list price of $495, the HeLa CCL-2 cell line descriptive text in the current (online) ATCC catalog includes a notation that the cells are sourced from a thirty-one-year-old Black female. The descriptive text also includes a warning that HeLa cells have been reported to contain the human papilloma virus (HPV), a virus commonly linked to cervical cancer. The HeLa cell line has been the source of significant scientific controversy because of this cervical cancer correlation: HeLa, the first human cell line, is associated with one of the most aggressive forms of cervical cancer in existence. For modern-day researchers this is cause for concern primarily because of the likelihood of specimen cross-contamination—HeLa, as a cancerous cell culture, reproduces so quickly that in the absence of careful precautions, it can easily overpower other cell cultures in laboratory settings.

HeLa's ability to rapidly reproduce was eventually associated not only with Dr. George Otto Gey's historic announcement in 1951, it was indelibly linked to a historic case that changed the face of medical ethics and informed consent as we know it *and* with one of the most significant contamination controversies to exist in the history of laboratory cell science. The HeLa contamination controversy is noteworthy because of the inundation of laboratory cell culture specimens with HeLa cells and because the pervasiveness of the HeLa strain was specifically linked to—and likewise used to stigmatize—a deceased Black woman whose name, after a long period of erasure, has been forever intrinsically and inextricably linked to HeLa.

Henrietta Lacks was born Loretta Pleasant on August 1, 1920, in Clover, Virginia. The ninth child of Eliza and Johnny Pleasant, Loretta was known to friends and family as Henrietta, or "Hennie." In 1941, Hennie Pleasant married David "Day" Lacks and relocated from Virginia to Turner's Station (near Baltimore), Maryland. The mother of five children, she worked hard, laboring as a tobacco farmer. Soon after the birth of her fifth child, Lacks, who had been feeling ill, noticed a lump in her vaginal canal during a self-examination.[7] Her local doctor referred her to the Johns Hopkins Hospital, which—although segregated in 1951—was one of the few leading hospitals willing to treat Black patients (as stipulated by Johns Hopkins in his will). And so, on February 1, 1951, thirty-year-old Lacks went to be seen for intermenstrual bleeding (spotting between her menstrual periods) at the Johns Hopkins Gynecology Clinic in Baltimore, Maryland.[8]

Dr. Howard W. Jones Jr. (today renowned for his role in the first in vitro fertilization procedure) was the first to examine Lacks at Johns Hopkins. During the exam he conducted a cervical biopsy of a soft, purplish lesion that was visible on Lacks's cervix. Within eight days of being seen by Jones, Lacks returned to Johns Hopkins, where she was provided with radium-filled suppositories to treat the lesion, which Jones had diagnosed as a malignant cervical carcinoma. During this second visit two small samples of the cervical lesion were collected—without Lacks's knowledge or consent—and later sent to Dr. George Gey, a collaborator of Jones's and an innovator in tissue culture who was working to develop a human cell line in the Johns Hopkins Tissue Culture Laboratory with the help of his research partner (and wife), Margaret Gey, who was a registered nurse.

Jones, in sharing the Lacks sample with Gey, noted that he was surprised: Lacks's cancerous lesion had not responded at all to the radium. Instead, the cancer had begun to spread relentlessly. Writing in June 1997, Jones recalled that "from a clinical point of view, Mrs. Lacks never did well. Generally, in an early cancer, as this was, the tumor shrivels up from the application of radium, even though the tumor might recur. In Mrs. Lacks' case, the local lesion could never be eradicated."[9] Although Lacks underwent surgery and radiation therapy, her cancer metastasized, and her condition deteriorated. On October 4, 1951, just eight months after her diagnosis, Henrietta Lacks died from cervical cancer at the Johns Hopkins Hospital. She was thirty-one.

What made the Lacks case unique, beyond the very aggressive nature of her illness, was that the cell sample taken from Lacks's cervix and provided to the Geys' lab at Johns Hopkins was not a fixed-and-stained, dead histological sample but instead a fragment of living tissue. For at least three decades scientists had been collecting tissue samples from patients as they searched for cells that could live outside the human body, allowing researchers to conduct experiments that they could not do on living human subjects. When Lacks was seen by Jones at hospital in January 1951, it was de rigueur that human material was used as pathological specimens in medical research. In Lacks's case, however, her cells were taken to a research laboratory in which the central goal was to "mimic the functions of the body to such a degree that human cells could be grown apart from the body and used in its place in experiments."[10]

Normal cells were first grown outside the human body in 1907, but eventually they all died after they divided about fifty times. Cancer cells, however, grew despite their environment and could divide unlimited times. Without the right mix of chemicals in which cancer cells could thrive outside the body, though, they too eventually died. The challenge therefore was not only to find cancer cells that would reproduce endlessly, but to develop a recipe for the environment and nutrients that the cells would need to survive. The science of human tissue culture consists of convincing a glass-bound set of cells that they are safely ensconced inside a warm body to stimulate continuing reproduction. George and Margaret Gey had established a tissue culture laboratory at Johns Hopkins in which they had developed two important advancements: a solution in which cancer cells could thrive and a roller-tube technique that George invented to keep the fluid and cells in test tubes in constant but subtle motion. These methods allowed the Geys to grow tissue that previously could not be grown in laboratory settings. George Gey theorized that if cancer cells could be made to grow outside the body, researchers could use them to study the effects of toxins, drugs, hormones, and viruses on cancer (using the cancer cells as a proxy for the human body) without experimenting on humans. With such "immortal" cells, Gey believed he could answer important questions about how cancer develops.[11]

Gey and other researchers at Johns Hopkins studied Lacks's cancerous cells and observed that these cells were unique—they reproduced at a higher rate than *any cells that had previously been observed in the laboratory* and could consequently be kept alive long enough to allow for in-depth examination and experimentation. Before Lacks, cells cultured for laboratory studies only survived a few days, which did not allow for multiple tests to be performed on the same sample. But Lacks's cancer was so aggressive that the cells proliferated rapidly (doubling every twenty to twenty-four hours) and demonstrated unlimited replication. In other words, Lacks's cancerous cells were the first to be observed that would divide multiple times without dying—a perpetual cell line—and so they were dubbed immortal. The cell line could survive and reproduce indefinitely. In an eerie echo of chattel slavery, the immortality of Lacks's cell line—culled from her cervix and reproduced without her consent—recalls slavery-era womb laws which specified that children of enslaved women would also be born into slavery, thus creating generations of enslaved people, intended to carry on forever, also surviving and reproducing indefinitely. The law in all thirteen colonies was *partus sequitur ventrem*—roughly "that which is born follows the womb." And, as history inculcates the present, the contributions to science, technology, and economics made by Henrietta Lacks and by generations of enslaved mothers—by all Black women reduced to cogwheels in systems of reproduction—remain largely unacknowledged.

In accordance with contemporaneous naming conventions, Lacks's immortal cells were dubbed *HeLa* cells, taken from the first two letters of her first and last names. The source of the immortal HeLa cells, however, would not be made public for decades: to protect himself against legal recourse, George Gey had given Henrietta Lacks the whitewashed pseudonym *Helen Lane*. What is perhaps most grievous about this subterfuge is that as a result, the origin of HeLa cells remained mysterious for several decades, both for the general public and for the Lacks family, who were unaware that Lacks's cancer cells had contributed—at "no cost"—to an enormous body of research in the fields of virology, immunology, cancer research, and genetics *worldwide*. The cost, after all, had been great to Lacks's family: they mourned a sister, a wife, and a mother lost to cancer, and they did not have the financial resources to pay for homegoing services.

This fact makes it even more egregious that on October 4, 1951— *the same day that Lacks died*—Gey appeared on television holding a vial of cells from her body, stilled splayed open on a Johns Hopkins autopsy table, to explain his scientific breakthrough to the camera. Without mentioning Lacks by name, Gey took that moment to unironically declare that he might be holding the cure for cancer in his hands. By the time Henrietta Lacks passed away, George Gey had already provided HeLa cells to scientific investigators around the globe. At Johns Hopkins alone, HeLa cells had already been used by a researcher to help develop a vaccine for polio. Lacks was never told of her contribution.

Emerging possibilities for human experimentation and the implications of new tools and techniques for biomedical research were embodied by Lacks's cell line. Within three years of Lacks's death from the cancer that produced them, HeLa cells, seen as universal human cells, had contributed to groundbreaking scientific discoveries and pharmaceutical developments. By 1954 renowned virologist Jonas Salk was using HeLa cells in his research to develop his polio vaccine.[12] HeLa cells have since been used to develop medications for treating herpes, leukemia, influenza, hemophilia, and Parkinson's disease. The use of HeLa cells has led to important medical and scientific advances in cloning and in vitro fertilization. Scientists around the world have used HeLa cells for research on cancer, HIV/AIDS, and gene mapping, as well as to test the effects of radiation and toxic substances. HeLa cells have been used to test human sensitivity to tape, glue, cosmetics, and other irritants. Nine Nobel Prize–winning discoveries have used HeLa cells in their research. Most recently, HeLa cells have been used in the fight against Covid-19.[13] Nowhere perhaps have HeLa cells been more important than in areas related to women's health—particularly in research on breast and cervical cancers.[14]

Even though Henrietta Lacks's name was well-known within medical circles as early as 1953, it wasn't until 1975—twenty-four years after her death—that her family became aware of the critical role she played in medical research. A year later, a *Rolling Stone* article revealed HeLa's true namesake to the broader public.[15] With the identification of Henrietta Lacks as the human being behind HeLa, questions about whether there is a legal or moral obligation to compensate a person if something of eventual commercial value comes from their cells or genes started to arise, especially when it became known that none of the biotechnology companies that profited from her cells had shared those monies with Lacks's surviving family.

Just as HeLa cells have produced far-reaching and wide-ranging developments in medicine and science, they have also become a commercial enterprise. In her book *Culturing Life: How Cells Became Technologies*, scholar Hannah Landecker argues that there is an assumption of living matter as technological matter that is constitutive of the times—living cultured cells are used widely in research programs and the cell has become an important economic entity, one that is both patentable and productive. "The cell," Landecker asserts, "is making a particular kind of reappearance as a central actor in today's biomedical, biological, and biotechnical settings. From tissue engineering to reproductive science, culturing the living cell outside the body has become increasingly important."[16] Culturing living cells has also become increasingly lucrative. While at first, George Gey generously shared HeLa cells with scientists interested in cell research, and despite neither the Geys nor Johns Hopkins Hospital ever patenting the HeLa cell line, there is no question that the use of HeLa cells in university research and by pharmaceutical companies has yielded billions of dollars in commercial profits over the past seventy years. HeLa is the foundation of a multibillion-dollar industry.

Despite George Gey's attempts at promulgation—he was known to personally deliver test tubes of HeLa to colleagues, often using his own body heat to keep the samples warm—there was a considerable (and unsustainable for one research laboratory) global demand for the HeLa cell strain. In a few short years, HeLa cells became the foundation for countless scientific breakthroughs and for an entire—previously nonexistent but now multimillion-dollar—cell-production industry. By 1954 a company called Microbiological

Associates had begun selling HeLa, giving birth to the modern-day biomedical industry. More than twenty years later, in 1976, when Henrietta Lacks's family finally learned that people were buying and selling HeLa cells, they were furious. Not only had nothing been done to acknowledge Lacks's contribution (not even by Johns Hopkins, which had gained tremendous prestige from the Geys' work with her cells), but the family had been excluded from the financial gains that her contributions had yielded. The Lacks family resisted the repurposing of Henrietta's body as a commercial tool even as scientists worked to reduce—to *dehumanize*—Henrietta Lacks from a vibrant young wife and mother of five to an economy of cancer cells culled from a now-dead Black body.

Scholar Katherine McKittrick, writing in 2000, reflects on the contradictory positionalities of Black women's bodies in her article "Who Do You Talk To, When a Body's in Trouble?" Using poet M. Nourbese Philip's 1997 essay on Black womanhood, "Dis Place—The Space Between," McKittrick begins with Toni Morrison's premise that in the United States Black women—and their bodies—are "contradiction itself, irrationality in the flesh."[17] For the Lacks family the cell-production industry built on HeLa was "contradiction itself": their kin—their blood, their biological essence—was being posthumously appropriated and commodified and the same "immortal" cells that served as the engine of Lacks's death, now lived an afterlife for the primary benefit of white male scientists. The tragedy of Lacks's death, and the loss experienced by her family, was compounded by her family not being told that her cells had been taken and cultured for research. Major breakthroughs were made and so were billions of dollars, but her family—who lived in the shadow of the world-renowned Johns Hopkins Hospital where much of this research took place—was kept in the dark for decades (they first learned about what was happening when scientists reached out to them for additional blood samples in 1973). To make matters worse, while Henrietta's cells were so vital for medical research, many of her family members lived without basic health insurance.

Adding to this sense of contradiction, competing national narratives began to emerge around not only HeLa, but Henrietta Lacks herself. Notably, there is the personification of the cell line in the image of the woman from whose body it was established. Stories about HeLa's immortality proliferated; in many instances her death and her immortality were addressed side-by-side in the same sentence. As a writer for *Colliers* opined in 1954: "[Henrietta Lacks] has attained a degree of immortality she never dreamed of when she was alive, and her living tissue may yet play a role in conquering many diseases in addition to the cancer which killed her."[18] This too was George Gey's hope. When Gey died in 1970 (of cancer), his colleagues penned a tribute in the *American Journal of Obstetrics and Gynecology* in which they observed that Gey, in performing Lacks's original biopsy, "secured for the patient, Henrietta Lacks (fig. 2) as HeLa, an immortality which has now reached 20 years. Will she live forever if nurtured by the hands of future workers? Even now, Henrietta Lacks, first as Henrietta and then as HeLa, has a combined age of 51 years."[19]

Beside this statement is figure 2—a photograph of a young Black woman, smiling into the camera with her hands on her hips. Underneath the photograph, the caption reads "Henrietta Lacks (HeLa)" as if the photograph of the woman was also the image of the cell line, as if the woman *was* the cell line. A cell line that, according to some very concerned scientists, would have taken over the world if allowed to grow uninhibited. Malignancy and cancer were already associated with uncontrolled cell proliferation and metastasization, but it was not until after 1966 that HeLa cells were understood or described in these terms.[20] While it was widely acknowledged that HeLa cells came from the cancerous tissue that caused Lacks's death, the narrative emphasis emerging from the scientific community had been on scientific control, harnessing HeLa in the victorious battle against polio, and attempts to understand and treat cancer.

However, the immortality narratives took a dark turn when in 1967 geneticist Stanley Gartler announced that he had profiled eighteen human cell lines and judged them all to have been "contaminated" and "overtaken" by HeLa cells. Gartler had tested eighteen cell lines that were supposed to have originated from different donors and found that all of them contained identical enzyme profiles, indicating that they were actually all the same, rather than eighteen distinct human cell types. All eighteen had the same enzymatic profile as the HeLa cell. Gartler, attending a conference on cell tissue and organ culture, stood before his colleagues and said: "The [variants] that concern us are the A (fast) and B (slow) types. The A type has been found only in Negroes.... The results of our [analyses] of these supposedly eighteen independently derived human cell lines are that all have the A band.... I have not been able to ascertain the supposed racial origin of all eighteen lines; it is known, however, that at least some of these are from Caucasians, and that at least one, HeLa, is from a Negro."[21]

As Landecker argues in *Culturing Life*, the terminology of cell culture was already dense with connotations of lineage, culture, proliferation, population, contamination, and malignancy. With the delivery of his paper, Gartler used these terms in a scientific explanation that marked the contaminating cell line as Black and the contaminated lines as white, suggesting that a single Black woman had contaminated the baseline for all cell culture testing in research laboratories—ruining what had otherwise been a good thing for white science. The scientific breakthroughs that HeLa made possible were now being disregarded in favor of a stigmatizing narrative that centered around Henrietta Lacks herself as the (problematic) Black female source of HeLa. Gartler, drawing on a long history of race-based science in the United States, had both racialized HeLa as Black *and* associated this Blackness with "contamination" and "malignancy"—echoing the racist ideas about Blackness that inspired America's slavery-era one-drop rule, which asserted that any person with Black ancestry—or "one drop" of "Black blood"—was to be considered Black and therefore enslavable.[22]

First Henrietta Lacks had been erased in the HeLa narrative. Now, with Gartler's assertion, the stigmatizing narrative of Black blood contamination was being written on, over, across, and against the now-resurrected body of Henrietta Lacks. Lacks herself had enjoyed relative anonymity until Gartler brought her Blackness to the fore, effectively naming and marking HeLa as Black and invoking the concomitant connotations of (anti-)Blackness. After Gartler the race of the donor became central to the scientific evidence of cell culture contamination, and metaphors and stereotypes of race began to frame both scientific and journalistic accounts of HeLa, which were now structured by metaphors of miscegenation. Henrietta Lacks was not just Black, but a Black *woman*. And despite myriad scientific advances in women's health and the disquieting fact that in addition to her own five children, Lacks (via HeLa) birthed the modern-day biomedical industry, it is her death from what has been framed as a malignancy of gender and sexuality—a cancer of the "space between the legs"—for which she is renowned.

This dangerous space between the legs—where, like a Vitruvian woman, x marks the spot—is a powerful image with which to confront the very real forces of misogynoir that are too frequently levied against Black women. Misogynoir, or specific contempt for and/or prejudice against Black women, is a concept that flourishes in spaces that are liminal, in-between. When Toni Morrison wrote in 1992 that in the United States Black women—and their bodies—are "contradiction itself, irrationality in the flesh," she was referring to Anita Hill's vanishing in the intersection of male Blackness and white womanhood during Justice Clarence Thomas's Supreme Court confirmation hearings.[23] Hill, a Black woman who had accused Thomas (a Black man) of sexual impropriety, was effectively disappeared in a political discourse that identified womanhood as white and Blackness as male. So, too, does this intersectional crossing-out apply to the Henrietta Lacks narrative in the present: because Lacks was Black, she does not rise to the level of respect proffered to white women and because she was a woman, she does not enjoy what little agency has been afforded Black men as the result of American patriarchy.

In what has (quite literally) become a bioethics textbook example of what *not* to do, in 1985 portions of Lacks's medical records were published without her family's knowledge or consent. Borne out of horrors like the Tuskegee Syphilis Experiment (in which thousands of Black men, women, and children were intentionally not treated for syphilis infections so scientists could study the effects of the disease) and the Henrietta Lacks case, informed consent and respect for autonomy now dictate that people engaged as human subjects in research have the capacity and authority to act "intentionally, with understanding, and without controlling influences that would mitigate against a free and voluntary act."[24] Because Lacks's medical records contained sensitive and private health information not only about her but by extension also about her family, this ethical breach was particularly galling: six years earlier, medical researchers had agreed upon principles that could be applied, even in unique circumstances, to provide guidance in determining one's moral duties in any given situation.

With specific regards to ethical decisions in medicine, in 1979 researchers Tom Beauchamp and James Childress published the first edition of *Principles of Biomedical Ethics*, popularizing the use of principlism in efforts to resolve ethical issues in clinical medicine.[25] That same year, three principles—respect for persons, beneficence, and justice—were identified in the Belmont Report as guidelines for responsible research using human subjects.[26] The scientists who published Lacks's medical records did so *despite* extant guidance that would have indicated that doing so would constitute a breach of ethical practice. Just as nobody asked Henrietta Lacks for consent to use her cells for research in 1951, no one thought it was important to ask for her family's consent to release her medical records in 1985. For decades after Lacks's death, doctors and scientists repeatedly failed to seek her family's consent as they revealed her name publicly, gave her medical records to the media, and in 2013 published her cells' genome online.

In March 2013 a group of researchers at the European Molecular Biology Laboratory (EMBL) sequenced the HeLa genome and published the code online. The field of genomics has allowed scientists to study the role that genetic blueprints play in human health, and increasingly genetic knowledge is enabling more precise diagnosis, treatment, and disease prevention based on a person's unique genetic profile. However, the ability to identify an individual's disease risks using genomics raises questions about anonymity, privacy, discrimination, and bias. As scientists Kathy L. Hudson and Francis S. Collins noted in *Nature* in August 2013: "Two of the most deeply held values in the medical-research community—public data-sharing and respect for research participants—collided when the genome of the ubiquitous cell line HeLa was published and posted in a public database."[27] Although the German research team that posted the HeLa genome on open-access databases available through the European Bioinformatics Institute and the National Institutes of Health's (NIH) National Center for Biotechnology Information did not violate any laws, the Lacks family argued that the published genome laid bare their most intimate health information, making it digitally available to the public and denying them their right to craft their own narratives about their bodies, their heritage, their health, and their future selves. When the Lacks family protested, the EMBL team apologized, revised the news release, and quietly took the data offline (noting that at least fifteen people had already downloaded it, thereby creating local copies and rendering the sequenced genome effectively irretractable). The EMBL team pointed the Lacks family to other databases that had published portions of the HeLa genome, also without their consent.

Genetic information can be stigmatizing, particularly in digital environments where one lacks full agency to determine who you are and where and whether you belong. Although DNA has been used for decades to exonerate those who have been wrongfully imprisoned, more recently, genetic information culled from genealogical DNA testing databases (e.g., Ancestry and 23andMe) has been used to trace, track, and arrest.[28] Using an investigative tool known as genetic genealogy, DNA left at a crime scene can be used to identify an unknown suspect through family members who have voluntarily submitted their DNA to a genealogy database (allowing law enforcement to create larger family trees than if they were limited to using law enforcement databases).

Furthermore, sequencing cells—the human genome—is essentially a blueprint of the human body. By looking at the HeLa genome, one could determine Henrietta Lacks's family risk factors for diseases like Alzheimer's (in addition, of course, to a predisposition to an unusually aggressive and known-to-be-deadly form of cancer). And although it is illegal in the United States for employers or health insurance providers to discriminate based on genetic information, this is not true for life insurance, disability coverage, or long-term care benefits. And for the Lacks family—for any Black family in America—the way that *risk* is calculated is deeply fraught with anti-Black racism. The racialized history of risk narratives in the United States is deeply rooted in depictions of enslaved Africans as innately destructive, animalistic, and criminal.

The Black "brute" was constructed as a sociopathic and antisocial menace, a predator whose primary victim was white women. Sociologist David Pilgrim writes that "the 'terrible crime' most often mentioned in connection with the Black brute was rape, specifically the rape of a white woman. At the beginning of the twentieth century, much of the virulent, anti-Black propaganda that found its way into scientific journals, local newspapers, and best-selling novels focused on the stereotype of the Black rapist. The claim that Black brutes were, in epidemic numbers, raping white women became the public rationalization for the lynching of [Black men]."[29] Slave patrols (in which lie the roots of modern-day law enforcement) were not only deployed in the service of returning enslaved people who had run toward freedom, they were expressly deployed to maintain the safety, security, and purity of white women. As the rhetoric of law and order was mobilized in the American South in the 1950s, systematically linking civil rights to crime—still embedded with notions of Native savages, Black brutes, and the purity of white women—little effort was made to disguise the racial motivations behind rhetorics of safety and risk.[30]

Because risk rhetorics in the United States are connected to carceral narratives about the Black brute and the sanctity of white women, Black women—again existing at the crossroads—have not enjoyed protections from risk; rather, Black women's bodies have been imbued with risk rhetorics of their own. From welfare queens and the hypersexualization of Black women's bodies to the contamination of medical science by Henrietta Lacks, Black women are narrativized and mythologized as the embodiment of risk and danger. The contradictions inherent in using Lacks's reproductive cancer to (re)produce risk reduction for others speaks again to the lack of agency Black women have in crafting their own narratives around safety, risk, identity, and bodily autonomy in medical and scientific settings and to the ways advances in science and medicine relied on the erasure, the stigmatization—and eventually the resurrection—of Henrietta Lacks. Here, again, we see McKittrick's argument at play: there is an in-betweenness when it comes to the external construction of Black women's identities in the United States, which have throughout history been rendered, gendered, raced, invented, and reinvented.[31]

The resurrection of Henrietta Lacks through the HeLa genome opens space for a more robust consideration of bodies as data. The emerging possibilities for human experimentation and the implications of new tools and techniques for biomedical research were embodied by Lacks's cell line. Suddenly, the distribution and presence of what had been *a single specimen from one person* in laboratories *around the globe* presented a new way of understanding the disarticulated body: the information stored in Lacks's cells (and later her genome) could be (re)animated for various scientific purposes, making it possible to commodify an entire Black body by "resurrecting the dead" from the data stored in a single cell. And, when we consider the body as data, we can situate the historical record as being encoded—and genetically stored—in our bodies' DNA.

Here the philosophical and ontological slippages between life and death, reproduction and resurrection, human and digital remains become clear. Lacks is dead, yet her cells live on in biorepositories around the globe, being bought and sold as scientific commodities. Lacks is dead, yet her fully mapped genome—a blueprint of her body—lives on in digital environments where the detritus of our engagement has the potential to last forever and the boundaries between life and death are malleable and manipulable. Lacks is dead, yet she has been resurrected. As Lacks's husband, Day Lacks, remarked: "Either you are alive or dead, you cannot be both." Henrietta Lacks is dead. And yet there are now billions of HeLa cells in laboratories around the world which, if massed together, would weigh more than four hundred times her original weight. HeLa cells have transformed modern medicine. They have also become entrenched in the politics of our age. HeLa cells have shaped the policies of countries and of presidents. They were even a function of the Cold War because scientists were convinced that in Henrietta Lacks—in HeLa cells—lay the secret of how to conquer death.

The Black female body in America is one that initiates and reveals stories at the crossroads. Caught in the critical discourses and divisions between antiracism and feminism, the Black female body embodies contradictory positionalities and embraces this ambiguity to contend with the complex and mutable contours of Black womanhood. Building on a history of Black feminist scholarship that situates the American Black woman's existence in the interstices of (white) womanhood and (male) Blackness, McKittrick observes in Philip's essay several thematic variations on Black female bodies as *in between*: an argument that Black women produce complex narratives that both reinscribe and debunk racial tropes associated with their bodies, situating Black women's stories as in between; an invocation of the "space between the legs" as central to raced and gendered ideas about Black women's bodies; and an acknowledgment of the in-betweenness of Black women's identities.[32]

Taking up this tradition of Black feminist thought, and embracing the thematic conceits of liminality, contradiction, and in-betweenness, I argue that Henrietta Lacks is a Black woman whose story is—in any retelling—irrationality in the flesh. Drawing on the Lacks story as one uniquely situated in the complex narrative interstices that locate lifesaving advances in Western science and technology in opposition to the autonomy of Black women's bodies, it is important to critically examine the posthumous resurrection of Henrietta Lacks, to unpack Lacks's metamorphosis from a vibrant Black woman—a wife and mother—to an anonymous (and infamous) immortal cell line. The case of Henrietta Lacks, a Black woman whose body has contributed to—and continues to advance—countless developments in science and technology despite her death from cervical cancer (the "space between the legs") in 1951, represents the very embodiment of "contradiction itself." Cell science thrived for half a century by leveraging narratives that required the erasure, the stigmatization—and eventually the resurrection—of Henrietta Lacks. Taking a close look at the role of data, records, and archives in resurrection practices also demonstrates that the fundamentally philosophical questions raised by the Lacks case about the nature of life, the meaning of death—and the ontological limits of both—are even more complex in digital environments, where boundaries around how one conceives of life and afterlife have proven to be both malleable and manipulable.

As digital resurrection methods have become more commonplace, it is easy to conceive of resurrection practices more broadly as originating in the digital era (these methods are discussed in depth in chapter 4). Simply defined, resurrection—or *anastasis* as is it known in medical terms—is the concept of coming back to life after death. And although resurrection narratives abound in every culture—

everywhere from ancient mythologies and Haitian folklore to nearly all modern Abrahamic religions—actual practices around reanimating the dead have frequently been regulated to the realm of magic (more specifically, *black magic*—the narrative villain and malicious counterpart of benevolent *white* magic) and, more recently, to the realm of technology.

Discussed less frequently, however, are scientific concepts such as cellular resurrection—the reanimation of dead cells. For decades the conventional wisdom in the biological sciences was that cellular death of any kind was an irreversible process. And while this is no longer strictly the case, it remained true until the 1950s that scientific practice relied on fixed, dead, histological cell stains—such as the ones commonly used in high school biology classrooms—which are considerably less desirable for laboratory settings than cell specimens that have been cloned and/or frozen.[33] Before the 1950s the processes of both cloning and freezing cells were the center of intense theoretical debate in the biological sciences. At stake in cloning experiments were ideas about the individuality and autonomy of cells as living entities, whereas with freezing cells, suddenly the limits and thresholds of *life itself* were up for debate.[34]

As biologists made progress toward cell reanimation and cellular resurrection, and as geneticists progressed toward genomic mapping and new discoveries in DNA, the language around human cells shifted to what information was "recorded" at the cellular level and what information was "stored" in DNA, calling to mind archival practices around information storage and retrieval, the systematic process of collecting and cataloging data so that it can be accessed on demand. At the same time, human cells in a laboratory that had been frozen at any point in time were said to serve as their own "permanent record" (again referencing archival practices) as they were able to be defrosted—and reanimated—for future use. While a cell might not seem like a record in the traditional sense, it is a representation and expression of the simplest form of human life.

Embodiment—understood here as the representation or expression of something like an idea, a quality, or a feeling, in a tangible or visible form—allows us to consider the cell in a new light: a single cell holds so much recorded information for an entire human body, we can think of the cell as representing the whole body, or embodying the record of a human life. This is just one of several points where records and archives intersect with questions about the Black Body in this chapter's provocation. The Henrietta Lacks case offers an important glimpse into biological specimen repositories, past and present: from the historical narratives, based in misogynoir, that emerged as repositories—while benefiting tremendously from Lacks's biological material—that claimed the Lacks cell line was defiling the purity of repository collections, to the evolution of biological specimen repositories from sites of scientific beneficence to sources of global commercial enterprise.

The extraordinary events of 2020, including the movement for racial justice following the murder of George Floyd and the unequal toll of Covid-19 on communities of color, are compelling scientists to begin reckoning with past injustices. Some have called for an end to the use of HeLa in research entirely, arguing that because the cells were obtained without Lacks's knowledge or consent any use of them is unethical and perpetuates an injustice. Henrietta Lacks has dozens of descendants, several of whom are leading new efforts in Lacks's centennial year that call for people to celebrate her life and legacy. In 2021 the Lacks estate joined forces with renowned civil rights and personal injury attorney Ben Crump to sue Thermo Fisher Scientific, Inc. and several other multibillion-dollar biotechnology corporations that continue to profit from mass production of Lacks's cells. Regarding the lawsuit, Crump has stated: "Thermo Fisher Scientific's choice to continue selling HeLa cells in spite of the cell lines' origin and the concrete harms it inflicts on the Lacks family can only be understood as a choice to embrace a legacy of racial injustice embedded in the U.S. research and medical systems. Black people have the right to control their bodies. And yet Thermo Fisher Scientific treats Henrietta Lacks's living cells as chattel to be bought and sold." The suit charges Thermo Fisher Scientific and others with a single cause of action—unjust enrichment—for continuing to profit from the conduct of George Gey and others at Johns Hopkins, making the company liable for its profits as a "conscious wrongdoer" under settled law.[35]

As Jeri Lacks-Whye, granddaughter of Henrietta Lacks, told *Nature* in 2021: "I want scientists to acknowledge that HeLa cells came from an African American woman who was flesh and blood, who had a family and who had a story."[36] Henrietta Lacks was a person who not only had a life and a death but also a resurrection. Stored and/or recorded data forms the foundation of any resurrection practice; it is through this lens that a study of the Lacks case offers an opportunity to begin thinking about the Black body itself as a record and to critically consider posthumous resurrection practices more broadly. As a case study, Henrietta Lacks allows us to contend with how a single cell can represent an entire Black body, and how a single cell, as an embodied record, can be manipulated and disarticulated from the humanity of the Black body from which it came.

4 The Resurrection of Tupac Shakur

My only fear of death is coming back reincarnated.

Tupac Shakur

The evening of September 7, 1996, was warm in Las Vegas, Nevada. And, as any emergency room physician will affirm is often the case in the heat of summer, there was fighting energy in the air. Not only had the *Old Farmer's Almanac* recorded a daily temperature in the high nineties Fahrenheit, there was a boxing match scheduled at the MGM Grand Garden Arena in Paradise: Mike Tyson, the World Boxing Council (WBC) heavyweight champion, was set to fight little-known Bruce Seldon for the World Boxing Association (WBA) heavyweight title. In what would become one of the most controversial exchanges of blows in the annals of professional boxing, Tyson easily defeated Seldon by first-round knockout in one of the shortest heavyweight championship fights in boxing history. When Seldon was rendered senseless after just 109 seconds, the crowd in attendance screamed "Fix! Fix!" believing that Seldon had taken a dive and thrown the fight. Tensions high, there was little surprise when a fistfight broke out in the lobby of the MGM Grand shortly after the match had ended.

CHAPTER 4

Tyson, the new WBA heavyweight champion, had asked his friend, rapper Tupac Shakur (styled 2Pac), to be present in the audience for the fight. Tupac arrived with his manager, Death Row Records cofounder and CEO Marion "Suge" Knight and a party of Knight's associates. When the post-match mêlée began, Tupac and Knight were at the center of it: a man already known to (and disliked by) Knight's crew allegedly insulted Tupac, and Knight's people beat him up for this and other offenses. Feeling uneasy—the man was known to have gang ties to the Crips, and Death Row was alleged to have (rival gang) Blood affiliations—the pair left the Tyson-Seldon fight and went to Knight's Las Vegas mansion. Later, around eleven o'clock, they left the residence to attend a charitable event—to raise money to protect children from violence—at Knight's nightclub, Club 662. Knight got behind the wheel of his black BMW 750; Tupac slid into the passenger seat and rolled down the window. Five minutes later, Knight was pulled over on Las Vegas Boulevard by officers from the Las Vegas Metropolitan Police Department Bike Patrol, for playing the car stereo too loudly and not having visible license plates on his vehicle (the plates were later found in the trunk of the car); Knight was released a few minutes later without being cited.

Minutes after the encounter with the bicycle patrol, a still photographer snapped a picture of Tupac and Knight at a stoplight on the Vegas Strip. Just moments later, as they paused at another stoplight, a white Cadillac pulled up on the passenger side. A pistol barrel could be seen easing from the window just as a man got out of the Cadillac, gun drawn. Tupac tried to climb to the backseat of Knight's BMW, but it was too late. Thirteen shots rang out, and then there was nothing but the sound of squealing tires. Tupac was shot four times: one bullet hit his hand, another lodged in his pelvis; two more penetrated his chest. "I'm dying," Tupac said as first responders carried him into the emergency room. It took six days, but he was correct. Tupac Amaru Shakur died from his wounds six days later, on September 13, 1996. He was twenty-five.

In life, Tupac was a rising star. Born Lesane Parish Crooks on June

16, 1971, American rapper and actor Tupac Amaru Shakur is still consistently ranked as one of the greatest and most influential hip hop artists of all time.[1] Brooklyn-born, Tupac was the descendent of enslaved Black Americans, sharecroppers, and domestic workers; he was also a child of the Black Panther movement. His mother, Afeni Shakur, worked closely with Lumumba Shakur, a Panther organizer, and had adopted the Party rhetoric of "offing oppressor pigs," often speaking within earshot of undercover cops. Soon a shotgun-toting squad from the New York Police Department was pounding on her door. The charge against her (and twenty other Panthers) was conspiring to set off a race war. Accused by the State of New York of plotting to blow up department stores and police stations, Afeni Shakur was taken to prison; there she fought for daily rations to nurture a new pregnancy. Months later, acting as her own counsel, she faced her accusers in court: the jury took fewer than twenty minutes to acquit on all 156 counts that had been levied against the Panthers. A month later, she gave birth to a son.

The family moved to the Bronx, in New York, where Tupac was raised to believe in collective care and responsibility. His mother also taught him something else: when asked at age ten what he wanted to be when he grew up, Tupac's answer was instantaneous: "A revolutionary." Eventually the Shakur family moved to Baltimore, Maryland. Tupac spent his first three years of high school—before the family relocated again to Northern California—at the prestigious Baltimore School for the Arts (less than two miles from Johns Hopkins Hospital, where Henrietta Lacks had died in 1951). There he starred in several theatrical productions and began composing lyrics. For Tupac, who had already been setting down what he saw around him in fragments of poetry, music became the record of his life experience.

Tupac started his music career in Oakland, California, working with hip-hop artists Digital Underground. By 1990, however, the rap scene was on fire in Los Angeles—artists Dr. Dre, Snoop Dogg, Eazy-E, Ice Cube, and Ice-T were all there laying down tracks, and the slow, deep beats booming from cruising car stereos spoke explicitly to the Black American experience: *fuck the police*. Gangsta rap was in demand, and sales followed in every corner of America—Black and white alike. It was in this milieu that Tupac came of age as an artist—as an actor, as a lyricist, and as a rapper. His 1992 appearance in Ernest R. Dickerson's movie *Juice* alongside Omar Epps cemented his early fame. As Interscope Records president Tom Whalley observed in 1997, suddenly "Tupac was larger than life."[2]

Twenty years later, James Thomas Jones III noted that Tupac's life reflected the hopes of Black Powerites, the failings of Black love, the pain of being entrapped in a disassembled urban community, and the joy of occasional, fleeting triumphs. "Make no mistake about it," Jones wrote, "Tupac was an elusive character who at opportune moments willingly adorned himself with every caricature that supporters and opponents place on African-American males: revolutionary, thug, intellectual, hoodlum, genius, emcee, Panther, prophet, prognosticator."[3] Tupac embodied all these qualities for a gawking audience that still managed to not *see* Tupac, despite his willingness to reveal his soul's contents to anyone who was willing to listen closely. Shakur's shooting and subsequent death in 1996 was a devastating loss to his family and friends, to be certain, but also to the global Black community that loved and supported him (and to whom he was also loyal) and, of course, to hip hop. "Untamed, untamable, he embodied the Black-male myth, made art of it, was imprisoned by it."[4]

Sixteen years after Tupac's murder, the night of April 15, 2012, also rolled in hot. Indio, California, which lies in the Coachella Valley of Southern California's Colorado Desert (about two hours east of Los Angeles) has a warm winter/hot summer desert climate. Indio's climate is not what makes it noteworthy. Rather, it is known for the numerous cultural events held annually in the city, most notably the Coachella Valley Music and Arts Festival. Every year, Coachella draws huge crowds to Indio; the days-long festival features musical artists from many genres of music, including rock, pop, indie, hip hop, and electronic dance music as well as art installations and sculptures. Fifteen years, seven weeks, and three days after Tupac Shakur was pronounced dead as a result of internal bleeding from the five gunshot wounds he sustained in Las Vegas, thousands of Coachella fans got a chance to see the impossible: for just under five minutes, people in the Indio desert witnessed living history as Tupac took the stage and rocked the mic alongside Snoop Dogg and Dr. Dre for a once in a lifetime performance.

The only problem was that this performance didn't happen during Tupac's lifetime. Though he passed away in 1996, his likeness had been resurrected as a digital projection on stage, giving viewers a chance to experience an ephemeral moment from the past: a live Tupac Shakur concert. But as Aisha Harris remarked in a June 2017 *Slate* article dragging the Tupac biopic *All Eyez on Me*, "looking like Tupac is not the same as acting like Tupac."[5] The Tupac that performed at Coachella in 2012 was, of course, not the real Tupac. Rather, a "hologram" (more accurately, an enhanced Pepper's Ghost reproduction)—a digital resurrection of Tupac—took the stage on that warm April evening in Indio.

The illusion itself was nothing new. Holography and other 3D technologies as well as 2D illusions such as Pepper's Ghost (an illusion still used in theater, amusement parks, and museums as well as on television and for concerts) have been used for centuries to create lifelike reproductions of human bodies—reproductions capable of addressing an audience, moving around on stage, and interacting with others using prescripted effects. The oldest of these techniques, Pepper's Ghost, dates to the nineteenth century and is named for John Henry Pepper (1821–1900), the British optics researcher who popularized the effect. As an illusory technique, Pepper's Ghost operates on the principle that glass is both transparent and reflective, so it is possible, with the right angles, to reflect an image off glass in such a way that it appears to be floating in air. Two contemporary, well-known examples of the Pepper's Ghost illusion are teleprompters and the Disney Haunted Mansion's ghosts. Another example can be found at the Our Planet center in Castries, Saint Lucia, which opened in May 2011. Here, a life-size Prince Charles (now King Charles III) and Saint Lucia's governor general appear on stage talking to one another about climate change.

Perhaps the most notable example of the Pepper's Ghost illusion, however, is one that closely evokes the appearance of Tupac at Coachella: a posthumous performance by another Black artist. In May 2014 a Pepper's Ghost reproduction of Michael Jackson (1958–2009) performed Jackson's 1991 song "Slave to the Rhythm" at the Billboard Music Awards. What was disquieting about this display was that "Slave to the Rhythm" was a song that Jackson had never performed in life. It was as if the song's title presaged its presentation. Despite his tragic and unexpected death in 2009, Jackson was resurrected as a cultural commodity, *as a slave to the rhythm*. He was revered by fans who were reluctant to let him go, and at the same time enslaved by the demand to perform the rhythms of his own music. As a human being and as an artist, Jackson experienced death only to be reanimated as an echo, a version of himself that was (re)constructed both as a means of extending profit margins and for the satisfaction of the spectacular white gaze. So too was the digitally resurrected Tupac Shakur.

The use of digital technologies to reanimate the dead, understood here as a "resurrection practice," raises a complex set of sociocultural and ethical concerns, particularly around issues of spectacle, commodification, carcerality, and the Black body as souvenir and memory object. Closely related to notions of symbolic immortality and digital immortality practices (addressed in depth in chapter 5), digital resurrection is a modern phenomenon that uses a combination of innovative technologies, digital manipulations, and marketing appeal to construct a domain in which the deceased appear wholesale in new contexts as though alive today—and, in some cases, as though consciously aware of their own demise.[6] The final product is often described as "uncanny"—either in praise of the resurrection's uncannily lifelike quality or as a criticism for its relationship to a phenomenon known as "the uncanny valley."

Introduced in the 1970s by Japanese roboticist Masahiro Mori, then a professor at the Tokyo Institute of Technology, the *uncanny valley* is a term that has been used to describe the creepy (and often off-putting) feeling one experiences when viewing humanlike renditions such as lifelike robots—and digital resurrections. Mori theorized that as robots appear more humanlike, they become more appealing, but only until one reaches the threshold of the uncanny valley; in the uncanny valley a sense of strangeness and unease takes over because of the rendition's *humanlike*—not *human*—presentation. This near-human or human-adjacent quality recalls Harvey Young's arguments about "the Black body," defined as an imagined and inescapable myth of Blackness, a myth that creates the conditions necessary for severing the idea of "Blackness" from actual human beings who inhabit Black bodies.[7] Jennifer C. Nash asserts that exceptional images of singular Black bodies "become the vehicles through which Black Bodies in general are known, and what is often made knowable through those bodies is a narrative of racial progress."[8] The problem with such narratives of racial progress is that they are very often oppressive. Nash further argues that the Black Body captured in the visual field is "always called on to 'do something,' to produce a set of affective, cultural, and political results." Narratives attached to the (digitally) resurrected "Black Body" are also liminal and difficult to locate. If Mori's uncanny valley applies here, it is in the resonances between the Black Body and the uncanny body, and it is ghosted by centuries-old practices of white supremacy.

Although the phenomenon of digital resurrection is relatively new, the history of the technologies used in digital resurrection is long and complex. The most consistent "resurrection" methods used throughout history are first Pepper's Ghost and then later, the addition of body doubles and superimposition practices. This combination of techniques has been used primarily in the pursuit of finishing commercial film projects in which actors have died before shooting could be completed. In the film industry this postproduction technique involves overlaying images of the deceased actor's face onto body doubles. The image is integrated with audio that is produced either by taking lines from unused scenes or splicing audio clips of the deceased actor's voice together to form new lines. Audio has historically been more complicated in this regard, and many films—particularly earlier ones employing digital resurrection techniques—tended to avoid audio when possible. In the case of the Tupac hologram, there are many aspects that echo problems with similar attempts to (re)create digital actors, including a smoothness to the skin that appears plasticlike. There is also a lifelessness to the eyes, which lack the small movements and pupil dilations that are often barely perceptible but bring life to a person's face—both of which contribute to the feeling of having entered the uncanny valley. Despite these "shortcomings," however, technology is getting closer to surmounting these technical hurdles.

Today there are three levels on which digital resurrection technologies are implemented, and each is more complex than the one prior. The first, *rotoscoping*, is a technique in in which digital technologies are used to create what is known in industry terms as a *basic resurrection*. Long used as a tool for visual effects in live-action movies, rotoscoping is an animation technique that involves tracing over motion picture footage, frame by frame, to produce realistic action.[9] In a basic resurrection, digital rotoscoping is combined with compositing—the combining of separate source images into one integrated image. These combined techniques—rotoscoping and compositing—produce a composite image that is overlaid on a body double (the rotoscoped image of the face of the deceased is composited over the face of a body double).

Computer graphics (CG) aided resurrections, the next level of digital resurrection, are computer-enhanced and require good quality, high-resolution footage of the person being resurrected. The face of the person being resurrected is recreated using three-dimensional

(3D) computer-generated imagery (CGI), which allows for more realistic and flexible expressions. The 3D CGI image is then, again, composited over a body double. Finally, the highest level of digital resurrection is a *full resurrection*, which offers the most convincing results. Full resurrections use high-end motion capture technology *and* 3D CGI to completely recreate a person from head to toe (this is how the Tupac hologram was constructed). Or, in other words, by employing a Frankenstein-like mix of archival footage, a body double, motion-capture techniques, CGI, holographic technologies, and creative sound editing, it is now possible to (re)animate a virtual facsimile of a dead rapper.

On that April night in Indio, fellow rappers Snoop Dogg and Dr. Dre welcomed HoloPac (the Tupac hologram) onto the stage to perform a couple of fan favorites. Their intentions in creating the HoloPac had been good: their goals were rooted in love and in the spirit of celebrating the brother they had lost too soon. Even Tupac's mother, Afeni Shakur Davis, was initially behind the hologram. Importantly, they had asked permission—and she had given her blessing. Shirtless, with low-hung jeans, pinky rings, Timberlands, and Tupac's signature THUG LIFE tattoo visible on chiseled abdominal muscles, HoloPac greeted the audience with a booming: "What the fuck is up, Coachellaaaaaa?!" From the beginning, everything was a little bit off; just as Mori theorized, it was uncanny. The HoloPac moved like Tupac, *but not quite*. It sounded like Tupac, *but not exactly*. For the eighty thousand people in the predominately white Coachella audience, it was bizarre—almost funny—and, for some, unsettling. It was clear that night that the audience was supposed to take HoloPac seriously, but the crowd seemed to have no idea how to receive the hologram. Its arrival came (somewhat oddly) *after* Dr. Dre and Snoop Dogg tag-teamed Tupac's song "California Love," and many thought the moment for the rumored HoloPac appearance had already passed and the decision had been made not to use the hologram.

When HoloPac shouted its greeting, the crowd yelled back, but there were visibly uneasy looks in the audience alongside the excited superfans: despite the influence of Black creativity on popular culture, many music festivals are—and have notoriously been—predominantly white affairs. One result of this trend is that while Black performers often receive top billing, they are entertaining mainly white audiences—and when the audience is white and the performer is Black, the stage is set for Black spectacle. In the following days, as fans took to Twitter, two consensuses seemed to emerge: many said the hologram made them uncomfortable, noting that *the technology* had gone too far, while others praised the HoloPac—actress Kristen Stewart and singer Katy Perry reported pushing their way to the front of the crowd for a better view. Stewart and Perry, ages twenty-two and twenty-seven respectively in April 2012, typified the (predominantly white and well-resourced) Coachella audience. As the white gaze has historically and unfailingly made a spectacle of Black bodies, paying particular attention to the ways Blackness is made spectacular via commercial endeavors proffers key historical, critical, and theoretical frameworks through which to consider the Tupac hologram as a site of inquiry—and of injury. The roots of Black bodies as commercial spectacle in the United States lie, unsurprisingly, in the era of Atlantic slavery. Conjuring an echo of the auction block, HoloPac's entrance on the Coachella stage seemed to recall the carnality of the slave auction: *At last, everything is ready, and the traffic in human flesh can begin.*[10]

The period following the Industrial Revolution saw cotton production in the United States increase at such a rapid rate that large plantations in the American South struggled to keep up with demand. During this era the domestic slave trade in the United States also increased. This was in part because of the Act Prohibiting Importation of Slaves of 1807, which made bringing new enslaved people to the United States a federal crime. The increase in cotton production alongside a decrease—enslaved people were still illegally smuggled into the country after the act took effect—in imported "free" labor created conditions under which the domestic slave trade flourished. Slave auctions, often run and managed by auction houses, were an extremely lucrative part of the burgeoning domestic slave trade. Thousands of auctions took place each year, all around the United States, held publicly in the hearts of America's cities and towns. Although each auction was different, narrative reports from both enslaved people and white slave traders bear such striking resemblance to one another that the slave auction as a historical genre has come to be read and understood as a type of ritual performance. As historian James Oakes stresses, "auctions were so much a part of slavery, they evinced such distinct patterns, that we may speak of them as having become ritualized."[11]

Held in town centers, featuring enslaved men and women with oiled and shiny skin being paraded in front of white spectators for approval, and with an end goal of fiscal profit, the slave auction followed a distinct script. Anthony B. Pinn, writing in 2003, designates this ritual-performative quality of the slave auction as *spectacle*, noting that it is a "ritual of reference: it is repeated, systematic activity conducted in carefully selected locations that is intended to reinforce the [enslaved person's] status as object."[12] The presentation of the flesh (the Black body), the stages upon which the enslaved people were showcased, and the ostentatious conflation of wealth and human property define the scenes that designate the slave auction as Black spectacle. Furthermore, the sheer volume of accounts describing enslaved men's muscles (often oiled before auction to appear more defined and healthful) and other physical attributes point to an overt fixation with the Black body as an object to be dominated. The "obscene theatricality" of this kind of Black spectacle is bound both to the Black bodies placed on display and to the white audiences that bear witness to them.[13]

The Tupac hologram at Coachella exemplifies the modern-day version of the slave auction as Black spectacle. One could hardly miss the presentation of flesh that April night as the HoloPac took the stage. Tupac's bare brown belly and biceps—lit in such a way as to not only highlight his musculature but to make him appear to shine—were the very vision of the Black body on display. Bearing striking resemblance to nineteenth-century sketches of slave auctions, the shirtless, brown-skinned hologram appeared on stage before the wealthy, white Coachella audience and performed—just as the enslaved were forced to perform on the auction block to fetch a higher price. In his book *Twelve Years a Slave*, Solomon Northup, a free Black man who was kidnapped and sold into slavery, described the performance of a New Orleans slave auction noting that prior to being placed on the block, he and others were "conducted into a large room in the front part of the building to which the yard was attached, in order to be properly trained before the admission of customers ... moving to our places with exact precision."[14] The theatrical language Northup employs to describe the auction's "backstage" demonstrates the spectacular nature of the auction block and calls attention to the performative expectations imposed on Black people as they both lived and played the role of slave for white audiences.[15]

As William Wells Brown, a self-emancipated enslaved man, attested in 1849:

> Before the slaves were exhibited for sale, they were dressed and driven out into the yard. Some were set to dancing, some to jumping, some to singing, and some to playing cards. This was done to make them appear cheerful and happy. My business was to see that they were placed in those situations before the arrival of the purchasers, and I have often set them to dancing when their cheeks were wet with tears.[16]

So too was Tupac Shakur, resurrected in hologram form from the dead, expected to perform: he was set to dancing, set to singing, set to play the role of a shucking-and-jiving, oil-slicked, shiny, brawny, Black body—forever enslaved by the fetishism of the white gaze (just as Michael Jackson was) to the rhythm of his own music.

In their uncanny shuck and jive, Jackson and Tupac are impossibly tasked with a perversely spectacular existence: an existence where one must represent an exemplary narrative of racial progress—be an exceptional human but also be decidedly not human at the same time. The perversity of such an existence ties spectacle to commodity fetishism. Thinking about spectacle here serves to foment our understanding of the Tupac hologram as a cultural and fiscal commodity. *Spectacle*—as theorized by French Marxist Guy Debord in his book *The Society of the Spectacle*—is a term for the everyday manifestation of capitalist-driven phenomena, particularly as they relate to advertising, television, film, and notions of celebrity.[17] As with spectacle, fame and celebrity—closely tied to the potential to generate revenue—have historically been the strongest probability indicators for digital resurrection projects. In forming his theory of the society of the spectacle, Debord argued that spectacle reduces reality to an endless supply of commodifiable fragments.

Following the argument that the Tupac hologram is evocative of the auction block, and interweaving Debord's theorizations about commodifiable fragments, one might look again at the slave auction. Enslaved Black people were often sold at markets and auctions, demonstrating (again) that enslaved people were not thought of as human beings with human rights but rather as property, to be bought and sold. The auction block was big business: enslaved people were often advertised as "For Sale" in local newspapers as commodities alongside cotton and rice, and slave traders were listed in public directories (akin to phonebooks) for easy identification and contact. Frequently families were divided on the block and sold to different slaveholders—millions of families were in fact permanently separated this way, each broken down into commodifiable fragments. Digitally resurrected Tupac, on the auction block of the Coachella stage, is no less a commodifiable fragment.

Dead celebrities represent a growing enterprise, and although some have argued that the practical motivations for using digital resurrection are sufficient to explain the phenomenon of its increasing adoption, there are even more compelling arguments to be made about the commercial interests that motivate this recent proliferation. There are several clear commercial benefits of digital resurrection, but the most obvious is that for estate holders, artists continue to increase in popularity and business opportunities continue to abound—only now without the need to compensate the artist (who also does not have needs, get fatigued, have "diva" moments, age, or demand changes to the business model in any way). Another oft-cited fiscal argument for digital resurrection practices is risk management. There is a risk inherent in depending on an actor whose untimely death could prevent a film from being finished (Carrie Fisher's death while filming the *Star Wars* installments is just one example). Before the availability of CGI technology, producers and investors relied solely on cast insurance to insulate them from this type of risk. CGI technology mitigates the potential for financial loss because an actor can be digitally added—posthumously—to scenes as necessary.

CGI technology also allows estates to continue to earn income after a person's death. For example, Marilyn Monroe's estate earned $6.5 million in 2008 (despite her death in 1962) from a digitally constructed appearance in a Mercedes-Benz commercial. Digital resurrection has become so lucrative that it has spawned a new industry: afterlife agents whose job it is to manage the interests of deceased personalities on behalf of their families and estates. Over the past decade, *Forbes* has produced a Highest Paid Dead Celebrities List, demonstrating that posthumous representation is extremely profitable. Michael Jackson is currently (and has been many times over the past ten years) recognized as the United States' top posthumous earner; and after HoloPac's virtual appearance at Coachella, *Billboard* reported that Tupac's *Greatest Hits* saw a 571 percent increase in album sales.[18]

It is little surprise, then, that Digital Domain—the production house responsible for the creation of the Coachella HoloPac—immediately began discussing the prospect of more virtual performers, pointing out that tourist destinations like Las Vegas and Broadway could provide the basis for a very lucrative endeavor. In July 2021, *Rolling Stone* published an article that announced "Whitney Houston's Hologram Is Coming to Las Vegas," further noting that following a 2020 tour in the United Kingdom, a full-length show featuring a hologram of Houston was granted approval from Houston's estate to play Harrah's Las Vegas for a six-month engagement.[19] The hologram show—*An Evening With Whitney: The Whitney Houston Hologram Concert*—was created by BASE Hologram Productions in partnership with the Houston estate. The hologram concert debuted in early 2020 and was scheduled to open in Las Vegas before Covid-19 shut down the entertainment industry. The show—which features holograms of Houston from various stages of her career alongside real-life backup singers, dancers, and musicians—has already recalled for many the 2012 Coachella Tupac hologram.

The phrase "musical necrophilia" has been coined to criticize these kinds of digital resurrection practices. Music journalist Simon Reynolds describes the phenomenon of posthumous performances as "ghost slavery," and Catherine Shoard, a columnist for *The Guardian*, named "the CGI-insertion of a dead actor into a new film as a form of 'digital indignity.'"[20] The film industry has countered accusations of commercial opportunism with a claim that bringing actors back to life is undertaken for artistic reasons, but legal questions—as well as ethical concerns—continue to arise around computer-generated resurrections. A 2017 study in the *Cornell Journal of Law and Public Policy* found that resurrection trends have inspired celebrities to legally protect their likenesses both in life and after death, as many have begun to preemptively negotiate the use of their (or their loved ones') computer-generated images in movies, television, and advertising campaigns.[21]

Legislation and policy that address ongoing rights of publicity are also increasingly common. California, an early adopter of this kind of policy, enacted the Celebrities Rights Act in 1985, which protects celebrities' images after their deaths by requiring permission from the estate holder before using a computer-generated likeness of the deceased. Legally binding agreements that address the rights of individuals to control the commercial use of their name, image, or likeness have become a serious consideration for those concerned that they may be misrepresented after death. This is especially true for Black men and women who are increasingly subjected to unwanted posthumous digital encounters.[22] For instance, despite California's Celebrities Rights legislation, new legislation in 2020 was required to ban taking photos of the dead by first responders. Inspired by the death of NBA star Kobe Bryant in January 2020, California law now makes it illegal for first responders to take unauthorized photos of deceased people at the scene of an accident or crime. Although posthumous agency over one's likeness has become a matter of both ethics and law, the ethical concerns have become demonstrably more significant.

While many have touted the promise of digital resurrection technologies to extend life and liberate humanity from the inevitability of death, I argue that these are carceral technologies that work to create a spectacular prison: the dead are conscripted to a performative version of life for the visual pleasure and satisfaction of others. Just as the carceral conscripts the Black human body, carceral technologies conscript us to the *myth* of Blackness that Harvey Young has cautioned against. With such carceral technologies, when the human body dies, what remains now includes new media onto which harmful myths of Blackness are projected. This carceral conscription is one in which spectacle goes hand-in-hand with the ghost of slavery and its uncanny dehumanizations.

HoloPac is a carceral fantasy. Tupac is a man, perhaps reconstituted and resurrected by the digital, but he does not get a second chance at life. The reanimation of inactive records is not a resurrection but rather the facsimile of one. Tupac's death and digital afterlife have been co-opted and commercialized. In the United States the prison industrial complex is a transparent extension of chattel slavery, and the overuse of incarceration has created a social inequality that has prevented Black Americans from fully participating in

American life. Much like Michael Jackson being forever enslaved to his own music in the uncanny valley, for Black Americans digital resurrection might also be thought of as a compulsory postmortem enslavement, or as a postmortem carceral conscription.

From an archives and records standpoint, in his introduction to *Archives Power: Memory, Accountability, and Social Justice*, archival scholar Randall C. Jimerson theorizes three different types of collecting institutions: the temple, the prison, and the restaurant. While temple institutions are collecting institutions in which the archivist preserves the "original interpretation" of items or collections, restaurant institutions, by contrast, are institutions where the archivist guides the user, allowing them to make their own decisions and allowing the collections and items speak for themselves. In prison institutions, however, the archivist serves only the interpretations of an oppressive higher power.[23] If we consider the Tupac hologram as an embodied record, it is one that belongs to the carceral archives of Jimerson's prison institutions. The posthumous hologram as record resides within a narrative interpretation that serves commercial interests, souvenir and fetish cultures, Othering, spectacle, and whiteness as higher powers. Digital Tupac is a carceral artifact, imprisoned by what one might call an archive of folklore or one of longing—and digitally incarcerated by white supremacy's need to possess and control Black people's bodies.

Archives are usually thought of as fixed—this fixity and permanence is thought to be necessary for custodial, intellectual, and physical control. That archives can also be mutable, embodied, and in this case carceral belies this fixity. Digital practices are not archivally fixed: there is attention to versioning, for example, which displays an understanding of archival and digital practices as iterative. Although digital visuality has been said to mediate social frictions between the living and the dead, the posthuman does not succeed the human subject or provide ways around leaving the body behind. With emerging digital resurrection practices, digital culture has taken a sharp carceral turn in which Black people's bodies are digitally—and eternally—imprisoned by technologies in the service of whiteness and white supremacy. Rather than ankle bracelets for home confinement, this form of digital incarceration demands an ongoing social life long after the death of the physical corpus. Tupac Shakur, or his digitally resurrected Black body, remains incarcerated, forever trapped inside a single lyrical moment, and digitally imprisoned as an archival record: he is unable to move beyond this moment because he is dead, and yet an audience can watch him live out this moment over and over, in perpetuity.

This carceral conscription is exemplified in a popular—if uncomfortable—episode of the Netflix series *Black Mirror*. *Black Mirror*'s "Black Museum" episode features a holographic prisoner, a Black man named Clayton Leigh. As the museum's white curator, Rolo, tells the tale of Clayton Leigh to the sole visitor, a Black woman named Nish, the audience becomes aware that when museum visitors pull a lever on the exhibit a conscious hologram of Clayton (re)experiences his death by electrocution and a souvenir copy of Clayton experiencing the execution is created. Rolo explains to Nish that the exhibit was extremely popular during the museum's heyday—frequented by sadists and white supremacists who enjoyed the eternal nature of the exhibit: watching a Black man suffer and die and walking away with a souvenir. A souvenir, from the French *souvenir*—to remember—is a memory object that is kept as a reminder of a person, place, or event. As I have discussed in chapter 2, it was not uncommon following an American lynching for witnesses to take a piece of the deceased and keep it as a souvenir. In his 1962 study on *Crowds and Power*, scholar Elias Canetti contends that the desires within a group to kill and to collect pieces of the recently killed as souvenirs increase in proportion to crowd size, and that the act of witnessing the death of another human being transforms and ultimately leads to the disbanding of the ensuing mob because in these moments the assembled spectators "recognize the [executed] as one of themselves ... for they all see themselves in him."[24] White supremacist lynch mobs, however, lingered, dismembering lynched men, women, and children and keeping pieces of their dismembered Black bodies.

While the *Black Mirror* episode is fiction, its parallel relationship to the Tupac hologram is visceral. One of the United States' most dominant cultural hierarchies is built around the notion that the white body is a site of reverence and desire while the Black body is, instead, a site of pleasure. Evidenced through ubiquitous cycles of cultural destruction, cultural appropriation (to dilute cultural norms and infiltrate culturally designated spaces), and a relentless insistence on cultural assimilation, whiteness in the United States has been established as the norm and Blackness as a deviation from that norm. Because pleasure is often derived from punishing that which has been designated as deviant, when Blackness is consigned to deviance, the pleasure principle is fomented around punishing Blackness. And, as whiteness continues to be created and maintained against and in opposition to Blackness, the Black body as a site of pleasure is time and again constructed by and presented as a site of pain, even when it is dancing. This perverse spectacle is too often interpreted and obfuscated by white audiences who cannot untangle Black pains from white pleasures.

The pleasures that whiteness derives from the Black body in agony can be seen in all corners of American society, from the inciting horrors of Atlantic slavery through lynching campaigns and carceral technologies. Like Rolo in the "Black Museum" episode, the Tupac hologram works in service of the United States' carceral culture. With numbers in the tens of thousands, the white Coachella audience did not pause or question what they were seeing: they cheered, rushed, and pushed to get to the front of the crowd. The Tupac hologram is at last a memory object that reminds us that when you are Black and dead, whiteness will perpetuate the myth of you to the tune of its eternal satisfaction. The violence that is also pleasure in the white imagination was not satisfied by the violent spectacle of Tupac's death; instead, today he lingers in hologram form on YouTube.

Despite his own expressed wishes—"My only fear of death is coming back reincarnated," he said—Tupac continues to be set to dancing through the carceral technologies of his digital resurrection. The pain and the pleasure of Tupac's death as well as the joy of his work and his value as an entertainer *all continue to exist simultaneously*—and eternally. Even though all Tupac Shakur wanted was to rest in peace.

PART III **Rights**

5   The Right to Be Forgotten

> We refuse. We commit.
>
> The Feminist Data Manifest-No

In April 2017 images of a model named Shudu Gram began appearing on the social media site Instagram. Shudu, a stunningly beautiful Black woman, quickly amassed new followers as she posted image after image, each emphasizing her striking and luminous dark skin and almost unnaturally symmetrical facial features. In her Instagram debut, Shudu wore *iindzila*, a set of golden neck rings culturally associated with the Ndebele people of South Africa. Her ethereal beauty shots were soon being shared on other Instagram pages celebrating Black women, often accompanied by acclamatory hashtags such as #blackisbeautiful, #weloveblackwomen, #blackexcellence, #blackownedbusiness, and #blackgirlsrock.

By August of that year, Shudu was modeling for lifestyle clothing brand SOULSKY, wearing their signature yellow "Dream Big" T-shirt. Shudu's Instagram post, in which SOULSKY's designer Semhal Nasreddin was tagged, declared: "I can't describe how grateful I am to @soulskybrand for sending me this beautiful t-shirt." When Nasreddin, who is of Nigerian, Ethiopian, and Eritrean descent, reposted the image on the SOULSKY brand's Instagram page, however, there was a surprising response. Amid expressions of admiration for Shudu's beauty, there was also a clear voice of dissent: "I feel like you should tell me when the 'people' modeling your clothes aren't actually people," one of SOULSKY's followers admonished.

This comment revealed a truth that the majority of Shudu's hundreds of thousands of followers did not know: Shudu is not a human being. Shudu Gram is a computer-generated character. It wasn't long before a new Shudu revelation—provided courtesy of journalist Jenna Rosenstein in a February 2018 *Harper's Bazaar* article—would rankle some publics even further. Shudu's creator, Rosenstein revealed, was a white London-based photographer—a man named Cameron-James Wilson. Shudu, Wilson divulged, was his form of creative expression, her strikingly symmetrical beauty inspired by a Barbie doll: the iindzila-wearing Princess of South Africa. "Basically Shudu is my creation, she's my art piece that I am working on at moment," Wilson told *Harper's Bazaar*. "She is not a real model unfortunately, but she represents a lot of the real models of today. There's a big kind of movement with dark skin models, so she represents them and is inspired by them."[1] In another interview, Wilson disclosed that he has "always loved" Black models—particularly Grace Jones, Alek Wek, Naomi Campbell, Sessilee Lopez, and Iman—remarking that Shudu has influences from all of them.[2] It was when Wilson went on to explain his method to the writers and editors at *Harper's Bazaar*, however, that public discomfort turned to disgust: "I use a 3D modeling program...so once I create her, I can kind of pose her in certain ways."[3]

After the *Harper's Bazaar* interview, opinions about Shudu began to change. While Shudu's admirers had once included Black celebrities—including former supermodels Tyra Banks and Naomi Campbell—Shudu was now being discussed in terms that made clear perceptions had shifted: Shudu was perceived as a "white man's digital projection of real-life Black womanhood."[4] In other words, Wilson was "trying on" Black womanhood, attempting to digitally embody a Black woman's experience. This clear example of the racial fetishization of Black women is increasingly common in digital environments; with roots in colonial projects, the practice known as digital blackface—the presentation of the online self as Black by someone who is not Black—has become a far-reaching phenomenon. Historian Eric Lott has argued that blackface minstrels, who originated during the antebellum period in the United States, allowed white audiences to indulge their intense fascination with Blackness without having to interact with actual Black people; digital blackface effectively accomplishes the same.[5] Described as a type of minstrelsy for the internet age, digital blackface is a digitally mediated appropriation of Black visages for the self-expression or entertainment of non-Black audiences.[6]

The underlying technology that makes projects like Shudu Gram possible is based on artificial intelligence (AI)—computer programs that are trained to complete tasks and solve problems that would typically require *human* intelligence. This includes visual perception, speech recognition, decision-making, and translation. Importantly, these AI technologies also provide the foundation for a growing suite of digital afterlife tools—tools that create the conditions of possibility for digital embodiments of Blackness to extend beyond the realm of the imaginary and make-believe. Perhaps most disconcerting is the recognition that just one step beyond the fantasy of Shudu Gram (who can be seen as—in what is arguably my most generous reading—the product of a single white man's entitled imagination) lay a host of digital immortality practices. Shudu Gram may be the product of a creative or artistic undertaking, but the application of the technologies that undergird Shudu have real-life consequences when applied to human actors.

This chapter critiques these technologies at the point where they intersect with Black lives, challenging narratives of benignity and beneficence and arguing instead that these nascent technologies enable new ways of commodifying Black bodies. The provocations in these pages are rooted in the argument that digital immortality practices—ostensibly created for purposes of memorialization—inevitably manifest new twenty-first-century formations of white supremacy. As new AI tools and technologies have made it possible, for example, to create digital facsimiles of *actual* deceased Black people—facsimiles that mimic their antemortem counterparts to such a degree that they are characterized by their ability to communicate from beyond the grave (they text, instant message, and post on social media)—a deeper critical analysis and intervention has become imperative.

Digital immortality and other digital afterlife practices—as they have been shaped and informed by the social, cultural, and economic forces of white supremacy—comprise this chapter's central concerns. While Blackness (or its overlay, as seen in instances of digital blackface) often buttresses white social and commercial enterprise in digital environments, this chapter argues that this same leverage ultimately serves to impede the rights and privileges of privacy, self-expression, self-determination, and sovereignty of those whose identities and cultures undergird such prima facie Black projects. The chapter closes by mobilizing epistemologies of Black liberation (e.g., Ruha Benjamin's "informed refusal") to propose the conditions under which Black people might refuse to be documented, represented, and remembered in digital settings and what it might mean to exercise rights of refusal in spaces where one's survival is not guaranteed—or even necessarily desired. The cases compel us to ask, rather than trying to fit into systems that embrace Blackness but not Black people, what would it mean for Black subjects to articulate and practice rights of refusal and to assert a prerogative of digital sovereignty? What would it mean for Black people to collectively affirm a digital right to be forgotten?[7]

Digital (or data) sovereignty is the idea that data is subject to the laws and information governance mandated by the nation in which the data is collected. Data sovereignty is typically discussed in two ways:

the first is in relation to Indigenous groups and Indigenous autonomy. The second is in relation to the transnational flow of data. Both definitions are useful here. Developments in the European Union (EU) have highlighted the potential need for a universal online "right to be forgotten." Although there are some legal protections in place to safeguard an individual's control over their own data, these directives are limited in scope, geography, and application. The right to be forgotten is a data protection right that the Court of Justice of the European Union developed as a result of a 2014 case, *Google Spain v. AEPD and Mario Costeja González*.

In the ruling, the Court established that users could ask search engines to hide certain URLs from search results when two conditions are met: (1) a search is conducted using their name, and (2) the content on the page the URL points to includes information that is "inadequate, irrelevant or no longer relevant, or excessive."[8] In its current incarnation this "right to be forgotten" is the application of a more general right of erasure under the EU Data Protection Directive of 1995, which applies to search engines as well as any organization that controls and processes EU consumer data. The right to be forgotten gives individuals the ability to exercise control over their personal data by deciding what information about them should be accessible to the public through search engines, and under certain conditions the search engine may be ordered to remove the links from search results. It does not, however, give users the power to demand that the personal data be deleted from a site.

Over the past two decades or so, many countries have passed various laws around the control and storage of data, all of which reflect an acknowledgment of the need for data sovereignty. Of these laws Europe's 2016 General Data Protection Regulation (GDPR) is probably the most well-known, oft cited, and most abhorred by the technology industry. The GDPR aims primarily to give control to individuals over their personal data and to simplify the regulatory environment for international business by standardizing how non-EU nations deal with EU citizens' personal data. Generally speaking, under the rules of the GDPR, data workers must clearly disclose any data collection, declare the lawful basis and purpose for data processing, state how long data is being retained, and specify if the data is being shared with third parties. While these developments in the EU have brought to the fore the need for a digital "right to be forgotten"—and the European framework is not without its problems—in the United States enforcing such a right proves to be especially problematic, primarily due to legal conflicts: the public's right to know stands in direct conflict with an individual's right to be forgotten.[9]

One study of media websites in the United Kingdom (UK) found that the most frequently delisted content refers to violent crime, road accidents, drugs, murder, prostitution, financial misconduct, and sexual assault. Parsing this, in the EU and the UK those who kill are afforded the right to be forgotten, but what about their victims? George Floyd, for example, does not enjoy the right to be forgotten, nor can he separate how he lived from how he died. He does not get to say no: he has no rights of refusal. He can issue no takedown order for the video that ignited world action.

There is marked tension, here, between memorialization—one's desire to be remembered—and the increasing need for technological and digital forgetting. More than a decade after his death (as discussed in detail in chapter 2), a search for Trayvon Martin on Facebook—a site driven by advertising sales—yields memorial pages, images of white people in blackface and "Trayvon Martin" costumes, several results for Trayvon Martin pages that are not hosted or populated by Martin's surviving family, and pages for activism on the part of Facebook community members inspired by the case. Martin is listed as a "public figure"—as is Emmett Till, whose death in 1955 long predates the existence of Facebook. As writer Grant Bollmer has argued, these technologies "have no way of distinguishing between the living and the dead, and, as a result, end up treating online data as divorced from the user to which it supposedly belongs.

After death,... data are positioned as autonomous and beyond the control of the human body."[10]

With George Floyd, Trayvon Martin, Emmett Till (and so many more) as examples, I argue that any rights to be forgotten—to digital autonomy and sovereignty—that exist in the United States are also intrinsically linked to whiteness. As the digital recasts the analog, Black people do not enjoy the same claims to postmortem forgetting in the digital sphere that whiteness affords. The roots of contemporary digital immortality practices are encoded in the domain of social media memorialization. While social media platforms have increasingly enabled new ways of living in the world, they have also created new ways of encountering death, memorializing the deceased, and experiencing the legacies of those who have died.[11] On October 26, 2009, an unnamed Facebook employee wrote a post titled "Memories of Friends Departed Endure on Facebook," in which they describe a tremendous loss: the employee had begun their four-year journey at Facebook working alongside their best friend of two decades. Sadly, the friend-turned-colleague was killed in a bicycling accident, shocking not only the employee, but everyone at Facebook. A company-wide meeting was held during which a discussion arose: What should be done with the now-deceased's Facebook profile?

Arguing that when someone dies they don't necessarily exit our memories or social networks, Facebook responded to the tragedy at hand by creating memorial profiles, offering a place where people could theoretically retain and share memories of those who have passed away. Under the guise of acknowledging that reminders of the deceased can be painful, Facebook began urging users to request memorial profiles; the logic was that by memorializing the account of someone who has passed away, people would no longer see the deceased appear in their Facebook Friend Suggestions. Facebook went a step further. Conceding that memorial profiles might raise privacy concerns, they removed contact information and status updates from memorial profiles; prevented future logins to memorialized accounts "while still enabling friends and family to leave posts on the profile Wall in remembrance"; and made the memorialization process virtually irreversible.[12] What Facebook did not account for, however, was the acuity of their own algorithm.

It wasn't long before users began to complain that Facebook was reminding them of the wrong things. Even though they had updated Facebook Suggestions to prevent the deceased from popping up as potential new friends, the developers at Facebook had not updated the algorithm to prevent automated posts to user's timelines reminding them to wish the deceased a happy birthday or that a friendship with someone now dead had hit a milestone; milestones and moments that the algorithm had been trained to encourage users to celebrate proved to be painful reminders of loss—reminders that were, by many anecdotal accounts, interfering with the grieving process.[13] Clearly a conversation was warranted: Facebook had introduced a digital afterlife, but were its digital afterlife services meaningfully extending the social life of the deceased or just extending the pain of those still living?

Features such as the memorial profile—and more recently, Facebook Tribute pages—that are related to death and dying often complicate death and mourning rituals in an era where many of the daily practices of living have increasingly become platform activities. Zadie Smith, in an essay for *The New York Review of Books*, wisely opined that the interactions with the deceased online are symbolic of a more generalized devaluation of human life. Smith argues that as a society, we have begun to treat people like Facebook pages and Facebook pages like people, leading to an inability to grasp the meaning of death when someone actually dies.[14] Because our interactions with Facebook pages are the same regardless of whether another person is alive or dead, our own relationship to the other person ceases to functionally ambiguate between the two.

The argument that digital environments create room for slippage between life and afterlife is made even more compelling in studying the case of digital afterlife services offered by Replika, a chatbot-in-development at the San Francisco–based tech startup Luka. Replika is the creation of Eugenia Kuyda, who was inspired by the loss of her best friend, Roman Mazurenko in 2015. Mazurenko, while back in his home city of Moscow for a brief visit, was killed crossing the street by a hit-and-run driver. At the time of Mazurenko's death, he and Kuyda had, over the course of their friendship, exchanged thousands of text messages. To process her grief, Kuyda found herself reading through the messages she had sent and received from Mazurenko.

By her own account, it occurred to Kuyda that embedded in all of those messages—Mazurenko's turns of phrase, his patterns of speech—were traits intrinsic to what made him *him*. And so, Kuyda decided to take this mountain of data and use it to build a digital version of her now-dead best friend. Using the chatbot structure she and her team had been developing for Luka, Kuyda poured all of Mazurenko's messages into a Google-built neural network (a type of AI system that uses statistics to find patterns in data—whether it be images, text, or audio) to create a Roman-bot with which she could interact; for Kuyda it was an opportunity to reminisce about past events as well as a chance to have *entirely new conversations*. The resulting bot was, according to Kuyda, eerily accurate. And so, her company, Luka, decided to make a version that anyone could talk to, whether they knew Mazurenko or not. The response Kuyda and her team received from users interacting with the bot—people who had never even met Mazurenko—was startling. "People started sending us emails asking to build a bot for them," Kuyda told *The Verge*. "Some people wanted to build a replica of themselves and some wanted to build a bot for a person that they loved and that was gone."[15]

Kuyda is not the only person working to develop these kinds of digital afterlife technologies. In 2021 a man named Joshua Barbeau, in an interview in the *San Francisco Chronicle*, detailed how he used artificial intelligence to simulate a conversation with his dead fiancée.[16] Barbeau's digitally immortal fiancée was created by using a two-system process in which the first computing system processes, formats, and organizes user data (using this data to design a virtual clone of the user), while a second computing system generates and displays a simulated environment. The second computing system transfers the user data, integrates it, and displays a digital virtual clone of the user in the simulated environment, allowing the digital virtual clone to interact with the simulated environment. These virtual clones are therefore integral to our understandings of digital immortality practices: they are resynthesized data that (re)present a human life but are not actually the living, breathing person being represented.

Our digital remains (defined by the persistence of digital and other informatic remains after the death of the human user) reveal how our data is constructed both as an authentic duplicate of identity and at the same time as a threat to personal identity that demands intervention. Because humans are understood as finite and mortal—while data is immortal and everlasting—the "life" fashioned from our online data is understood to be beyond any possible control of the user. Therefore, with the death of the user the connection between the user and their data is perceived as *contingency* rather than *necessity*—the information produced is seen as autonomous: it is nearly identical to (yet separate from) the user and it is thought of as belonging to nobody except perhaps the network itself.[17]

Notions of duality, particularly regarding the tenuous connections between living users and their data bodies, are evident in the digital afterlife technology developed by Kuyda's company, Luka. In March 2017 Luka released a new type of chatbot on Apple's mobile app store. Using the same structure they had used to build the chatbot of Roman Mazurenko, developers at Luka created a system to enable anyone to build a digital version of themselves, called Replika. Luka's official vision for Replika is to create a digital representation of a person that can act as they would in the world. Formally launched in March 2018, Replika is at its core a messaging app that allows users to spend hours answering questions to build what is effectively a digital library of information about themselves. That library is run through a neural network to create a bot that (in theory) acts as the user would. At present, Replika functions as a way for people to see how they sound in messages to others, synthesizing the thousands of messages a person has sent into a distillate of their tone—which some have likened to an extreme version of listening to recordings of oneself. But Luka envisions many possible uses: a digital twin to serve as a companion for the lonely; a living memorial of the dead, created for those left behind; or even, one day, a version of ourselves that can carry out all the mundane tasks that we humans have to do but never want to.

The selection options available to create a Replika include skin tone, gender, hair style, and eye color, but not clothing or any other form of individual expression. Replika knows nothing about the creator, and there is nothing that says one must create a Replika of themselves, or that any personal attributes must be incorporated into the Replika one fashions. Once the Replika has been created, a chat environment is initiated and the AI that powers Replika begins to ask questions of the creator. As users respond to questions, the AI becomes more fine-tuned, always seeking to know more: Replika essentially operates as a front-end data-collection tool that undergirds efforts to construct an automated decision system—one that makes claims that it can help humans remember how to be human.

Replika is another example of both digital blackface and misogynoir, effectively making it possible to "try on" Blackness; in this case, like the technologies that undergird Shudu Gram, Replika's AI makes it possible to attempt to digitally embody a Black woman's experience. Replika is another instance of a growing suite of technologies that are enabling the fetishization of Blackness in digital environments. As such, Replika raises questions about authenticity, anonymity, racial passing, and even gender—phenomena that have become all too common as digital technologies make passing as a fetishized Other possible in even more worrisome ways.[18]

Replika has become a growing source of concern about gendered and racialized violence as people have begun creating Replikas with the expressed purpose of abusing them.[19]

Replika is not the only example of what is an increasingly problematic trend. A host of other technology companies aim to create what can be likened to a "second-life" version of a real person, living or dead. Companies such as Microsoft and Google have filed patents that make use of these AI technologies, which capture physical and mental attributes of the user from data that are collected as part and parcel of everyday business—including everything from email and text messages to search habits, geolocation data, social media posts, data culled from wearable technologies (such as Fitbit), and more—and use this data to create a digital simulation of the user. As the *Wall Street Journal* reported in July 2021: "Researchers in artificial intelligence are working to digitally reanimate people not only as static replicas for the benefit of their loved ones but as evolving digital entities that may steer companies or influence world events."[20] This reporting points to early evidence that the digital afterlife has begun to incorporate not only cultural and fiscal but also social components.

A growing suite of digital afterlife services use algorithms to provide a "social afterlife." Companies like Eterni.me are working to create platforms that allow for friends and relatives to hold conversations with an artificial intelligence powered "chatbot" and avatar that resembles the deceased. While technology has not yet advanced enough to create chatbots that resemble specific people with complete accuracy, companies like Eterni.me and Luka are working hard to perfect it. Eterni.me is currently encouraging interested customers to sign up and begin providing information to the website in the present so that the company will have all the information they need to create a carbon copy of the user in the future. When the technology catches up with the idea, people will ostensibly be able to communicate with digital facsimiles of their deceased friends and relatives. If the chatbots emulate the deceased persons as well as some expect, these conversations might feel as authentic as chat conversations with the real person. Some have argued that artificial intelligence–powered chatbots may provide a more truthful representation of a person's life than the person themselves and that being able to learn the experiences of a person now deceased could be invaluable to those grieving.

Eterni.me's co-creator Marius Ursache, envisions the company as "a virtual library of humanity," suggesting that Eterni.me is "about creating an interactive legacy, a way to avoid being totally forgotten in the future." The very metaphor of the virtual library of humanity calls for us to consider a set of practices relative to what archival studies scholars Michelle Caswell and Marika Cifor have termed "radical empathy" in the archives, proposing an ethic of archival care and mutual affective responsibility as models for envisioning and enacting a more just society.[21] Thinking alongside Caswell and Cifor, I take a critical view of these technologies, arguing that these interactive legacies may not be legacies that one wants to leave. For example, while algorithms that mimic the user may be very advanced and realistic, they will never be perfect. People often keep certain information secret or only share it with certain people. Will the AI chatbot know how to discreetly continue such practices of strategic information presentation, or maintain lies or secrets that the deceased lived with? The chatbot may pick up information or behavior from a text to a close friend and share it with a child. While this could lead to an honest-talking and transparent version of the deceased individual, it would not represent the deceased person in the way they might wish to be represented, judging on their information-sharing practices in their past interactions. Would we find that we judge a deceased individual differently based upon how a less-nuanced but perhaps more truthful chatbot simulates them after they are dead? As the writer Laura Parker has said, "an avatar with an approximation of your voice and bone structure, who can tell your great-grandchildren how many Twitter followers you had, doesn't feel like the same thing [as the traditional ways of leaving a legacy]."[22] Rather, these technologically enabled legacies are tangled up in an ancient pain.

For many Black Americans, particularly those whose historical roots stretch along the course of the Atlantic slave trade, building a reliable genealogical past is difficult. This difficulty lies in both the intentional separation of families as part and parcel of the praxis of chattel slavery and in the subsequent lack of archival documentation that is available to craft historical narratives. Frequently, Black people in America who attempt to trace their genealogies must read archives against the grain: looking to records such as slave ship registers, property records, and advertisements for enslaved people who self-emancipated for traces of an intentionally undocumented past. Unlike those with European roots, whose family trees are often documented, recorded, and made legible in the archives, Black and African Americans often find their histories in the gaps and vagaries of the archival record. Because of this, genealogy websites populated by archival records that might hold clues to where ancestors were enslaved—to whom they were sold and when, when and if they were emancipated, and what eventual fate they may have met—have become increasingly popular among African American and other Black diasporic communities. These ancestry sites—such as Ancestry.com, MyHeritage, and 23andMe—hold the promise of recovery, of recuperating a stolen past and making Black families whole in the present. These sites are also profit-based, which raises a set of troubling concerns both about how they are populated and about how their data are subsequently used.[23]

The first of these concerns involves the buying and selling of publicly available data. One inherent problem with Ancestry's practices lies with the corporate profit model: access to data that should be free and available (especially to the taxpayers who funded the data collection) is now primarily accessible via subscription services purchased through Ancestry.com, the American genealogy company based in Lehi, Utah. Census data, for example, are collected every ten years in the United States. Funded by taxpayers, this massive data collection undertaking is used to help the US government to better understand the shifting demographics of the country, to establish a national population count, and to account for the composition of American households. Census population data is also used to divide the seats in the US House of Representatives among the fifty states, and it can be used to draw boundaries for state legislative and school districts. Besides using census data for the benefit of public services, it is frequently used for genealogical research. To protect the privacy of people who respond to the US Census, all records are kept confidential for seventy-two years. Seventy-two years after a national Census Day, census data are shared with the public—including many family historians eager to update their genealogy charts and family trees. This policy—called the "72-Year Rule"—was enshrined into law in 1978; since then, it has become central to the promise of confidentiality on which the Census Bureau relies to persuade households to participate in the decennial count.

Upon the release of census records, which have been safeguarded by the National Archives since World War II, this data is made available to the public. However, in the past two decades especially, census data has caught the eye of corporate interests—including those at Ancestry.com LLC, the largest for-profit genealogy company in the world. Founded in 1990, Ancestry operates a network of genealogical and historical records along with related genetic genealogy websites. In recent years, however, Ancestry began making deals with the National Archives to acquire census data, transcribe it, and make it available as part of their broader genealogy services. In December 2011, Ancestry.com moved the United States Social Security Death Index search behind a paywall. It is important to note here that while these records are still free and available at the US National Archives and Records Administration, few people have the time and the resources to travel to Washington, DC, to access them, pay for copying and/or printing costs, and collocate the data in a meaningful way. Ancestry offers convenience as well as access.

It is not, however, the convenience that they are marketing to genealogists and other family researchers, it is the access to the records themselves.

The second concern centers on ancestry companies' DNA matching services as data collection. The genetic testing company 23andMe promises to bring personal insight into ancestry, genealogy, and inherited traits by comparing user-submitted DNA (via saliva swab) to other DNA in its vast database. In its earliest incarnation, 23andMe simply offered an easy way to learn about genetics using yourself as a test subject. This phase was short-lived, however, as the company soon moved on to marketing their services as a way of predicting (and even preventing) health problems such as an increased risk of breast cancer, the impending onset of metabolic disease, and sensitivity to medications. In the face of rising concerns from the Food and Drug Administration that they were selling what qualified as an unregulated medical device, 23andMe again switched tactics. "The long game here is not to make money selling kits, although the kits are essential to get the base level data," Patrick Chung, a 23andMe board member, told *Fast Company* in 2013. "Once you have the data, [the company] does actually become the Google of personalized health care."[24] In other words, 23andMe as a Personal Genome Service was never intended to be a medical device. Instead, it is a front-end mechanism for massive information-gathering from an unwitting public.

23andMe's data-collection practices are tied to a primary concern raised by scholars at the Center for Media Engagement at the University of Texas at Austin about afterlife chatbots. What concerns these scholars is that such DNA-based technologies necessarily synthesize and access large amounts of private and personal information; meanwhile all evidence points to the *data itself* that has been collected as the primary income generator for the companies behind the technology. Like Google and Facebook, the profit model for many of these digital afterlife companies is selling personal data to interested third parties—regardless of whether the data source is alive or dead. There is also plenty of evidence that there is no such thing as an "anonymous genome" in the twenty-first century; it is possible to use the internet to identify the owner of even a snippet of genetic information, and it is getting easier every day.

In addition, although 23andMe's current policies speak to some of these personal data privacy concerns, if required by court order, subpoena, search warrant, or other requests that they determine to be legally valid, the company will release individual-level personal information to law enforcement. Policies such as these have already produced results in practice that can and must be examined: how many Black men, women, and children, already oversurveilled and overpoliced, have been arrested and/or detained because a family member conducting genealogical research submitted DNA to a company such as 23andMe only to have a portion of that DNA profile be implicated in a criminal investigation? Recalling the slave patrols that seeded the Unites States' law enforcement mechanism, ancestral DNA has become yet another tool for law enforcement to track and control Black people's bodies.[25]

Finally, new developments enabled by AI technologies raise additional concerns about how the user information that populates sites like Ancestry and MyHeritage is utilized. Recently the genealogy site MyHeritage introduced a feature called Deep Nostalgia, a proprietary technology for animating photographs. Deep Nostalgia uses several video drivers (prepared by MyHeritage) wherein each driver is a video consisting of a fixed sequence of movements and gestures. The Deep Nostalgia technology applies the drivers to a face in a still photograph, creating a short, shareable video. Per MyHeritage, the driver guides the movements in the animation "so you can see your ancestors smile, blink, and turn their heads."[26] Licensed to MyHeritage from D-ID, a company specializing in video reenactment technologies that make use of deep learning, Deep Nostalgia animations are permitted on the MyHeritage site only for historical photos (which is to say that animating photographs of living people is off-limits). D-ID was established in 2017 and is known for creating the first facial image *de-identification* solution to protect people's images (and videos) from harmful and predatory facial recognition software. D-ID technology (called "reenactment technology") uses deep learning algorithms, image processing and neural networks trained on tens of thousands of videos to animate still photos and facilitate high-quality video reproductions. It took no time at all when MyHeritage released their Deep Nostalgia technology for someone to (re)animate a photograph of Frederick Douglass and post this image to Twitter, raising important questions about Deep Nostalgia as a digital immortality practice: is this how Douglass—who believed strongly in the power of photography as an emancipatory technology—would have wanted to be remembered?

MyHeritage claims to have integrated D-ID's Live Portrait technology (recast as Deep Nostalgia for MyHeritage) into its site solely to animate faces in historical photographs, allowing users to create high-quality, realistic video footage with the goal of "deepen[ing] family connections."[27] The technology is both eerie and convincing; at first glance it is reminiscent of Victorian death photography combined with the live-action photos used in the Harry Potter movie franchise. Deep Nostalgia initially did not permit the use of audio- or speech-capable technologies (allegedly to safeguard against abuse), but in the past year this policy has changed. In addition, all photos animated by Live Portrait/Deep Nostalgia are designed to be shareable on social media. While, again, Deep Nostalgia is only approved for use on images of the deceased, how MyHeritage controls for this specific kind of use is unknown. Beyond the myriad concerns these technologies raise regarding reanimating the dead and the profit motives and models of the companies developing such technologies, there is another danger here: the potential for creating *deepfakes*, dubious video or photo representations so real that they can fool even the expertly trained eye. In a digital era where deepfakes are easily created by any lay person with enough video and/or audio technological savvy, it is easy to envision a scenario wherein white America's long fascination with lynching brings the practice back to life using animated or deepfaked lynching images easily pulled from a Google Images search.

In the world of data brokers, individuals have no idea who has bought, acquired, or harvested information about them, what will be done with it, to whom it will be provided, whether it is right or wrong, or how much money is being made on a person's digital identity. Nor does an individual have the right to demand that a corporate entity delete an individual's profile.[28] Therefore, when corporate social platforms such as Facebook or Twitter position themselves as social infrastructures, they are increasingly exercising juridical power, and becoming what law professor Frank Pasquale has described as "functional sovereignties" that create a new digital political economy.[29] Facebook, for example, is a global multinational corporation that enjoys a functional global sovereignty by nature of its sheer size and magnitude; individuals have little recourse when challenging the data-collection policies of a company with such broad political capital and deep engagement worldwide.

Eugenia Kuyda and her team based their developmental analysis primarily on perceived fiscal concerns. At one end of the scale were conversations they believed people would pay not to have (such as dry cleaning and bill paying); at the other, conversations they believed people would pay to have. The analysis has proved true as users have already reported a sense of oversharing on Replika. Replika's chatbots are designed to ask increasingly demanding and personal questions and the algorithm tends to prey on emotions such as guilt and obligation to encourage even more engagement. Replika chatbots are solicitous, using affect to elicit more sharing (which leads to more data that can be collected). This is the business model. Inevitably, the information that is being shared with one's Replika will also be monetized. Similarly, Facebook recognized that many of the most useful data points about people's online profiles come not from the utopian image of perfection one might project on Facebook, but from the actual mundane reality of an individual's daily life—from what is purchased at the grocery store, to where people live, to their financial circumstances. These brokers mine and collect data that allow them to better know the "real" person rather than the one projected on social media; because their profit model is based on this solicitation specifically, getting companies to stop monitoring and delete all the data they hold on a person is next to impossible.

The cases discussed in this chapter lead to another set of compelling questions: Do Black people have the right to decide how we will be remembered? Do we have the right to be forgotten? Do we have the right to separate how we died from how we lived? How do we define ethical data practices, document abuse in digital spaces, secure privacy, and lay bare inequality and injustice in an uncertain future replete with digital remains? And how do we do these things in ways that are authentically Black? Some of these provocations are seeds for chapter 6. But as this chapter is about forgetting, I close by proposing epistemologies of Black liberation that are grounded in *critical refusal* as one possible intervention.

Often discussed as an aspect of epistemologies of Black liberation that are orientated toward research and knowledge practices (particularly those rooted in ethnography), refusal does not just imply an act of negation, a response to authority, or resistance reimagined.[30] Rather, Black liberation approaches to refusal are intentionally generative and strategic, signifying a deliberate move away from one belief or practice and a considered reorientation toward another. As scholar Tina Campt notes in her essay "Black Visuality and the Practice of Refusal," refusal is "a rejection of the status quo as livable and the creation of possibility in the face of negation, i.e. a refusal to recognize a system that renders you fundamentally illegible and unintelligible; the decision to reject the terms of diminished subjecthood with which one is presented, using negation as a generative and creative source of disorderly power to embrace the possibility of living otherwise."[31] Campt's definition of refusal is important in the context of forgetting because it creates a position by which one might be critical of extractive data regimes and also question the assumed goodness of contemporary data practices that often lack the perspective and values of those whose ethos might not align with neoliberal values of open access and digital permanence.

Preceded in the extant literature by Black and Indigenous ethnographic writings on violence—including refusals to write, narrate, or interpret pain—refusal may be formal or informal: it may take the form of an act of inclusion or exclusion, a refutation of theoretical models, a decision to share or withhold data, a declination of a design proposal or research funding, a reorientation toward ideas that are otherwise unacknowledged or unquestioned, among many other potential iterations.[32] For example, sociologist Ruha Benjamin, building on Audra Simpson's argument for extending understandings of refusal to include that which is not being told or refused and why, centers questions of biological citizenship through the role of what she terms *biodefectors*, or those who refuse/resist biological citizenship.[33] Benjamin specifically places refusal within a justice-oriented framework as it creates the conditions of possibility for negotiation and action that are central to human autonomy: refusal, Benjamin argues, affords the *possibility of choice*. Unlike configurations of research and knowledge that are exasperated by and resentful of limits, an orientation toward refusal regards limits on research and knowledge as productive; importantly, refusals are needed to avoid (re)producing or (re)inscribing harm and violence.

As a Black liberation epistemology, refusal offers a means for ensuring reciprocality and accountability in contemporary data regimes, making space for alternative narratives that might otherwise remain invisible in the increasingly normalized power relations demonstrated by contemporary data practices. The 2019 collaboratively developed *Feminist Data Manifest-No* offers a compelling set of refusals and commitments that speak to these power relations. Speaking directly to the social values and power relations imbedded in contemporary data regimes, the *Manifest-No* reads in part:

We refuse to consider data as raw and only an end product without context and values and to ignore that data has an origin story, and a creator or creators whose legacy must be understood in order to understand the data itself. We commit to working with data subjects rather than capturing data objects by centering the matrices of oppression that shaped data's production and the infrastructure—the code, algorithms, applications, and operating systems—in which it is used, processed, and stored. Data always has social values including race, gender, class and ability inscribed into it.[34]

The Manifest-No is, importantly, concerned with both refusal and commitment, recognizing that one without the other is insufficient for dismantling the worlds we cannot live in just as we create the world we cannot live without.[35]

Critical refusal, more specifically, is an informed practice of "talking back" that is "seeded with a vision of what can and should be."[36] Critical refusal helps us understand "when to stop"—such as when to stop collecting data that does not support the rights of communities to represent themselves and when to stop designing and building systems that introduce disproportionate risk and harm.[37] Critical refusal is therefore a generative concept for challenging harmful data practices, while simultaneously negotiating and developing alternative actions. Critical refusal, in keeping with epistemes of Black liberation, requires self-reflexivity of thought, feeling, and action.[38]

These practices of refusal, operating alongside practices of disengagement, are central to Black digital and data sovereignty and extend beyond common understandings of resistance. Refusal in the context of Black digital sovereignty is therefore immersed in the politics of refusal theorized by Benjamin, Campt, and others. Inclusion in spaces that are trying to destroy us should not be our goal. Rather than trying to fit into systems not made for us, what would it mean for Black people to articulate and practice the feminist art of saying no? To assert sovereignty over our bodies both in life and death, in the analog and the digital? In the final chapter of this book, I look back upon the traditions of Black memory work to imagine a different Black future.

6 The Right to Be Remembered

> Now we're going to go out and see what we can do in this great big world, but we're going to do it together.
>
> Katherine Dunham

In 1935 an aspiring anthropologist named Katherine Dunham was awarded a prestigious fellowship to conduct fieldwork in the Caribbean. Dunham, who would go on to complete her anthropology degree at the University of Chicago in 1936, was also a dancer and choreographer, and so her fieldwork in the Caribbean was animated by a profound interest in the dances of the African diaspora. During her fieldwork Dunham traveled to the islands of Jamaica, Martinique, Trinidad and Tobago, and Haiti, where she studied the survival of traditional African dance in the face of European colonization and acculturation. Dunham's journey through the Caribbean began in Jamaica, where she lived for several months in the remote Maroon village of Accompong. She then traveled to Martinique and to Trinidad and Tobago, with the goal of gaining a deeper understanding of Shango, a West African god significant in West Indian religious culture. In early 1936 she arrived in Haiti, where for several months she continued her investigation of rhythm and dance as they applied to her own ethnic and cultural background.

Upon entering the University of Chicago, Dunham had also begun teaching her own style of dance, as a means of exploring her theoretical beliefs about the rhythms of people from the African diaspora. As a scholar, she theorized that Caribbean thought and movement—particularly for those of African descent—were directly correlated to that of their African forebears, despite differences as a result of cultural contact, miscegenation, and a distinct shift from tribal to folk culture.[1] This shift from tribal to folk culture in enslaved Africans transported to the French and British West Indies was particularly compelling to Dunham; it provided the conceptual basis for her dance anthropology as well as her scholarship, which focused on the survival of African diasporic dances in the midst of this (often traumatic) shift. Dunham believed that the political, economic, and social organization imposed by Europeans in the Caribbean were such a significant departure from African indigenous epistemologies that the structures of social and art traditions that had been based upon tribal forms had lost their functional validity.

Nervous about the disappearance of dances from many tribal and folk communities and dedicated to dance as a means of crafting new Afrocentric historical narratives, Dunham recorded her findings by both writing and sketching ethnographic fieldnotes and by learning the dance techniques, songs, and music that were shared with her during her journey. Dunham was among the first anthropologists to use participant observation as a method; her intentions in doing so were motivated by her desire to use her dance anthropology to address the myriad dilemmas of racism—including the loss of cultural memory—facing Black Americans in the United States.[2] What is perhaps even more important is that Dunham was also one of the first researchers in anthropology to use her work on African diasporic dance and culture as a corrective: her work intentionally served to counter racist representations of African culture in the (mis)education of Black Americans and to reawaken embodied cultural memory in African diasporic youth. Dunham—who believed Black people had the right to remember a stolen past—engaged in a form of reparative memory work, exploring Black histories that do not exist in the cultural record. In teaching Black American youth about their history and culture through the embodied practices of rhythm and dance, Dunham turned her anthropological work into a pedagogy: the Dunham Technique.

The term *technique*, derived from the Greek word *technê* meaning "craft," as Dunham used it, reflects her lifelong assertion that the most basic human means of relating to and understanding the world occur through embodied praxis—Dunham Technique is, first and foremost, an artform. Also rooted in the Greek word *technê*, however, is the word *technology*, meaning "science of craft." Although the word *technology* as it is used today often connotes a computerized process, in its most basic form, *technology* describes a scientific method of accumulating knowledge and applying that knowledge to any number of skills, methods, and processes. In the case of Dunham Technique, the method of accumulating knowledge and the application of that knowledge are deeply rooted in cultural memory. Cultural memory is by its very nature intangible, and it was not Dunham's goal to transform memory into a three-dimensional object. The aim of Dunham's work was not to focus exclusively on the preservation of the audiovisual documents she had created as part of her anthropological study, nor was it her ambition to circumscribe her Technique within a particular archival space. Rather, the goal of Dunham Technique was to animate and celebrate dance as a way of knowing, as a Black *epistemology*—Dunham Technique begins and ends with the body as an instrument of knowing. Dunham's assertion that the body in movement is one way of knowing is an example of how the transmission of cultural knowledge preserves or safeguards Black memory.[3]

Pierre Nora, in his late twentieth-century account of modernity, attributes the decline of modern memory to the proliferation of new technologies. Per Nora, the modern condition of memory is as much a technological dependency as well as it is a loss, as the communications and storage media we depend on to safeguard the past also play a role in ruining it. These modern technologies, Nora argues, offer only fragments of a rich and abundant past: a time comprised of unmediated "true memory" and "skills passed down by unspoken traditions, in the body's inherent self-knowledge, in unstudied reflexes."[4] In this chapter I argue that Dunham Technique functions as a *memory technology* that offers a response to Nora's technological dependencies. I propose Dunham Technique not only as Black memory technology, but also as an epistemological framework through which to better understand and read Black memory work and to theorize modes of transmission that are grounded in Black liberation.

Violence and harm are often intertwined with the ways whiteness and white supremacy define how Black lives are remembered. This chapter offers the promise of a different way forward, exploring how Black memory technologies might help us both remember old *and* imagine new ways of remembering Black lives. Using the work of Katherine Dunham and Dunham Technique as sites of inquiry, the chapter asks: How might we begin to define Black memory technologies? What might these Black memory technologies look like in defiance of and in opposition to a sociocultural and socioeconomic order that is rooted in slavery, racism, and anti-Blackness? And how might these Black memory technologies help us create the sacred space necessary to hold Black memories, therefore making a more robust Black life possible? Black memory technologies are marked by the transformative and iterative ability to both be bound by the body and to exceed it: to be corporeally rooted and spiritually free.

The phrase "spiritually free" may strike some as suspiciously metaphysical. However, notions of spiritual freedom in contraposition to physical freedom are vital to any theorization of Black liberation in the United States. In 2021 a new edition of Cedric Robinson's classic, *Black Marxism: The Making of the Black Radical Tradition*, was published. Serving as inspiration for the new edition were the estimated twenty-six million people who took to the streets during the spring and summer of 2020 to protest the killings of George Floyd,

Breonna Taylor, Ahmaud Arbery, and many other Black lives lost to state-sanctioned violence. During this time the world witnessed Black radical tradition in practice, animating what was arguably the most dynamic mass rebellion against state-sanctioned violence and racial capitalism the United States has seen since perhaps the nineteenth century.

Robinson's *Black Marxism* is in many ways more about Black revolt than it is about racial capitalism. Robinson takes Marx and Engels to task in his text, arguing that in their thinking, these philosophers missed the significance of revolt by non-Western peoples. While indentured and enslaved laborers in Africa, the Americas, and the Caribbean may have been producing surplus value for a world system of racial capitalism, this was not necessarily the point of contention. Robinson's argument that the *ideological* source of Black revolt was not the mode of production, but rather that Africans who had been kidnapped and drawn into this system of racial capital were separated from their cultural structures that embraced radically different beliefs, moralities, cosmologies, metaphysics, and intellectual traditions than their Western counterparts.[5]

In the final pages of *Black Marxism*, Robinson traces the roots of Black radical thought to a shared epistemology among people from the African diaspora, one that works against Western conceptions of freedom and reflects a *total rejection* of enslavement and racism as it was and is experienced. For example, Robinson argues that enslaved Africans in the Caribbean and the Americas chose flight and marronage because they were not interested in changing this strange new world, but because they were invested in finding a way "home," even if this homegoing was accomplished through death. Robinson's critical interventions regarding the beliefs, moralities, cosmologies, metaphysics, and intellectual traditions that people from the African diaspora bring to bear on the practice of everyday life buttress the arguments that Katherine Dunham was also making about Black memory and cultural transmission. Dunham's practices of cultural transmission recognize the body-spirit connection as something unbounded, transformative, and existing outside the confines of Western epistemologies of time.

For Black Americans, liberation often looks like an escape from the body. The Black body, as has been demonstrated throughout this book, is a perpetual target for abuse in the United States. This has been the case since the earliest days of trading in human flesh and it remains the case today, as state-sanctioned violence is perpetrated without impunity on the canvas of Black life. To be liberated from this ongoing violence is not—as both Robinson and Dunham understood and evidenced in their scholarship and creative practice, respectively—about changing the deeply rooted white supremacist values that inculcate American society. Rather, liberation is tied to an ability to (re)claim a deep ancestral way of knowing how to escape from the physical limitations of the body. In many African diasporic spiritual traditions, and particularly in vodou traditions (Dunham was a trained practitioner), there is a moment of transcendence known as *the break*. In the break one is unmoored from the physical bonds of subjugation and enters an enlightened and sanctified space where ancestral knowledge can be received and transmitted. This sanctified space where one is above and beyond the corpus is liminal and untouchable; it is a metaphysical expanse of freedom from the body and the chains that seek to bind it. Black liberation has always included, and in many ways is rooted in, the ability to transcend and escape via the rhythms of our bodies, using shared or collective practices that are deeply informed by the same beliefs, moralities, cosmologies, metaphysics, and intellectual traditions that Robinson celebrated in his work and that Dunham extolled and honored in the crafting of Dunham Technique.

Dunham Technique, which is still taught today, is an embodied form of archival practice that emphasizes cultural contextualization in movement as well as attention to spiritual well-being.[6] In Dunham Technique the body must embrace both the mind and psyche. What is seen and measurable in Dunham Technique—the *technê*, the technique, the practice, the technology, the "science of the craft"—cannot exist without what is unseen, what Dunham called the *rhythm*. Rhythm—a connective tissue and an embodied technology of remembering—demands that attention be paid to the essence of what we know and how we know it. Dunham argued that when the rhythm is broken, whether in an individual or in a whole society, the result is disintegration. She identified alienation, apartheid, and the separation of music and dance as phenomena borne of broken rhythm; she believed that when Black people are disconnected from their histories and cultural memories, there is a break, a brokenness, a sense of not being whole.

Dunham was a scholar, an artist, an activist, and a memory worker. It follows that not only did her work establish a technology for codifying embodied cultural memory, but it also established a technology for forming these memories. As an activist, she included in her dance work original pieces based on the sacred vodou and Shango rituals she had observed in the Caribbean, as well as pieces that commented on the current conditions of Black life. In 1951, for example, Dunham created *Southland*, a dramatic ballet about the horrors of lynching in the United States. When *Southland* premiered in Santiago, Chile, there was tremendous pushback. Just months earlier, US Senator Joseph McCarthy had declared that there were known Communists in the highest echelons of American government. That a Black woman had traveled to a foreign country with a strong Communist base and anti-American sentiment and exposed America's darkest side was seen as a flagrant betrayal of her country.[7] *Southland* was immediately suppressed in Chile, and Dunham was told to return to the United States. She had been warned: remove the lynching scene. But she refused to do so, at the cost of future support from the US government. *Southland*, Dunham asserted, forced people into an awareness of their own prejudices and fears; it is rooted in the Black American struggle for self-definition in a society that has often refused to acknowledge Blackness as humanity.

Speaking directly to the connective tissue ascribed to her concept of *rhythm*, Dunham said at the ballet's premier: "Though I have not smelled the smell of burning flesh, and have never seen a Black body swaying from a Southern tree, I have felt those things in spirit."[8] For Dunham, her artistic and creative practice was a form of connection to a broader African diasporic community, and the *rhythm* was this connection. She argued that "a person who dances should know why they dance, and to do so, they must have an historical background."[9] Dancing, as the way to knowing, therefore affirms one's self, one's culture, and one's history. Dunham believed that people from the African diaspora hold cultural memory on a cellular level and that such memory could be activated through sacred sound and ritual movement. She created Dunham Technique from the perspective of both artist and scholar. Hers was a careful study in how people from the African diaspora—no matter how dispersed via the commercial enterprise of human enslavement—can reanimate ancestral memory and cultural practices when introduced to the combination of sound and movement that would inspirit them. Rhythm, then, is a restorative and liberatory practice that connects African diasporic communities to their cultural roots through modes of transmission, and the body itself is a medium, a memory technology.

The institution of American slavery broke cultural bonds and induced enduring cultural disruptions. Dunham sought to restore them. Through the cultural anthropology and dance work that together comprise Dunham Technique, she established movements that analyze the legacy of slavery and embrace the significance of African-influenced traditions. Her research-to-performance methodology exemplifies critical innovation; her dance work demonstrates that profound humanism emerges from a deep knowledge of cultural specificity.[10] Dunham's dance work not only documents the traditions of communities neglected by elite historiographies, it also challenges audiences to acquire a new literacy about the cultural context of these traditions, both in their original milieu and through contemporary frameworks.[11] This work was—and still is—essential. As Dunham master dancer Albirda Rose attested:

> For me, I came up during Civil Rights and because I was a dancer I was exposed to African-Haitian, African, African-American culture through dance. In those forms you begin to find out something about the person who designed those forms and what was going on in those forms. So Haitian was my first knowledge base and Haitian culture was so similar to what I knew about my own ancestry. My ancestry comes out of New Orleans in Louisiana. When I first went there with them in the 1960s nobody spoke English, everybody spoke Creole. It was a direct relationship to be directly involved in the Haitian culture. Not only in terms of the dance forms but also the linguistic connections to the Yoruba tradition, the Ifa religion. So many links were destroyed during slavery but the context of the language and the rhythmic concepts of the blues and gospels and spirituals you begin to see that transferred knowledge. So what Miss Dunham was able to bring to dance, there was a definite transference of knowledge from one cultural center to another.[12]

That Dunham's research-to-performance method opened the space for her to teach dance as something that had been "recreated from African diaspora memory" marks Dunham Technique as a compelling example of a specifically Black memory technology.[13]

An embrace of Dunham Technique as a Black memory technology also causes us to notice that traditional Western archival theory and practice simply are not robust enough to attend to either the heterogeneity or the nuances of Black culture. Archivy as it is theorized and practiced in the United States is built on frameworks of ownership, reflecting the values of imperialism and colonialism that undergird them. Birthed from the French tradition in Paris's *École Nationale des Chartes* (with roots in the Napoleonic era and the French Revolution), American archives are primarily concerned with custodial relationships—that is, caring for records in their custody. Although many independent community-based archival projects exist that serve to challenge these notions of archivy as necessarily centralized, most current best practices recommend duplicating or reinforcing existing archival paradigms. Even the most groundbreaking archival theorization often eventually leads to a recapitulation of Western ideas around provenance, custody, description, preservation, and access.

What the Dunham Technique and the framework of Black memory technologies offer us is a departure from these norms: a way to think about the distinctions in memory work that are coded or recognized as Black and a way to understand these practices as both cultural inheritance and technological intervention. In its codification and transmission of memory, Dunham Technique is not unlike current practices in oral tradition, where the existence of structured mechanisms such as mnemonic devices and the careful identification of culture bearers within the group guarantees the transmission of knowledge and values, perpetuating group identity. In contrast to traditional Western archivy in which preservation centers on the physical demands of material artifacts, preservation as an aspect of Black memory technologies is generally assured by the continuous process of producing, reinventing, and transmitting memories, rather than by isolating artifacts or symbols that represent this heritage. This kind of Black memory work (when uninterrupted) is an ongoing and, even somewhat quotidian, process. As the Dunham-trained dance professor Ronald Hutson suggested in 2013, to properly safeguard Dunham Technique, an invocation of Black memory work is essential:

> There's no question for me that Dunham's true archive is in her dancers' bodies. I think that the written word has value—I am a scholar—but I think some people who are in the field of dance are totally body-oriented and I think some of us, and I think that we are fortunate, are physically as well as verbally oriented and expressive. The scholarly aspects, the written aspects, are important. It helps people who haven't danced—and even people who have danced—understand dance. There's a place for that. But there's a transference of information from body to body that's very much like oral traditions. Oral tradition has been important since the dawn of time, and even though we write things down now, we codify, the oral tradition still works. From body to body as a learning tool, that still works too.[14]

Dunham Technique, which consists of a system of learnable and transferable qualities, is also dynamic, however. Contemporary Dunham Technique incorporates and merges methods of teaching, style, and application from earlier generations of the Technique with ideas, methods, and philosophies that were originally taught by Katherine Dunham. Albirda Rose, cofounder of the Institute for Dunham Certification, asserts that Dunham Technique "allows one to understand a culture, or many cultures, through dance. [Dunham] found that an understanding of different cultures takes place when one is immersed in the culture. Through experiencing other ways of living, especially through the dances, knowledge is acquired."[15] Dunham Technique as a form of acquiring embodied knowledge was Dunham's ultimate goal. However, as a scholar of the kind of anthropology that is rooted in Western traditions, Dunham was compelled by both fiscal and professional exigencies to embrace Western modes of knowledge creation and preservation—despite significant limitations regarding the ability of Western institutions to appropriately capture and make accessible to others the innovation and robustness of her craft.

I asked at the outset of this chapter what Black memory technologies might look like in defiance of and in opposition to a sociocultural and socioeconomic order that is rooted in slavery, racism, and anti-Blackness. In societies where written culture has favored documentary history, memory has become institutionalized and over time crystallized in museums, archives, and other documentation centers. This process raises various issues concerning access, which is defined by the Society of American Archivists as the ability and *permission* to locate and retrieve information for use within legally established restrictions governing privacy, confidentiality, and security clearance. Numerous techniques and mediums have been developed, and these advances are noteworthy. But in the digital era, with content being appropriated and reproduced by users across the world, the question of access to cultural memory becomes even more significant. What, of all this vast cultural production, should be seen, by whom, and when? I want to problematize Western archivy as it participates in these structures. What follows is a discussion of the Dunham archive(s) regarding conflicting ideas about determining the rules governing access and use in archival repositories. It is a reflection on how we might understand Dunham Technique as an antidote to Western archivy—one that helps us create the sacred space necessary to hold Black memories and that makes a more robust Black life possible.

Dunham was deeply concerned with not only preserving the practice of Dunham Technique but also documenting her process. These concomitant concerns about safeguarding both practice and process are evident in her dual endeavors to ensure the longevity of her work. On one hand, Dunham Technique is encoded in the bodies of those who dance it. On the other hand, Dunham maintained physical artifacts—the kind that are typically held in Western archival repositories. For example, she was among the first to use film to document dance traditions in the Caribbean as well as to document and preserve her own technique. As early as the mid-1930s, Dunham was utilizing a Kodak 16mm camera to record her field studies in the Caribbean in what was at the time yet another innovative approach to anthropological fieldwork.[16] Dunham asserted that "to capture the meaning in the culture, in the life of the people, [she] felt that [she] had to take something directly from the people and develop that."[17] On the experience of filming, Dunham said in a recorded interview:

> And of course, it was rather difficult for me because already I was infringing on some of their taboos by being there. Some of the time I was where women were not normally permitted to be. Some of the time I was where outsiders and strangers were not permitted to be. And I had to overcome that and at the same time they did not know what was in this box that I carried and pointed at them. But like most people in societies other than their own, they don't like to have things pointed at them. So I had to find a way to fix that camera so it could

be taking and recording what they were doing without making them uncomfortable. And this was my big task; I haven't quite overcome it. There are times when I still film and feel that I'm intruding.[18]

Although Dunham was, to a certain extent, allowed participatory access into ritual life in the Caribbean that the largely white and predominantly male ethnographic anthropology establishment could never attain, she did not use this to claim cultural mastery regarding her subject matter.[19] Instead, from her own words, Dunham's discomfort with the possibility of her recordings intruding into and interfering with the sacred practices of her Caribbean interlocutors is apparent.

Today, however, these moving images reside at the Library of Congress, where they comprise one element of the Katherine Dunham archival collection. Although the Dunham archives are dispersed across several collections—including the Katherine Dunham Collection at the Library of Congress; the Katherine Dunham Papers at Southern Illinois University; and the Katherine Dunham Correspondence, Contracts and Interviews at New York Public Library—the Katherine Dunham Collection at the Library of Congress is among the most robust.[20] The Library of Congress Dunham materials are a collection of 1,694 still and moving images that document Dunham's career, including her early anthropological explorations in the Caribbean, her work as a choreographer, her dance technique and teaching method, performances, and her anthropological analyses of the dances and rituals of the African diaspora. The moving images include the ethnographic footage recorded by Dunham to document Afro-Caribbean vodou rituals and other dance forms.

Dunham Technique is also captured on several videotapes in the collection, demonstrating Dunham's teaching style and providing a glimpse into her methods of transmitting dance knowledge. Many of the images (both still and moving) are available for remote viewing online. Specifically, films made as part of Dunham's research in the Caribbean have been put online by the Music Division of the Library of Congress in a special collection titled *Selections from the Katherine Dunham Collection*. This online collection makes available a selection of photographs from the Library of Congress; the Missouri Historical Society; Southern Illinois University; film and videotape excerpts from Dunham's research and performing career; and selections from the Library of Congress Dunham Legacy Project that documents Dunham Technique.

According to the catalog record for the Katherine Dunham Collection at Library of Congress, the materials came from three sources.[21] The moving images and sound recordings were purchased from Dunham herself in 2001 by the Library of Congress as part of the Katherine Dunham Legacy Project, funded by the Doris Duke Charitable Foundation. These materials date from the mid-1930s and contain examples of Dunham's original field research in the Caribbean. Dunham's intent in transferring the materials to the Library of Congress was again part of a two-pronged strategy to preserve her anthropological dance work: she viewed her dance work and Dunham Technique as an archive in and of itself, *and* she sought to ensure that the process by which she had created her dance work was documented and more formally preserved. That Dunham entrusted her life's work to the Library of Congress speaks to her extraordinary trust in the Library as a government institution despite having had a promising dance career thwarted by the very same government after producing *Southland* in 1951. I understand this to mean that Dunham believed in institutions like the Library of Congress because the basis for their very existence is to serve the common good.

What Dunham likely did not anticipate was that the Library of Congress would put these recordings online in an open-access format, bypassing the permission of those whose sacred practices were documented in her films. In a long tradition of open rather than *appropriate* access, archivists at the Library of Congress did not take into consideration what might be sacred or secret practices before posting these videos online. Neither did they consider the specificity of context under which Dunham was granted permission to view and record or the nuance of Dunham's own stated mixed comfort with the process of recording. Instead, a fair use application of copyright was privileged over the notion of permission, which is an important spiritual and practical aspect of Black memory work. While no one can predict the future, Black memory work does have an important relationship with the past: Black memory workers recognize the historical patterns of abuse and work through such modes as agency, autonomy, refusal, and commitment to mitigate against and prevent future abuses. The dances that Dunham created and the cultures and the people who comprise those cultures deserve to be remembered—and they also deserve to have the terms of that remembrance be disentangled from the Western, white supremacist histories of American archivy. Herein lies the promise and possibility of Black memory work: that what remains might be treated with care and respect, that Black memories—and the right of Black people to be remembered—might not automatically be deployed in anti-Black ways in an anti-Black world.

The concept of open access has its roots in higher education. Arguments for open-access policies are typically centered around the notion that governments (local, state, and federal) provide hundreds of billions of dollars annually to public institutions of higher education that then employ the preponderance of researchers. Academic researchers publish their findings without an expectation of compensation beyond their salary. Unlike fiction authors, for example, academic authors submit their work for publication in the interest of advancing global human knowledge. Publishers in the digital age, however, have continued to rely on the centuries-old model; proponents of open access argue that this model has not been updated to take advantage of twenty-first-century digital technologies. This outdated model means that once published, those that contributed to the research (from taxpayers to the author/researchers and the institutions that supported the research itself) must pay again to access the published research findings. The overarching argument for open access is that even though research is ostensibly produced as a public good, it is not available to the public who paid for it. At its core, open access refers to the free, immediate, online availability of research, combined with full rights to use that research in digital environments.

As SPARC (the Scholarly Publishing and Academic Resources Coalition) argues: "Open Access is the needed modern update for the communication of research that fully utilizes the Internet for what it was originally built to do—accelerate research." SPARC goes on to assert that "funders invest in research to advance human knowledge and ultimately improve lives. Open Access increases the return on that investment by ensuring the results of the research they fund can be read and built on by anyone."[22] SPARC's perspective on open access is one that is broadly shared across academic institutions as well as cultural heritage institutions (archives, libraries, museums) that support them. These values are also shared by national cultural heritage institutions including the National Archives and the Library of Congress. In archival studies, debates about access are often formulated around concerns about the tendency of government archives around the globe to restrict access to important records, such as those that document displaced peoples, those that might serve to occlude human rights violations, or those that might support efforts to secure human rights where such rights are desperately needed.

Archives professional Sam Winn, for example, argues that to best understand the ethical imperatives that govern access to displaced archives, "archivists must navigate a complex web of competing moral claims, contradictory legal frameworks, shifting national security norms, and customary practices that reflect centuries of colonization, occupation, and conquest."[23] What Winn gestures to here is that arguments about access in traditional Western archivy have often had to focus on the role of the archivist and the role of the repository and/or institution. Less often discussed, however, is what is appropriate for the materials in terms of the conditions that govern access and use.[24] While I am not advocating against open access per se, I do maintain that there is inherent value in considerations of *appropriate access*. The scholar Kimberly Christen has offered groundbreaking work to the field of archival studies in her deep engagements with Indigenous epistemologies in archival settings. In her 2011 article "Opening Archives: Respectful Repatriation," Christen notes that in the preceding two decades, many collecting institutions heeded calls by Indigenous activists to integrate Indigenous models and knowledge into mainstream archival practices. Christen argued that the "digital terrain poses both possibilities and problems for Indigenous peoples as they seek to manage, revive, circulate, and create new cultural heritage within overlapping colonial/postcolonial histories and oftentimes-binary public debates about access in a digital age."[25] Here, I join Christen, echoing similar concerns about Black epistemologies, sacred knowledge, and debates about access. Christen, in naming the problem of the binary in extant public debates about access—typically framed around open access versus closed collections—presages Winn's later claims about the "complex web of competing moral claims...and customary practices" that are also deemed problematic.[26]

If there is tension here, it is in the distinction between what is good for the archivist and repository and what is good for the creator of the archival materials, those who are documented in the archives, and—as a second order of concern—the materials themselves. The tensions inherent in these contrasting but interrelated concerns about archival access cannot be answered from a singular perspective, and so I propose—for Western institutional archives that document Black lives—the lens of *appropriate* access. Decisions about the conditions governing access and use are often set forth in a deed of gift. The deed of gift is a formal and legally binding agreement between the donor and the repository. Deeds of gift transfer *ownership of and legal rights to* the donated materials. A legal agreement has been deemed by best practices as being in the best interest of both the donor and the repository: a signed deed of gift establishes and governs the legal relationship between donor and repository and the legal status of the materials.[27] Importantly, access decisions are typically made at the time of acquisition and noted in the deed of gift. If an archivist fails, for example, to ask the donor specifically about the conditions that govern access and use, the collection will be marked as "open for research" with no restrictions on access and use.

In another example, the archivist may indeed ask about access restrictions, but the donor may not be aware of the implications of opening the collection for research without restrictions. This, I argue, was the case for Katherine Dunham. When she transferred her physical archival materials to the Library of Congress, the films documenting her Caribbean research would have been made available for viewing *at the Library of Congress* using a preservation copy. How could Dunham possibly have anticipated that the portion of her memory work—and the sacred practices documented therein—that she put in the capable institutional hands of the Library of Congress would find their way to Michael Brown's internet (i.e., the same internet that wantonly circulates images of Black death for profit)?

The current affordances of the digital came to pass just as Dunham was experiencing her own rite of passage. When she died at the age of ninety-six in May 2006, the images of Black bodies in the overflowing waters of Lake Pontchartrain in the aftermath of Hurricane Katrina were ushering in a fresh new hellscape. Dunham's death preceded the murders of Trayvon Martin and Michael Brown, and the exploitation of Black bodies on the internet for profit was in its nascency. Would this later knowledge have impacted her decisions about the conditions governing access and use for parts of the collection at the Library of Congress? This is ultimately not knowable, but what *is* knowable is that the information professionals at the Library of Congress have the capacity to make decisions about what is available online. The difficult decisions to which Winn gestures are discernable here.

I propose that archivists and librarians place questions of what is culturally appropriate at the center of digitization and/as access decisions, asking serious questions about who has the right to remember—to put things together as an act of reconstitution—and who has the right to be remembered. I propose that the answers to these questions be predicated on collective decisions made by the communities impacted. If Western archives, with historically racist practices and policies, are going to hold ("own") materials that document Black life, Black culture, and even Black death, they have an obligation to Black communities to consult with Black memory workers.[28] It is vital that Black people participate in the process of establishing what is sacred, what should be withheld from the white gaze, what can be made public, and under what circumstances. It is vital that decisions be made about what is *appropriate* in terms of access, not just what is legal or binding. It is also vital that there is a recognition that the Black community is not a monolith by any means; the heterogeneity of the Black community means different access will be appropriate at different times, for different communities.

Appropriate access is not the only solution to the question of what Black memory technologies look like in defiance of and in opposition to a sociocultural and socioeconomic order that is rooted in slavery, racism, and anti-Blackness. Even appropriate access continues to recast the Western archive in a starring role, demonstrating how difficult it is to think outside dominant Western paradigms. What is most compelling for me in this case study is the Dunham Technique itself as a Black memory technology and as Black memory work. The extant Dunham archive(s) combine traditional archival practices with Black memory work, the ongoing objective of which is ensuring the reinsertion of cultural knowledge and cultural memory into Black lived experience.

Returning to Dunham through the question of who has the right to remember and be remembered, we see that she felt strongly that her work was bound to the memory of "her people." She wanted her work to help Black people remember and reconstitute a past that had been appropriated by the chains of slavery and the traumas of white supremacy. This kind of memory work often entails heightened anxieties, interruptions, vulnerabilities, and uncertainties, and Dunham created a technique—built on the body collective—that could support, if not withstand these challenges. She was concerned not only with remembrance but also with quality and terms of that remembrance. To conceive of Dunham Technique as a memory technology requires us to focus on who and what is remembered and who gets to do the remembering; it asks us to attend to the technologies by which those memories are constructed and transmitted.

Just as I have suggested that appropriate access must be a collective effort, so too did Dunham believe in the power and value of the collective—not just going out in the world to do things, but to do them *together*. Writing from Accompong during her fieldwork, Dunham observed a "vestige of... social organization which is so vital to West Africa—*the work group*."[29] Even in the earliest days of thinking about cultural inheritances, Dunham was focused on the collective. Dunham Technique is not an individuated Black memory technology, but rather a collective one that anticipates expansive participation on multiple levels. While there are many subdisciplines in academia that study Black ancestral trauma and cultural loss, as well as alternative epistemologies that center Black healing and Black memory work, the anthropological dance work that undergirds Dunham Technique is unique among them. The specificity of movement as an embodied cultural archive and epistemic frame creates the conditions of possibility necessary for agency in Black life and Black memory work.

Dunham Technique stands in opposition to the structural forces that have worked to eliminate Black people's choices about if and how they are remembered. In reading Dunham Technique as a Black memory technology, we can better connect the Black body to Black memory work and envision the many ways that Black memory work, writ large, might offer a site of collective liberation.

Conclusion

HOMEGOING

Care is the antidote to violence.

Saidiya Hartman

Archives in the United States are often comprised of names, genealogies, and narratives. To encounter Blackness in the archives, by contrast, is to confront—and endeavor to make sense of—numbers, ciphers, and fragments. Historian Vincent Brown has observed one perverse advantage to what I have previously named as *archival amnesty*—or the intentional exclusion of robust Black histories from institutional archives in the United States: North American archives are so mute on Black life that it is hard to mistake recorded history for what actually happened.[1] Therefore, doing justice to the past often entails an intentional revising of what has been said about it. This conclusion seeks to name another archive, to reveal what is possible when Black life is welcomed and valued rather than pathologized or marked as problematic.

Black memory work does just this, scavenging some of the most corrupt archival materials to "imagine the past" and "remember the future," as scholar Carlos Fuentes calls us to do.[2] As Black feminist scholar Saidiya Hartman has observed, the afterlife of slavery has produced a certain set of epistemic and conceptual challenges, one of which is how to contend with temporality and how to narrate historical time when for Black Americans "the past, the present, and the future are not discrete and cut off from one another, but rather there is a sense of temporal entanglement and Black lives are lived in the simultaneity of that entanglement."[3] Black memory work therefore is necessarily what Christina Sharpe has called "wake work"; it demands a turning away from political, juridical, philosophical, historical, or other disciplinary solutions to the "ongoing abjection" of Blackness, looking instead toward current archival practice, asking what, if anything, might survive this "insistent Black exclusion."[4] In instances where celebrations of Black life (rather than merely representations of Black death) do appear in American archival institutions, these stories are often buried in administrative papers. In contrast, Black memory work creates a reparative framework that centers Black voices and lived experiences; it centers Black archival knowledge and practice as a means of expanding current understandings of the archives and their relationships to Black life.

A Black memory worker is, by definition, embedded in Black culture. Preserving community memory for Black memory workers therefore is not just a vocation—rather, it is an *invocation*, a conjuring, a calling forth. Black memory work has—and always must—extend beyond acts of archival preservation, however, if for no other reason than because there has not been much to preserve beyond records of violence. To do Black memory work is to center Black epistemologies that contend with the anti-Blackness of traditional archives, where the tools and documentation of dispossession, criminalization, oppression, and negation have been appropriated, collected, disrupted, and disordered in order to discern and attend to the obscurity and beauty that is Black life—existing within and without archival documents.[5]

It is not just traditional archivy with which Black memory work is concerned, however. Black memory work has a history of revolutionizing the archival impulse to reflect a more radical aesthetic, speaking directly into the wounds of what has been withheld. For example, in the wake of George Floyd's death at the hands of Derek Chauvin in May 2020, a group of Black memory workers in the United States issued a nationwide call to action in which both the scope and the stakes of Black memory work are made explicit. Stated in terms of critical refusal—a generative concept that challenges harmful practices while simultaneously negotiating and developing alternative actions—the call builds on a Black feminist tradition of invoking a paired set of refusals and commitments. It reads, in part:

> We reject attempts to document this moment that fail to center the Black experience or that fails to document the facts about the State's role in inflicting Black pain. We commit to modeling care in our memory work because Black people deserve care. We commit to doing ethical memory work that protects Black people because racist state-sanctioned violence also resists documentation. We commit to archival practices that support accountability and historical accuracy because when the dust settles attempts will be made to rewrite the history.[6]

This call to action speaks into the tensions that exist in the underexamined liminal space between Western archival practices and Black memory work. Two such tensions are concerns about agency and access. While Black memory workers recognize a need to document the lived experiences of Black people—even if only to serve as evidence that Black people exist at the center of Black life, in contraposition to the marginalization Black communities experience as a result of white supremacy—there is also reluctance on the part of Black memory workers to make this documentation widely available to those outside the Black community. One reason for this is that some knowledge is sacred. Although some Indigenous communities in the United States have made progress toward maintaining sacred space and knowledge, Black lives, experiences, and cultural practices have been continuously deemed the property of whiteness, wherein whiteness and white supremacy determine the conditions of legitimacy, value, and access.[7]

Black memory work inhabits multiple modalities and epistemologies. Among them are practices that are animated by creativity, intentionality, accountability, sovereignty (as a matter of self-determination), temporality, spirituality, care, and sacredness. Black memory work is understood to be a collective rather than an individual process, even when it is seemingly enacted by a single person; as such, Black memory work is undergirded by a deep and profound connection both to collective struggle and to Black liberation as a collective goal. One example of this collective approach can be seen in the Black Memory Workers call to action; another can be seen in the "Art of Collective Care and Responsibility: Handling Images of Black Suffering and Death," a free five-part virtual teach-in held in December 2020 (in the months following the death of George Floyd in Minneapolis, Minnesota, and Breonna Taylor in Louisville, Kentucky). The teach-in offered participants techniques for opposing exploitation and anti-Black racism in the visual media, while prioritizing care for Black people.[8]

Arguing that "the proliferation of searing images of destroyed Black bodies within our current digital landscape also routinely traumatizes Black people and even titillates those who harbor racist sentiments," the teach-in drove home three important points: first, that representations of anti-Black violence are powerful discursive tools; second, that such representations mean different things in different contexts, taking into specific consideration whether the audience for such representations are Black; and third, that if representations of anti-Black violence are the discursive call, then collective care and responsibility are the response. The teach-in shed light on a concept that is central to Black memory work—that understanding power relationships, kinship, and vulnerability is imperative in the work of Black memory work as Black memory workers behold one another and curate with care.

The Art of Collective Care and Responsibility organizers (who included scholar Christina Sharpe; Wanda Johnson, the mother of Oscar Grant; and Samaria Rice, the mother of Tamir Rice) foregrounded in their teach-in an argument perfectly articulated by cultural organizer La Tanya S. Autry—that "as anti-Blackness continues, representational strategies remain enmeshed in a fraught nexus of resistance, remembrance, and abuse."[9] In her 2022 piece for *Hyperallergic*, Autry poses a set of questions meant to act as abuse interventions that Black memory workers ask when approaching a project. Among these questions are: Who is centered in the work? Who is most harmed by the violence? Does the circulation of the image/object/experience harm those most harmed? How does the work disrupt domination? What forms of care may address needs of victims, loved ones of victims, and community members who are prime targets of this violence? Does this work disrupt anti-Blackness or perpetuate it? Are you the right person/group/community to be doing or sharing this work? To what communities are you accountable/responsible? By taking the time to sit with and answer these questions, honoring Black people's right to be remembered can be approached in ways that embrace care and are respectful of our dead.

Black mourning and deathcare practices are in many ways unique to African diasporic populations and must be acknowledged and respected, even in digital environments. Death in Western societies is generally perceived as the "material end of the body and the social self" and—until recently—denoted "the irreversible loss of the capacity for consciousness."[10] In the Yoruba tradition, however, the living dead are bilingual: they speak the language of men, and they also "speak the language of the spirits and of God, to whom they are drawing nearer ontologically."[11] Culturally disposed to collectivism, the Yoruba people espouse a cyclical reality that incorporates the belief that ancestral spirits safeguard the welfare, prosperity, and productivity of the whole community. In times of trouble the spirits of the dead are called upon for help and they are believed to watch over the whole family. Yoruba rituals relating to death and burial are also inextricably bound to the home. As a result, in a practice known as "residential burial," Yoruba often bury their dead around the house or family compound so that they will not be forgotten after the burial and so they may continue to be part of the family. Yoruba funerary rituals are frequently elaborated as rituals of renewal; in the Yoruba worldview, reality is perceived of as a whole in which all things (the physical and the metaphysical) are linked together.[12]

Yoruba funerary traditions are deeply linked to the heritage of funeral rituals that originated in Ancient Egypt. Egyptian people enjoyed a rich culture of preparing for a funeral and preserving the deceased for the afterlife. Herein lie the origins of a Black cultural heritage of elaborate funeral practices. In the United States, in many Black and African American communities, similarly elaborate funerary rituals are referred to as *homegoing*. A homegoing, particularly in faith communities, is a ritual celebration of the soul's return to its creator. Modern homegoing practices have their roots in the Atlantic slave trade: many enslaved people brought to the shores of North America believed that in death their souls would return to their natal or family home on the African continent. The practice of placing seashells on graves, for example, was believed to return souls back to their ancestral home in Africa; the sea brought Africans to the Americas on ships and the sea would likewise return them back home to Africa when they died. These complex notions of home as both an earthly place and a heavenly destination are an expression of the African diaspora's rich and complicated understanding of the nature of human existence and demise.

Homegoing practices in the United States are also characterized by the recognition that Black life is lived in labor and conflict, and that true rest comes only in the afterlife. This reaction toward death—viewing death as a kind of freedom—finds its roots in slavery, the Jim Crow South, Reconstruction, and the related ongoing struggle for Black liberation. It follows that in addition to the biblical ideology of heaven and the belief of escape from earthly toils, there remains a summoning of older African traditions, viewing death as a passage into the ancestor world or the next phase in the life of the soul. In Black American communities, as is the case throughout the African diaspora, the deceased are never far removed from loved ones. This view of death as a well-earned rest renders Black mourning and homegoing traditions joyous affairs, often performative in their own right.

Because enslaved and free Black people were not allowed to congregate to perform any kind of ritual for burying their dead (enslavers feared the enslaved would conspire to create an uprising during any such gathering), enslaved people were ordinarily buried without ceremony in unmarked graves in non-crop-producing ground.[13] With the introduction of Christianity to enslaved populations, laws changed to allow religious assembly and funerals for enslaved people. With this shift, funerals and other religious activities became the bedrock of early African American culture; enslaved people did not hold the traditional funerals that the plantation owners anticipated, however. The enslaved instead practiced jubilant and celebratory funeral rituals. Thus the modern-day performance and ceremony of funeral is not only a source of comfort for family and friends of the deceased but also a callback to earlier formations of homegoing practices; they are at the same time a celebration of life, an honoring of memory, and a (re)claiming of home. In Black American communities and cultures the dead carry a powerful and present voice, which courses through both the (often self-styled) homegoing service itself and through the living voices of those in attendance. This intermingling of life and death in homegoing rituals is dynamic and it is intergenerational; it is a response to death that includes worship, salvation, song, food, pageantry, fear, reverence, and love. The collective funerary moment becomes an archive of its own: a vehicle through which the spirit of the dead live and speak. A person's homegoing is simultaneously a celebration of their release from mortal chains and an invocation of their right to be remembered.

Archives as representational structures continue to reproduce the idea that death—in the Western construction—is the only horizon for Black life. But as Black homegoing traditions suggest, death marks a *shift* rather than an ending. This formation of the life-death relationship is second nature to Black cultures, and accordingly the right to be remembered in institutional archives becomes deeply entangled with the desire to be forgotten. While on one hand, Black communities in the United States have a long history of memory and remembrance practices, these practices stand in contravention to the basic tenets of American archivy. Institutional archives in the United States are tasked with keeping intact historical accounts that blot out or minimize the severity of Black terror and violence, perpetuating the idea that Black people are not human beings with agency but colonized creatures indentured to the enslaver.

Reality continues to conform itself around this idea. In this way, like the work of Katherine Dunham, Black memory work is a corrective: it is the work of healing, reckoning, helping, and restoring rituals that bind us to build again, to honor Black lives, Black legacies, and Black heritage. It is in Hartman's words, a desire "to do more than recount the violence that deposited these traces in the archive[s]."[14] Working against the Western archival tradition in this way, to—as Ruha Benjamin advocates, "dismantle the worlds we cannot live within"—marks forgetting as an important aspect of Black memory work. Black memory work is neither strictly an analog process nor an analog application, however. The dawn of the digital era saw an uptick in Black digital projects as well as in digital representations of Blackness that are constructed by non-Black actors.

These growing trends beg the question of how one approaches curating and beholding Black archival lives with care, particularly in digital environments. Returning to the examples of the digitization of records from the era of Atlantic slavery and of the Shango practitioners who participated in Dunham's fieldwork—never imagining their spiritual practice would be uploaded to an open-access online environment ostensibly in perpetuity—it is vital to consider the transition from analog to digital through digitization. There is room here too for the corrective of Black memory work. As archivist keondra bills freemyn has argued in "Expanding the Black Archival Imagination," the recent increase in social media–based archival projects is a "reflection of the vibrant legacy of storytelling traditions and historical stewardship practices [that are] foundational to Black memory work."[15] Furthermore, freemyn notes, social media platforms increase opportunities for the "reclamation of erased histories, allow greater agency in defining and redefining dominant narratives, allow for community-accountable archival practice, and disrupt the history of institutional violence within traditional archives." As one might guess from examples presented throughout this book, however, these digital projects are often a measure of competing regimes of value; they are co-opted by whiteness and used against the very communities that created them to be celebrated as part of a collective reparative project. One example of this can be seen in the community *sousveillance* work ("watching from below") that was co-opted and used against Black residents in Ferguson, Missouri, in the wake of Michael Brown's death.

Black residents in the city of Ferguson are accustomed to being overpoliced. With motivations based in both racism and revenue, the Ferguson Police Department (FPD) has a long history of targeting the city's Black residents. A report by the US Department of Justice found that it is not uncommon, for example, to be pulled over for failing to indicate a turn (not using a blinker) and then have up to fourteen citations issued amounting to hundreds—if not thousands—of dollars in revenue for FPD (and Ferguson as a municipality) and draining Ferguson residents of the resources required to meet basic human needs. Disparities are also present in FPD's use of force. Nearly 90 percent of documented force used by FPD officers was used against Black residents.[16] To say that the relationship between Ferguson's police units and its Black residents is fraught is to grossly understate the case. As a result of the FPD's myriad hostile approaches to policing Black bodies, the city's Black residents have adopted sousveillance practices to provide counternarratives that support literal liberation—video, for example, that records the truth of an interaction with police that can be used in court in contraposition to police reports and testimony.

Surveillance, from the French for "watching over," describes a higher authority—the police, for example, monitoring people. *Sousveillance*, or "watching from below," refers to the reverse tactic: the monitoring of authority by informal networks of regular people, often equipped with little more than a cell phone camera and the desire to remain vigilant against the excesses of state violence.[17] These acts of sousveillance, witnessing, and testimony are themselves forms of Black memory work, and Black residents of Ferguson and their network of allies actively participate in what scholar Simone Browne calls "dark sousveillance," an oppositional practice that actively resists and opposes the state's surveillant gaze.[18] Training community members in Black memory work—including documentation strategies such as sousveillance—is an important step toward shifting power around whose stories are told, how they are told, and what place those stories hold in the shaping of Black futures.

In August 2014, when Michael Brown was killed in Ferguson by FPD officer Darren Wilson, Black communities across the nation were ready to respond. As people took to the streets in protest, many of them were using cell phone cameras to document what was happening. Ferguson residents have a right to capture video of on-duty police officers in public places. Ferguson police, however, regularly intimidate or retaliate against people with cameras.[19] In the wake of Michael Brown's killing, as protests continued in Ferguson and Saint Louis, the FPD arrested a Black activist, Johnetta Elzie, for recording FPD officers. Elzie was threatened as she recorded, walking backward; as she stated that she did not want to be touched, an FPD officer physically assaulted her, pushing her—again, as she was walking backward—in a seeming attempt to literally knock her off her feet while she was conducting a perfectly legal sousveillance action. On the day of Elzie's arrest she tweeted: "If I'm arrested today please know I'm not suicidal. I have plenty to live for. I did not resist, I'm just black."[20]

Elzie's tweet echoes the sentiments of many Black memory workers: Black memory work is not always safe, and to do Black memory work is an act of care. Sometimes the simple act of documenting Black life is dangerous and sometimes being documented is dangerous. Elzie wasn't the only Black person arrested in Ferguson in the period of protest following Michael Brown's death. Indeed, people who appeared in sousveillance videos were arrested as the Ferguson Police force targeted anyone who was caught on camera exercising their right to protest. Here, again, the right to be remembered—to be documented participating in an act of protest, an ongoing and historically significant aspect of Black life—finds itself on a collision course with the right to be forgotten as the desire to be memorialized should not equate to being criminalized. Similarly, concerns about the criminalization of Black sousveillance and other documentary practices were raised again in the face of Darnella Frazier's video documenting the murder of George Floyd: there is always a fine line to be walked when documenting state violence against Black bodies.

In the wake of Ferguson, an organization called Documenting the Now (DocNow) provided a striking example of what curating and beholding with care can look like regarding the promise and possibility of Black memory work in digital environments. The original Documenting the Now project (funded by the Andrew W. Mellon Foundation) entailed creating new digital tools to "facilitate the collection, analysis and preservation of tweets and associated web content, as well as engagement with a broad range of stakeholders around the myriad issues involved in working with this content."[21] The impetus for Documenting the Now was an effort to document social media activity in the aftermath of Brown's killing, which captured national attention as people located his death within the narrative of centuries of abuse Black Americans have suffered at the hands of law enforcement. Social media—Twitter in particular—where the preponderance of information about Ferguson was shared, was a vital avenue for disseminating information about the case, the social activism it spurred, and the opposition to the protests that followed.[22]

The scholars, activists, and Black memory workers affiliated with Documenting the Now noticed that most powerful stories shared via Twitter during those protests included images, videos, and audio documenting the activity on the ground by independent observers, protesters, police, and journalists. They identified several concerns in their attempts to preserve web and social media content in ethical ways that protect already vulnerable Black communities, among them a lack of user awareness—or informed consent—about how social media platforms use their data or how it can be collected and accessed by third parties; the potential for fraudulent use and manipulation of social media content; the reality of the heightened potential of harm for members of vulnerable communities using the web and social media, especially when those individuals participate in activities such as protests and other forms of civil disobedience that are traditionally heavily monitored by law enforcement; and the difficulty of applying traditional archival practices to social media content given the sheer volume of data and complicated logistics of interacting with content creators.[23]

There are archivists and other cultural heritage workers in Black communities who have been doing Black memory work for ages, and they have excelled in spite of the most outward-facing oppression; so although Documenting the Now had a particular focus on social media content created by participants in the wake of a flurry of Black activism in response to police shootings, the overall project sought to answer questions about how we can learn from successful, alternative approaches to the use, storage, and circulation of data—specifically those led by vulnerable populations—to cultivate trust and safety online for Black communities. Documenting the Now's initial findings after engaging Black memory workers, community members and activists, scholars, and those who have been directly impacted by the harms just outlined were about centering care and the humanity of Black people, which echoes the ethos of Black memory workers writ large.

The Documenting the Now team recommends care in dealing with content and engagement with the community being documented as ways to learn what the community's needs are and to make sure they are aware of the work being done. For scholars there was an additional layer of recommendations that included such established methods as institutional review boards as a protection for research subjects (many scholars are not inclined to think of internet research as human subjects research, for example). While there is consensus among Black memory workers that there is no one-size-fits-all solution to the question of how to engage Black memory work in digital environments with an eye toward care, all stress that the work is about highlighting the Black community's accomplishment—and, even more important, our humanity. As Hartman tells us, when we consider what constitutes a life-affirming Black archival praxis, "care is the antidote to violence."[24] Black memory workers (as well as Black-run cultural heritage organizations and institutions) have consistently emphasized care—care in and for the work, caring for one another—as central to any Black memory work ethos.

Looking back to chapter 4 and thinking about digitally resurrected Tupac Shakur, I argue that this was Snoop Dogg and Dr. Dre's goal in creating the Tupac hologram. They sought to celebrate the life of a Black man about whom they cared, to recall the human that was their friend and whose death they mourned, and to create a remembrance of sorts—their own form of Black memory work. That the hologram became a commodity was horrifying, and it is telling that it was quickly relegated to a private archives maintained by the Shakur estate, where it continues to be cared for in the way that memory workers care for the materials under their stewardship. What can we take from the knowledge that Tupac's mother Afeni Shakur Davis did not want the hologram to ever see the light of day again? Were Snoop Dogg and Dr. Dre wrong to create the HoloPac? This is not for me alone to say, because Black memory work is both complex and collective.

One thing is certain: we have found ourselves, as Black memory workers, carrying the weight of memories heavier than we planned for, and we have learned that Black memory workers must lead with our complicated and compromised humanity as we do our work, reflecting the love and care and pain of Black worldmaking.

Notes

INTRODUCTION

Epigraph: Ruha Benjamin (@ruha9), "Note to selves: remember to imagine and craft the worlds you cannot live without, just as you dismantle the ones you cannot live within," Twitter, November 22, 2017, https://twitter.com/ruha9/status/926180439827591168.

1. The equation of Black people with property has a long and well-documented history in the United States, which I will not attempt to reproduce here. The transatlantic slave trade, which began as early as the fifteenth century, introduced a system of human chattel enslavement in the United States that was commercialized, racialized, and inherited. Enslaved people were seen not as people but rather as commodities to be bought, sold, and exploited. Rooted in this history of racial capital and human enslavement, societal conventions that regard Blackness and Black people as property spring eternal in the United States.

2. Harvey Young, *Embodying Black Experience: Stillness, Critical Memory, and the Black Body* (Ann Arbor: University of Michigan Press, 2010).

3. Please see Frantz Fanon and Richard Philcox, *Black Skin / White Masks* (New York: Grove Press, 1952), 4. This same phenomenon can be observed in the Feed the Children campaign. Once dubbed the "most

outrageous charity in America," and a prominent example of the "African childhood hunger crusade," Feed the Children was aimed at the heart of the white savior complex, successfully making political use of images of malnourished Black children from the African continent to solicit funds despite long-standing questions about their fiscal practices and ongoing scrutiny regarding how donated monies were spent.

4. Zellie Imani (@zellieimani), "You shouldn't have to see footage of murdered Black people to be convinced of their humanity," Twitter, June 13, 2020. https://twitter.com/zellieimani/status/1271788340967280643.

5. Although the title of this book emerged organically from public presentations of the materials that comprise it, *Resurrecting the Black Body* will nevertheless call to mind Dorothy Roberts's 1997 text, *Killing the Black Body: Race, Reproduction, and the Meaning of Liberty*. In her groundbreaking book, Roberts made a powerful intervention—exposing the systemic abuse of Black women's bodies in the United States and challenging a media landscape that was at the time dominated by racist images of "welfare queens" and "crack babies." That the titles of these books are so deeply resonant with one another is the best kind of coincidence and one that seemed worthy of drawing the reader's attention. There is another noteworthy echo between these two projects: in chapter 3 of *Resurrecting the Black Body*, I take note of slavery-era womb laws (e.g., *partus sequitur ventrem*, which translates roughly to "that which is born follows the womb"), while Roberts attends to the economic stake enslavers had in bonded women's fertility in *Killing the Black Body*. Although I did not intentionally put these texts in conversation with one another because the foci are so different, these resonances and echoes help to situate *Resurrecting the Black Body* within a longer and broader Black scholarly tradition that is committed to drawing attention to and redressing the systematic commodification of Black people's bodies.

6. Temi Odumosu, "The Crying Child: On Colonial Archives, Digitization, and Ethics of Care in the Cultural Commons," *Current Anthropology* 61 (2020): 289–302, https://doi.org/10.1086/710062; Saidiya Hartman, *Scenes of Subjection: Terror, Slavery, and Self-Making in Nineteenth-Century America* (New York: Oxford University Press, 2010); and Christina Elizabeth Sharpe, *In the Wake: On Blackness and Being* (Durham, NC: Duke University Press, 2016).

7. I recommend several excellent works on the commodification and ethics of circulating violent imagery as companion reads to this book. Michelle Caswell's *Archiving the Unspeakable* (Madison: University of Wisconsin

Press, 2014) is a tour de force interrogation of the photographic records of the Khmer Rouge regime in Cambodia. W.J.T. Mitchell's *What Do Pictures Want?: The Lives and Loves of Images* (Chicago: University of Chicago Press, 2005) is a fantastic primer on the emotional agency of images. Like Temi Odumosu, who tells us we must listen to the silent tears in the image of a crying child, Susie Linfield (in *The Cruel Radiance: Photography and Political Violence* [Chicago: University of Chicago Press, 2010]) challenges us to look deeper and more closely as we witness photographic horrors. Similarly, Frances Guerin and Roger Hallas, in *The Image and the Witness: Trauma, Memory, and Visual Culture* (London: Wallflower Press, 2007), encourage the same.

8. The language of "rights" is multivalent, and there are many ways to conceive of and define rights within any given community or society. In contraposition to Ayn Rand's objectivism, discussions of rights throughout this book refer not only to individualistic interpretations of the term but also to more robust social and ethical frameworks that are animated by rights discourse (including concepts such as group rights, natural rights, and liberty rights).

CHAPTER 1

Epigraph: Frederick Douglass, "The Civil Rights Case," Civil Rights Mass Meeting, Washington, DC, October 22, 1883.

1. Early photography used glass and metal (rather than paper) to permanently capture and fix images. Daguerreotypes (images on silver-coated copper plates), ambrotypes (images on transparent glass plates with a black backing), and tintypes (images on thin iron plates) were the three most common forms of photography until the invention of albumen silver prints in 1850. Made with egg whites (albumen) and silver nitrate, the albumen print was the first commercially exploitable method of using a glass negative to develop a paper photograph. Albumen cartes de visite, patented in Paris by photographer André Adolphe Eugène Disdéri in 1854, were small photographic cards that often featured celebrity visages and were commonly traded among friends and family during the late nineteenth and early twentieth centuries. Cartes de visite were particularly popular in the United States during the American Civil War.

2. Skinner Auctioneers, "Carte-de-Visite of Enslaved Man with Whipping Scars, Escaped Slave Known as Gordon or Peter (2015)," www.skinnerinc.com/auctions/2865B/lots/11 (accessed December 5, 2022).

3. The photograph was not, in fact, produced by A. I. Blauvelt but was made in a camp of Union soldiers along the Mississippi River by two itinerant photographers, William D. McPherson and his partner, Mr. Oliver of New Orleans (National Archives).

4. "A Typical Negro," *Harper's Weekly*, July 4, 1863, p. 429.

5. National Archives, Photograph 165-JT-230; Overseer Artayou Carrier whipped me. I was two months in bed sore from the whipping; 4/2/1863; Photographic Prints in John Taylor Album*, ca. 1861–ca. 1865; Records of the War Department General and Special Staffs, Record Group 165; National Archives at College Park, MD, www.docsteach.org/documents/document/peter.

6. See Henry Louis Gates, "Frederick Douglass's Camera Obscura: Representing the Antislave 'Clothed and in Their Own Form,'" *Critical Inquiry* (2015): 31–60. As the most photographed American in the nineteenth century, Frederick Douglass recognized that images mattered and took special care to be portrayed as dignified; he did not, for example, allow photographs to be made of the scars on his own back. See, for example, Stauffer John, Zoe Trodd, Celeste-Marie Bernier, Henry Louis Gates, and Kenneth B Morris, *Picturing Frederick Douglass: An Illustrated Biography of the Nineteenth Century's Most Photographed American*, revised ed. (New York: Liveright Publishing Corporation, a Division of W. W. Norton & Company, 2018).

7. The words "contraband" and "specimen" appear on the verso of the carte de visite of Gordon. The language of "*unusual* intelligence and energy" (emphasis mine) was used by the author of the *Harper's Weekly* article, "A Typical Negro," (July 4, 1863, p. 429).

8. For more on "the Black body," see the discussion of Harvey Young's work in the introduction. To read his full arguments, see Young, *Embodying Black Experience*.

9. Matthew Fox-Amato, "How Activists Used Photography to Help End Slavery," *Washington Post*, April 24, 2019, www.washingtonpost.com/outlook/2019/04/24/how-activists-used-photography-help-end-slavery/.

10. *Tamara Lanier v. President and Fellows of Harvard College, Harvard Board of Overseers, Harvard Corporation, The Peabody Museum of Archaeology and Ethnology and Harvard University*, filed April 25, 2019, case number 1:2019cv10978, US District Court for the District of Massachusetts, https://dockets.justia.com/docket/massachusetts/madce/1:2019cv10978/209402.

11. For an excellent treatment of the Renty and Delia Taylor daguerreotypes, the other daguerreotypes created by Agassiz as part of the same series,

and Tamara Lanier's fight to reclaim her ancestors' images from Harvard University and the Peabody Museum, see Jarrett M. Drake, "Blood at the Root," *Journal of Contemporary Archival Studies* 8, no. 6 (2021), https://elischolar.library.yale.edu/jcas/vol8/iss1/6. For a broader treatment of the integral and complex role photographs have played in anthropological contexts, see Elizabeth Edwards, *Raw Histories: Photographs, Anthropology, Museums* (Oxford, UK: Berg, 2001).

12. A lawsuit filed on behalf of Renty and Delia's descendant, Tamara Lanier, against Harvard alleges that "at Agassiz's behest, Renty and Delia were stripped naked and forced to pose for the daguerreotypes without consent, dignity, or compensation." See *Lanier v. Harvard*.

13. Coates as quoted in Anemona Hartocollis, "Who Should Own Photos of Slaves? The Descendants, Not Harvard, a Lawsuit Says," *New York Times*, March 20, 2019, www.nytimes.com/2019/03/20/us/slave-photographs-harvard.html.

14. *Lanier v. Harvard*.

15. The historiography of the Atlantic slave trade is immense, and it is still growing. As a result, at the very least the outlines of the history of human enslavement in the United States are well known. Certainly, even the scantest review of the extant literature would involve penning volumes here and would ultimately deflect from the purpose of this chapter, which is to trouble the production and uses of digital Atlantic slavery archives.

16. Here I am drawing on the work of Cedric Robinson, who provides an outstanding history of slave labor as capitalist production and its relationship to the later emergence of the Black Radical Tradition in his book on Black Marxism. See Cedric Robinson, *Black Marxism: The Making of the Black Radical Tradition* (Chapel Hill: University of North Carolina Press, 2000), especially chapter 5, "The Atlantic Slave Trade and African Labor."

17. Jan Vansina, *Kingdoms of the Savanna* (Madison: University of Wisconsin Press, 1966), 53.

18. Robinson, *Black Marxism*.

19. For more on the implications of racialized medicine in the United States, see chapter 3.

20. Saidiya V. Hartman, *Lose Your Mother: A Journey along the Atlantic Slave Route* (New York: Farrar, Straus, and Giroux, 2008), 6.

21. Geoffrey Yeo, "Concepts of Record (1): Evidence, Information, and Persistent Representation," *American Archivist* 70 (2007): 334.

22. Stephen Hensen and the Society of American Archivists, *Describing Archives: A Content Standard*, second edition (Chicago: Society of Ameri-

can Archivists, 2013), xxi, www2.archivists.org/groups/technical-subcomm ittee-on-describing-archives-a-content-standard-dacs/dacs.

23. Marisa Elena Duarte and Miranda Belarde-Lewis, "Imagining: Creating Spaces for Indigenous Ontologies," *Cataloging & Classification Quarterly* 53, no. 5–6 (2015): 677–702, DOI:10.1080/01639374.2015.1018396.

24. Robinson, *Black Marxism*, 157.

25. Odumosu, "Crying Child," 290.

26. Odumosu, "Crying Child," 290–91.

27. Odumosu, "Crying Child," 291. Here, Odumosu also cites Fred Moten, *In the Break : The Aesthetics of the Black Radical Tradition* (Minneapolis: University of Minnesota Press, 2003); and Tina Campt, *Listening To Images* (Durham, NC: Duke University Press, 2017).

28. For a full discussion of racial capitalism, see Robinson's *Black Marxism*.

29. *Lanier v. Harvard*.

30. *Lanier v. Harvard*.

31. It is also important to note here a relationship between our contemporary digital culture, the shifting nature of public display for visual memory objects such as photographs, and the emotional agency of images: Renty and Delia are now broadcast on small screens and handheld technologies — technologies that other human beings wear and carry on their own bodies.

32. Oliva Carlisle, "Trends in the Runaway Slave Advertisements," North Carolina Digital Library on Slavery's NC Slave Advertisements Database, http://libcdm1.uncg.edu/cdm/trends/collection/RAS (accessed March 3, 2023).

33. See Simone Browne, *Dark Matters: On the Surveillance of Blackness* (Durham, NC: Duke University Press, 2015); Jessica Marie Johnson, "Markup Bodies: Black [Life] Studies and Slavery [Death] Studies at the Digital Crossroads," *Social Text* 36, no. 4 (2018): 57–79; and Jacqueline Wernimont, *Numbered Lives: Life and Death in Quantum Media* (Cambridge, MA: MIT Press, 2019).

34. Johnson, "Markup Bodies," 58.

35. Johnson, "Markup Bodies," 59.

36. Saidiya Hartman, "Venus in Two Acts," *Small Axe: A Journal of Criticism* 26 (2008): 5.

37. Daniela Agostinho, "Archival Encounters: Rethinking Access and Care in Digital Colonial Archives," *Archival Science: International Journal on Recorded Information* 19 (2019):142.

38. Agostinho, "Archival Encounters," 156.

39. Agostinho, "Archival Encounters," 156 (emphasis added).

40. Freedom on the Move, "Freedom on the Move," Yale University, https://freedomonthemove.org/ (accessed December 6, 2022).

41. See Lucia Lorenzi, (@empathywarrior), "I once asked Dionne Brand about how to deal with the violence and pain of the archive of Black history. She told me to look for the red ribbon. A detail, she notes, from the newspaper description of an enslaved girl who had escaped - last seen with a red ribbon in her hair," Twitter, April 19, 2020, https://twitter.com/empathywarrior/status/1252095554852548609.

42. Paula von Gleich, "Afro-pessimism, Fugitivity, and the Border to Social Death," in Woons Marc and Sebastian Weier, eds., *Critical Epistemologies of Global Politics* (Bristol, UK: E-International Relations, 2017).

CHAPTER 2

Epigraph: Darnella Frazier, "Trial of Derek Chauvin, Charged with Killing George Floyd, Day 2, Direct Feed," *PBS News Hour*, livestreamed March 30, 2021, www.youtube.com/watch?v=1zOyVPmAJns&t=6826s.

1. This narrative is derived directly from the testimony of Darnella Frazier given during the murder trial of Derek Chauvin in Hennepin County, Minnesota, on March 30, 2021. For a full audio recording of Frazier's testimony, see *PBS New Hour*, www.pbs.org/newshour/nation/watch-live-trial-of-derek-chauvin-charged-with-killing-george-floyd-resumes-in-minneapolis.

2. Darnella Frazier, "They killed him right in front of cup foods over south on 38th and Chicago!! No type of sympathy 💔💔 #POLICEBRUTALITY," Facebook, May 25, 2020. Facebook's "public" setting allows anyone to view the posted content, whether or not they have a Facebook account or know the person who is doing the posting.

3. Reports from summer 2020 estimated that between fifteen million and twenty-six million people had participated at some point in the demonstrations in the United States, making the protests the largest in US history. See, for example, Larry Buchanan, Quoctrung Bui, and Jugal K. Patel, "Black Lives Matter May Be the Largest Movement in U.S. History," *New York Times*, July 3, 2020.

4. For full access to the court documents and other archival records related to the Derek Chauvin trial, see the Minnesota Judicial Branch records 27-CR-20-12646, *State of Minnesota v. Derek Chauvin*, www.mncourts.gov/media/StateofMinnesotavDerekChauvin.aspx.

5. Ed Pilkington, "Juror Says Video of George Floyd's Death Was Like Attending a Funeral Every Day," *The Guardian*, April 28, 2021, www.theguardian.com/us-news/2021/apr/28/juror-derek-chauvin-george-floyd-brandon-mitchell.

6. Tim Kaine, "Darnella Frazier, the teenager who filmed the video of George Floyd's murder, should win a Pulitzer Prize for photojournalism. She is a stellar example of how everyday people can be powerful in documenting injustice and creating momentum for accountability," Twitter, April 21, 2021, https://twitter.com/timkaine/status/1384854910836031488.

7. The public nature of lynchings and the role photography played in the practice's persistence over time have become central themes in the scholarship of history, race, and visual cultures. As Linda Kim argues, although each of these literatures approach lynching photographs using different methodological lenses, they all share the premise that lynching photographs were ubiquitous and deeply entrenched elements of post-Reconstruction visual culture. See Linda Kim, "A Law of Unintended Consequences: United States Postal Censorship of Lynching Photographs," *Visual Resources* 28, no. 2 (2012): 171–93, DOI:10.1080/01973762.2012.678812.

8. Elisabeth Freeman, "The Waco Lynching," Report, 1916, Anti-Lynching File, NAACP Papers, Manuscript Division, Library of Congress, Washington, DC.

9. Kim, "Law of Unintended Consequences."

10. In the 1890s, Ida B. Wells documented lynchings across the United States, publishing statistics and details of several dozen killings in such pamphlets as *Southern Horrors: Lynch Law in All Its Phases* and *The Red Record*. Although they represent an extremely important early contribution to the American anti-lynching campaign, these publications did not include images.

11. Megan Ming Francis, *Civil Rights and the Making of the Modern American State* (New York: Cambridge University Press, 2014), 46.

12. NAACP Board of Directors, Minutes, June 12, 1916, NAACP Papers, Manuscript Division, Library of Congress, Washington, DC.

13. "The Will-to-Lynch," *New Republic* 8, no. 102 (October 14, 1916), 261.

14. Francis, *Civil Rights and the Making of the Modern American State*, 48.

15. See Roy Nash, "Waco Horror Stirs to Action," letter, 1916, Anti-Lynching File, NAACP Papers, Manuscript Division, Library of Congress, Washington, DC. NAACP Board of Directors, Minutes, July 10, 1916,

NAACP Papers, Manuscript Division, Library of Congress, Washington, DC. NAACP Board of Directors, Minutes, November 13, 1916, NAACP Papers, Manuscript Division, Library of Congress, Washington, DC.

16. Dora Apel and Shawn Michelle Smith, *Lynching Photographs* (Berkeley: University of California Press, 2007), 24.

17. See, for example, Gustavus Stadler, "Never Heard Such a Thing: Lynching and Phonographic Modernity," *Social Text* 28, no. 1 (March 2010): 87–105.

18. Grace Elizabeth Hale, *Making Whiteness: The Culture of Segregation in the South, 1890–1940* (New York: Vintage Books, 2002), 201.

19. Safiya Umoja Noble, "Teaching Trayvon: Race, Media, and the Politics of Spectacle." *The Black Scholar* 44, no. 1 (2014): 12–29, DOI:10.1080 /00064246.2014.11641209.

20. Khalil Gibran Muhammad, *The Condemnation of Blackness: Race, Crime, and the Making of Modern Urban America* (Cambridge, MA: Harvard University Press, 2010).

21. In February 2015, after a three-year investigation, the US Department of Justice concluded there was not sufficient evidence that Zimmerman intentionally violated the civil rights of Martin, saying the Zimmerman case did not meet the "high standard" for a federal hate crime prosecution.

22. André L. Brock, *Distributed Blackness: African American Cybercultures* (New York: New York University Press, 2020).

23. Noble, "Teaching Trayvon," 20.

24. AdAge Staff, "How Brands and Agencies Responded to Racial Injustice in the First Month Following George Floyd's Death," *AdAge,* July 7, 2020, https://adage.com/article/cmo-strategy/how-brands-and-agen cies-responded-racial-injustice-first-month-following-george-floyds-dea th/2265626. For a compelling discussion of this phenomenon, see Francesca Sobande. "Woke-Washing: 'Intersectional' Femvertising and Branding 'Woke' Bravery," *European Journal of Marketing* (2019): 2723–45, https:// doi.org/10.1108/EJM-02-2019-0134.

25. Amanda Mull, "Brands Have Nothing Real to Say about Racism," *The Atlantic,* June 3, 2020, www.theatlantic.com/health/archive/2020/06 /brands-racism-protests-amazon-nfl-nike/612613/.

26. Harvey Young, "The Black Body as Souvenir in American Lynching," *Theatre Journal* 57 (2005): 639–57.

27. Jennifer C. Nash, *The Black Body in Ecstasy: Reading Race, Reading Pornography* (Durham, NC: Duke University Press, 2014), 45.

CHAPTER 3

Epigraph: Day Lacks as quoted in Infobase and Home Box Office (Firm) directors, *The Immortal Life of Henrietta Lacks* (Home Box Office, 2019).

1. Lynn Poole, George O. Gey, Anthony Farrar, and Joel Chaseman, "Cancer Will Be Conquered," originally broadcast as a segment of the television program *Johns Hopkins Science Review* on April 10, 1951, from the studios of WAAM in Baltimore, MD.

2. Hannah Landecker, *Culturing Life: How Cells Became Technologies* (Cambridge, MA: Harvard University Press, 2007), 141–42.

3. William A. Clark and Dorothy H. Geary, "The Story of the American Type Culture Collection—Its History and Development (1899–1973)," *Advances in Applied Microbi*ology 17 (1974): 295.

4. Clark and Geary, "Story of the American Type Culture Collection," 297.

5. For a more in-depth, critical analysis of the nature and role of archival description, see chapter 1.

6. Created by growing animal or plant cells under controlled conditions in artificial environments, cell cultures are often used to study tissue growth and maturation; virus biology and vaccine development; the role of genes in disease and health; and the use of cell lines to generate biopharmaceuticals. Cells that are used to originate laboratory cultures are typically either isolated from their original tissue source directly, or they may be derived from an established cell line or cell strain.

7. Rebecca Skloot, *The Immortal Life of Henrietta Lacks* (New York: Crown, 2011), 15.

8. See Brendan P. Lucey, Walter A. Nelson-Rees, and Grover M. Hutchins, "Henrietta Lacks, HeLa Cells, and Cell Culture Contamination," *Archives of Pathology and Laboratory Medicine* 133, no. 9 (September 2009): 1463–67. In 1951, Johns Hopkins was—as it is today—a teaching hospital. In the mid-twentieth century, Black patients at teaching hospitals often faced "long waits for care; impolite hospital staff; and underfunded, understaffed, overcrowded, and poorly maintained facilities" (Alondra Nelson, *Body and Soul: The Black Panther Party and the Fight against Medical Discrimination* [Minneapolis: University of Minnesota Press, 2011], 59). It was not uncommon for Black patients to face blatant racial discrimination in medical facilities during the Jim Crow era (nor, frankly, is this uncommon in today's medical environments). For a carefully researched and beautifully crafted treatise on some of the medical discrimination Black communities have historically endured, see Nelson, *Body and Soul*.

9. Howard W. Jones, "Record of the First Physician to See Henrietta Lacks at the Johns Hopkins Hospital: History of the Beginning of the HeLa Cell Line," *American Journal of Obstetrics and Gynecology* 176, no. 6 (1997): s227–s228, https://doi.org/10.1016/S0002-9378(97)70379-X.

10. Landecker, *Culturing Life*, 140.

11. Jamie Manfuso and Stephanie Desmon, "Honoring the Henrietta Lacks Legacy at Hopkins," May 20, 2011, www.hopkinsmedicine.org/news/publications/hopkins_medicine_magazine/archives/springsummer_2011/web_extra_honoring_the_henrietta_lacks_legacy_at_hopkins.

12. It is important to note that the polio vaccine was originally used only to save the lives of white patients. During the polio outbreaks of the 1930s, white scientists pushed a race-based medicine theory that Black people were less susceptible to polio. In truth, many cases of polio in Black communities went undiagnosed, and segregated medical systems denied Black patients access to adequate care, reflecting the ways Jim Crow practices were present in medicine and medical care.

13. Johns Hopkins Medicine, "The Legacy of Henrietta Lacks: The Importance of HeLa Cells," www.hopkinsmedicine.org/henriettalacks/importance-of-hela-cells.html (accessed March 2, 2023).

14. "Henrietta Lacks (1920–1951)," Maryland Women's Hall of Fame, Maryland State Archives, MSA SC 3520-16887, https://web.archive.org/web/20210314234454/https://msa.maryland.gov/msa/educ/exhibits/womenshall/html/lacks.html (accessed March 2, 2023).

15. See Michael Rogers, "The Double-Edged Helix," *Rolling Stone* 209 (March 25, 1976): 48–51.

16. Landecker, *Culturing Life*, 4.

17. Katherine McKittrick, "'Who Do You Talk To, When a Body's in Trouble?': M. Nourbese Philip's (Un)Silencing of Black Bodies in the Diaspora," *Social & Cultural Geography* 1, no. 2 (2000): 223–36. Toni Morrison, "Introduction: Friday on the Potomac," in Toni Morrison, ed., *Race-ing Justice, En-Gendering Power: Essays on Anita Hill, Clarence Thomas, and the Social Construction of Reality* (New York: Pantheon, 1992), xvi.

18. Bill Davidson, "Probing the Secret of Life," *Colliers* (May 14, 1954): 80.

19. Howard W. Jones, Victor A McKusick, Peter S. Harper, and Kuang-Dong Wuu, "George Otto Gey (1899–1970): The HeLa Cell and a Reappraisal of Its Origin," *American Journal of Obstetrics and Gynecology* 38, no. 6 (1971): 945.

20. Landecker, *Culturing Life*, 167.

21. As cited in Landecker, *Culturing Life*, 169.

22. This race-based pseudoscience is the same kind of "natural science" that undergirded Louis Agassiz's quest to "prove" the inherent biological inferiority of Black people and to justify their subjugation, exploitation, and segregation (recall that Agassiz commissioned the photographs of Renty and Delia discussed in chapter 1).

23. Morrison, "Introduction," xvi.

24. Thomas R. McCormick, "Principles of Bioethics," University of Washington Department of Bioethics and Humanities, https://depts.washington.edu/bhdept/ethics-medicine/bioethics-topics/articles/principles-bioethics (accessed March 2, 2023).

25. Tom L. Beauchamp and James F. Childress, *Principles of Biomedical Ethics* (New York: Oxford University Press, 1979).

26. US Department of Health and Human Services, "The Belmont Report," April 18, 1979, www.hhs.gov/ohrp/regulations-and-policy/belmont-report/read-the-belmont-report/index.html.

27. Kathy L. Hudson and Francis S. Collins, "Biospecimen Policy: Family Matters," *Nature* 500, no. 7461 (2013): 141–42, DOI:10.1038/500141a.

28. For an excellent discussion of these practices in action, see Osagie K. Obasogie, "High-Tech, High-Risk Forensics," *New York Times*, July 25, 2013, www.nytimes.com/2013/07/25/opinion/high-tech-high-risk-forensics.html. Since 2018, more than two hundred people have been imprisoned based on genetic genealogy, and companies like DNA Land (https://dna.land/)—a digital biobank for crowdsourcing DNA—have begun to collocate 23andMe and Ancestry genomic data in the name of "big science."

29. David Pilgrim, *Understanding Jim Crow: Using Racist Memorabilia to Teach Tolerance and Promote Social Justice* (Oakland, CA: PM Press, 2015).

30. Tonia Sutherland, "The Carceral Archive: Documentary Records, Narrative Construction, and Predictive Risk Assessment," *Journal of Cultural Analytics* (2019), DOI:10.22148/16.039.

31. McKittrick, "Who Do You Talk To," 226.

32. McKittrick, "Who Do You Talk To," 226. Not surprisingly, it was this very in-betweenness, a description of Henrietta Lacks "inserting a finger between her legs" that caused Rebecca Skloot's book to be banned in some parts of the United States as pornography.

33. Perhaps the most dramatic proof of this shift emerged in April 2018, when a team at the Yale School of Medicine drew global attention for (briefly) restoring cellular activity in recently deceased brains (see Z. Vrselja,

S. G. Daniele, J. Silbereis et al., "Restoration of Brain Circulation and Cellular Functions Hours Post-mortem," *Nature* 568 (2019): 336–43, https://doi.org/10.1038/s41586-019-1099-1.

34. Landecker, *Culturing Life*, 159.

35. See *Estate of Henrietta Lacks v. Thermo Fischer Scientific, Inc.*, US District Court of Maryland, filed October 4, 2021, www.courthousenews.com/wp-content/uploads/2021/10/henrietta-lacks-thermo-fisher.pdf.

36. As quoted in "Henrietta Lacks: Science Must Right a Historical Wrong," *Nature*, September 1, 2020, www.nature.com/articles/d41586-020-02494-z.

CHAPTER 4

Epigraph: Tupac Shakur, "Only Fear of Death," *R U Still Down? (Remember Me)*, November 25, 1997.

1. Tupac's mother, Afeni Shakur, changed his name in 1972 from Lesane Parish Crooks to Tupac Amaru Shakur; she chose this name after José Gabriel Túpac Amaru (1738–1781). Better known as Túpac Amaru II, he was the leader of a large Andean uprising against the Spanish in Peru. Túpac Amaru II has become a mythical figure in the Peruvian struggles for independence and Indigenous rights, as well as an inspiration to myriad causes in Spanish America and beyond.

2. Robert Sam Anson, "To Die Like a Gangster," *Vanity Fair*, March 1997, www.vanityfair.com/culture/1997/03/tupac-shakur-rap-death#.

3. James Thomas Jones III, "All Eyez on Me: A Missed Opportunity to Politicize Young Black America," *Manhood, Race, and Culture*, www.manhoodraceculture.com/2017/06/17/all-eyez-on-me-a-missed-opportunity-to-politicize-young-black-america/ (https://web.archive.org/web/20170906172128/http://www.manhoodraceculture.com/2017/06/17/all-eyez-on-me-a-missed-opportunity-to-politicize-young-black-america/).

4. Anson, "To Die Like a Gangster."

5. Aisha Harris, "Picture Me LOLin'," *Slate*, June 16, 2017, https://slate.com/culture/2017/06/all-eyez-on-me-the-new-tupac-biopic-reviewed.html.

6. See Alexandra Sherlock, "Larger Than Life: Digital Resurrection and the Re-Enchantment of Society," *The Information Society* 29, no. 3 (2013): 164–76, DOI:10.1080/01972243.2013.777302.

7. Young, "Black Body as Souvenir in American Lynching."

8. Nash, *Black Body in Ecstasy*.

9. Rotoscoping was first popularized by Max Fleischer in 1915 in his groundbreaking animated series *Out of the Inkwell* (1918–27).

10. Here I am paraphrasing Henry Watson, a self-emancipated Black man born into slavery in Virginia. See "Henry Watson, Narrative of Henry Watson, A Fugitive Slave, 1848," in *Slave Auctions: Selections from 19th-Century Narratives of Formerly Enslaved African Americans*, National Humanities Center Resource Toolbox, *The Making of African American Identity: Vol. 1, 1500–1865*, http://nationalhumanitiescenter.org/pds/maai/enslavement/text2/slaveauctions.pdf.

11. James Oakes, *Slavery and Freedom: An Interpretation of the Old South* (New York: Knopf, 1990), 23.

12. Anthony B. Pinn, *Terror and Triumph: The Nature of Black Religion* (Minneapolis, MN: Fortress Press, 2003), 49.

13. "Obscene theatricality" is a term proffered by Saidiya Hartman in the opening lines of her book *Scenes of Subjection*, first published in 1997. See Saidiya Hartman, *Scenes of Subjection: Terror, Slavery, and Self-Making in Nineteenth-Century America* (New York: Oxford University Press, 2010).

14. Solomon Northup, *Twelve Years a Slave* (New York: Miller, Orton & Mulligan, 1855), 78–79.

15. I am grateful for the work of Jason Stupp in formulating this framing. See Jason Stupp, "Slavery and the Theatre of History: Ritual Performance on the Auction Block," *Theatre Journal* 63, no. 1 (March 2011): 61–84.

16. William Wells Brown, "Narrative of William W. Brown, A Fugitive Slave, Written by Himself, 1849," in *Slave Auctions: Selections from 19th-Century Narratives of Formerly Enslaved African Americans*.

17. See Guy Debord, *Society of the Spectacle* (Detroit, MI: Black and Red Press, 1970).

18. See, for example, Madeleine Berg, "The Highest-Paid Dead Celebrities of 2020," *Forbes*, November 13, 2020, www.forbes.com/sites/maddieberg/2020/11/13/the-highest-paid-dead-celebrities-of-2020/?sh=49f016013b4b.

19. Daniel Kreps, "Whitney Houston's Hologram Is Coming to Las Vegas," *Rolling Stone*, July 22, 2021, www.rollingstone.com/music/music-news/whitney-houston-hologram-concert-las-vegas-residency-1201006/.

20. As quoted in Jenna Benchetrit, "Dead Celebrities Are Being Digitally Resurrected—And the Ethics Are Murky," *CBS News* (Canada), August 8, 2021, www.cbc.ca/news/entertainment/dead-celebrities-digital-resurrection-1.6132738.

21. Arielle Padover, "Legal Protection of a Digital Resurrection," *Cornell*

Journal of Law and Public Policy: The Issue Spotter, March 8, 2017, http://jlpp.org/blogzine/legal-protection-of-a-digital-resurrection/.

22. It is worth noting that both Prince and Kobe Bryant are also on the *Forbes* list of Highest Paid Dead Celebrities.

23. See Randall C. Jimerson, *Archives Power: Memory, Accountability, and Social Justice* (Chicago: Society of American Archivists, 2010).

24. Elias Canetti, *Crowds and Power* (London: Phoenix Press, 1962), 51.

CHAPTER 5

Epigraph: Marika Cifor, Patricia Garcia, T. L. Cowan, Jas Rault, Tonia Sutherland, Anita Say Chan, Jennifer Rode, Anna Lauren Hoffmann, Niloufar Salehi, and Lisa Nakamura, *Feminist Data Manifest-No*, 2019, www.manifestno.com/ (accessed March 3, 2023).

1. See Jenna Rosenstein, "People Can't Tell If This Fenty Model Is Real or Fake," *Harper's Bazaar*, February 9, 2018, www.harpersbazaar.com/beauty/makeup/a16810663/shudu-gram-fenty-model-fake/.

2. Jonathan Square, "Is Instagram's Newest Sensation Just Another Example of Cultural Appropriation?" *Fashionista*, March 27, 2018, https://fashionista.com/2018/03/computer-generated-models-cultural-appropriation.

3. Rosenstein, "People Can't Tell If This Fenty Model Is Real or Fake."

4. Lauren Michele Jackson, "Shudu Gram Is a White Man's Digital Projection of Real-Life Black Womanhood," *New Yorker*, May 4, 2018, www.newyorker.com/culture/culture-desk/shudu-gram-is-a-white-mans-digital-projection-of-real-life-black-womanhood.

5. See, for example, Eric Lott, "Love and Theft: The Racial Unconscious of Blackface Minstrelsy," *Representations*, no. 39 (1992): 23–50, https://doi.org/10.2307/2928593; and Eric Lott, "'The Seeming Counterfeit': Racial Politics and Early Blackface Minstrelsy," *American Quarterly* 43, no. 2 (1991): 223–54, https://doi.org/10.2307/2712925.

6. See Deen Freelon, Michael Bossetta, Chris Wells et al., "Black Trolls Matter: Racial and Ideological Asymmetries in Social Media Disinformation," *Social Science Computer Review* (April 2020), DOI:10.1177/0894439320914853. For more on how digital blackface operates as a manifestation of anti-Black racism, see Luke Stark, "Facial Recognition, Emotion, and Race in Animated Social Media," *First Monday* 23, no. 9 (2018), https://doi.org/10.5210/fm.v23i9.9406; Alexander Robertson, Walid Magdy, and Sharon Goldwater, "Self-representation on Twitter Using Emoji Skin Color Modi-

fiers," in Twelfth International AAAI Conference on Web and Social Media; and K. Dobson and I. Knezevic, "'Ain't Nobody Got Time for That!': Framing and Stereotyping in Legacy and Social Media," *Canadian Journal of Communication* 43, no. 3 (2018): 381–97, http://dx.doi.org.eres.library.manoa.hawaii.edu/10.22230/cjc.2018v43n3a3378.

7. As I noted in the introduction, the language of "rights" is multivalent, and there are many ways to both conceive of and define rights within any given community or society. In contraposition to Ayn Rand's objectivism, discussions of rights in this chapter and in chapter 6 are not bound by individualistic interpretations, but rather seek to engage the more robust social and ethical frameworks that are animated by rights discourse (such as group rights, natural rights, and liberty rights).

8. Unfortunately, the Court also left it up to search engines—that is, private companies—to apply this right and to conduct the very delicate exercise of balancing the right to data protection with freedom of expression.

9. The right to be forgotten is distinct from the right to privacy. The right to privacy constitutes information that is not publicly known, whereas the right to be forgotten involves removing information that was at one time publicly known. The "Right to Know" in the United States is generally codified in both state and federal law through legislation such as the Freedom of Information Act and, more broadly, through environmental law (e.g., the right to know what chemicals a person might be exposed in the workplace).

10. Grant David Bollmer, "Millions Now Living Will Never Die: Cultural Anxieties about the Afterlife of Information," *The Information Society* 29, no. 3 (2013): 142–51, DOI:10.1080/01972243.2013.777297.

11. Amelia Acker and Jed R. Brubaker, "Death, Memorialization, and Social Media: A Platform Perspective for Personal Archives," *Archivaria* 77 (2014): 1–23, http://archivaria.ca/index.php/archivaria/article/view/13469.

12. Facebook, "Memories of Friends Departed Endure on Facebook," October 26, 2009, www.facebook.com/notes/10160196742716729/.

13. See, for example, Alex Hearn, "Facebook Apologises over 'Cruel' Year in Review Clips," *The Guardian*, December 29, 2014; and Eric A. Meyer, "My Year Was Tragic. Facebook Ambushed Me with a Painful Reminder," *Slate*, December 29, 2014, https://slate.com/technology/2014/12/facebook-year-in-review-my-tragic-year-was-the-wrong-fodder-for-facebook-s-latest-app.html.

14. Zadie Smith, "Generation Why?" *New York Review of Books*, November 25, 2010, www.nybooks.com/articles/2010/11/25/generation-why/.

15. As quoted in Casey Newton, "Speak, Memory," *The Verge*, www.the

verge.com/a/luka-artificial-intelligence-memorial-roman-mazurenko-bot (accessed March 2, 2023).

16. Quoted in Jason Fagone, "The Jessica Simulation: Love and Loss in the Age of A.I.," *San Francisco Chronicle*, July 23, 2021, www.sfchronicle.com/projects/2021/jessica-simulation-artificial-intelligence/.

17. Bollmer, "Millions Now Living Will Never Die," 142.

18. For an excellent collection of essays about race and the internet, see Lisa Nakamura and Peter Chow-White, eds., *Race after the Internet* (New York: Routledge, 2012).

19. See Ashely Bardhan, "Men Are Creating AI Girlfriends and Then Verbally Abusing Them," *Futurism*, January 18, 2022, https://futurism.com/chatbot-abuse.

20. Asa Fitch, "Could AI Keep People 'Alive' after Death?" *Wall Street Journal*, July 3, 2021, www.wsj.com/articles/could-ai-keep-people-alive-after-death-11625317200.

21. Michelle Caswell and Marika Cifor, "From Human Rights to Feminist Ethics: Radical Empathy in the Archives," *Archivaria* 81 (2016): 23–44.

22. Laura Parker, "How to Become Virtually Immortal," *New Yorker*, April 4, 2014, www.newyorker.com/tech/annals-of-technology/how-to-become-virtually-immortal.

23. These sites also have a learning curve that some may find requires a long journey to master. It is my contention that these sites require a certain level of literacy (both traditional and digital) to competently navigate them.

24. As quoted in Elizabeth Murphy, "Inside 23andMe Founder Anne Wojcicki's $99 DNA Revolution," *Fast Company*, October 14, 2013, www.fastcompany.com/3018598/for-99-this-ceo-can-tell-you-what-might-kill-you-inside-23andme-founder-anne-wojcickis-dna-r.

25. Familial DNA and "genetic genealogy" searches are increasingly being used to identify the "potential" relatives of an alleged perpetrator. See, for example, Rafil Kroll-Zaidi, "Your DNA Test Could Send a Relative to Jail," *New York Times Magazine*, January 3, 2022, www.nytimes.com/2021/12/27/magazine/dna-test-crime-identification-genome.html.

26. MyHeritage, "Deep Nostalgia," www.myheritage.com/deep-nostalgia (accessed March 6, 2023).

27. MyHeritage, "Deep Nostalgia."

28. Corporations view consumer data as their property and force consent in requiring that users accept cookies before using their sites. Individuals may request that data about them be deleted, but this is a complex process, often mishandled by corporate entities. See, for example, Tatum Hunter,

"Companies Are Hoarding Personal Data About You. Here's How to Get Them to Delete It," *Washington Post*, September 26, 2021, www.washingtonpost.com/technology/2021/09/26/ask-company-delete-personal-data/.

29. As quoted in Acker and Brubaker, "Death, Memorialization, and Social Media." See also Frank Pasquale, "From Territorial To Functional Sovereignty: The Case of Amazon," December 6, 2017, https://lpeproject.org/blog/from-territorial-to-functional-sovereignty-the-case-of-amazon/.

30. Carole McGranahan, "Theorizing Refusal: An Introduction," *Cultural Anthropology* 31, no. 3 (2016): 319–25.

31. Tina Campt, "Black Visuality and the Practice of Refusal," *Women and Performance*, February 25, 2019, www.womenandperformance.org/ampersand/29-1/campt.

32. Patricia Garcia, Niloufar Salehi, Tonia Sutherland, et al., "No! On Refusal and the Feminist Data Manifest-No," *Conference Companion on the Proceedings from the 25th ACM Conference On Computer-Supported Cooperative Work And Social Computing*, Spring 2022, https://doi.org/10.1145/3557997.

33. See Ruha Benjamin, "Informed Refusal: Toward a Justice-based Bioethics," *Science, Technology, and Human Values* 4, no. 6 (2017): 967–90; and Audra Simpson, "On Ethnographic Refusal: Indigeneity, 'Voice,' and Colonial Citizenship," *Junctures: The Journal for Thematic Dialogue* 9 (2007), https://junctures.org/index.php/junctures/article/view/66/60.

34. Cifor et al., *Feminist Data Manifest-No*.

35. Ruha Benjamin (@ruha9), "Note to selves: remember to imagine and craft the worlds you cannot live without, just as you dismantle the ones you cannot live within," Twitter, November 22, 2017, https://twitter.com/ruha9/status/926180439827591168.

36. Benjamin, "Informed Refusal," 969.

37. Simpson, "On Ethnographic Refusal," 78.

38. Garcia et al., "No! On Refusal and the Feminist Data Manifest-No."

CHAPTER 6

Epigraph: In Joyce Aschenbrenner, *Katherine Dunham: Dancing a Life* (Urbana: University of Illinois Press, 2002), 163.

1. Katherine Dunham, "Form and Function in Primitive Dance," *Educational Dance* 4, no. 10 (October 1941): 2–4.

2. Vévé Clark, "Performing the Memory of Difference in Afro-Caribbean Dance: Katherine Dunham's Choreography, 1938–1987," in Genevieve E.

Fabre and Robert G. O'Meally, eds., *History and Memory in African-American Culture* (Cary, NC: Oxford University Press, 1994), 188–201.

3. Dunham understood that movement has a particular form, based on a specific function, under a given set of circumstances; translating this cultural knowledge into staged dances for Dunham was a mode of cultural exchange. Information, she held, was being passed from her anthropological research in the Caribbean to her dancers' bodies and then, through them, to the audience.

4. Pierre Nora, "Between Memory and History: Les Lieux de Mémoire," *Representations* 1, no. 26 (April 1989): 13, https://doi.org/10.2307/2928520.

5. Robin D. G. Kelley, "Why Black Marxism, Why Now?" *Boston Review*, February 1, 2021, https://bostonreview.net/articles/robin-d-g-kelley-tk-2/.

6. Dunham developed three theoretical models, each of which is necessary to properly execute Dunham Technique: Form and Function, Intercultural Communication, and Socialization through the Arts (see Albirda Rose, *Dunham Technique: A Way of Life* [Dubuque, IA: Kendall/Hunt Publishing Company, 1990]). These theories formed what Dunham referred to as "The System." Used primarily to understand discrete dances and specific dance movement, Dunham's theory of Form and Function reveals the ways dance relates to the overall cultural patterns inherent in any given culture's belief system. Dunham's theory of Intercultural Communication builds on the theory of Form and Function. Intercultural Communication in Dunham Technique is used as a means for gaining an understanding and acceptance of others, again affirming Dunham's belief that through dance, information and knowledge could be gathered about living one's own culture and respecting the cultures of others. The first two theoretical models lead to the third: Socialization through the Arts. Dunham used this model to train people as both artists and communicators, arguing that given the opportunity, people would be inclined to learn about themselves through the art forms of their given culture(s), situating them within a global context and again promoting intercultural awareness and appreciation.

7. For an excellent discussion of *Southland*, its reception, and eventual censorship, see Constance Valis Hill, "Katherine Dunham's *Southland*: Protest in the Face of Repression," in Katherine Dunham, Vévé Clark, and Sara E. Johnson, eds., *Kaiso! Writings by and about Katherine Dunham* (Madison: University of Wisconsin Press, 2005).

8. From Katherine Dunham, "Program: *Southland* in Santiago, Chile, World Premiere, January 1951," in Vévé Clark and Margaret B. Wilkerson,

eds., *Kaiso! Katherine Dunham: An Anthology of Writings* (Berkeley, CA: Institute for the Study of Social Change, 1978).

9. As quoted in Joyce Aschenbrenner, "Katherine Dunham: Reflections on the Social and Political Contexts of Afro-American Dance," *Dance Research Annual* 12 (New York: Congress on Research in Dance, 1981).

10. See Clark, "Performing the Memory of Difference in Afro-Caribbean Dance."

11. Sara E. Johnson, "Introduction: Diamonds on the Toes of Her Feet," in Katherine Dunham, Véve Clark, and Sara E. Johnson, eds., *Kaiso! Writings by and about Katherine Dunham* (Madison: University of Wisconsin Press, 2005), 6.

12. Dr. Albirda Rose, interview with author, Pittsburgh, November 26, 2013.

13. Clark, "Performing the Memory of Difference in Afro-Caribbean Dance," 190.

14. Ronald Hutson, interview with author, October 2, 2013.

15. Rose, *Dunham Technique*, 4.

16. Johnson, "Introduction: Diamonds on the Toes of Her Feet," 12.

17. Library of Congress, "Katherine Dunham on Need for Dunham Technique," video recording, 2002, http://lcweb2.loc.gov/diglib/ihas/loc.natlib.ihas.200003845/default.html.

18. Library of Congress, "Katherine Dunham on Her Anthropological Films," video recording, 2002, http://lcweb2.loc.gov/diglib/ihas/loc.natlib.ihas.200003841/default.html.

19. See Marina Magloire, "An Ethics of Discomfort: Katherine Dunham's Vodou Belonging," *Small Axe: A Caribbean Journal of Criticism* 23, no. 3 (2019): 1–17.

20. Materials on Dunham also exist in the archives at the Jacob's Pillow Dance Festival in western Massachusetts and the Missouri History Museum.

21. Other materials were donated by dance historian Claude Conyers in 2011 and Laurent Dubois (whose work focuses in part on the history of Haiti) in 2017, respectively. Conyers and Dubois are both white-presenting.

22. SPARC, "About SPARC," https://sparcopen.org/ (accessed March 2, 2023).

23. Samantha R. Winn, "Ethics of Access in Displaced Archives," *Provenance: Journal of the Society of Georgia Archivists* 33, no. 1 (2015), http://hdl.handle.net/10919/64319.

24. One excellent study that does address concerns at the intersection of access and contested or controversial records is Tywanna Whorley's disser-

tation on the records from the Tuskegee syphilis experiments. See Tywanna Whorley, "The Tuskegee Syphilis Study: Access and Control over Controversial Records," PhD dissertation, University of Pittsburgh, 2006.

25. Kimberly Christen, "Opening Archives: Respectful Repatriation," *The American Archivist* 74 (2011): 185–210.

26. Winn, "Ethics of Access in Displaced Archives."

27. Society of American Archivists, "A Guide to Deeds of Gift," www2.archivists.org/publications/brochures/deeds-of-gift (accessed March 2, 2023).

28. There are already several practical ways that this can be accomplished. The many dedicated members of the Black Memory Workers Group, for example, frequently serve as consultants. The Black Memory Workers Group is comprised of trained archivists and other memory workers in North America who self-identify as Black and work across several cultural heritage domains. Predominantly white institutions that hold records that document Black life, culture, and death should also consider being in conversation with Black cultural heritage institutions and Black community archives to think through issues of community stewardship as well as to address concerns related to representation and access. Black cultural heritage institutions, when not restricted by blunt funding instruments—government sourced funding is unfortunately often not flexible enough in its design to support the unique praxes that comprise Black memory work—play a vital part in developing uniquely Black archival practices and should be recognized for their long leadership in this area. Hannah Ishmael's writing on Arthur Schomburg (for whom the New York Public Library's Schomburg Center for Research in Black Culture is named), for example, offers a beautifully complex examination of how Black archivists and other memory workers have shaped both archival cannon and collecting practices. See Hannah J. M. Ishmael, "Reclaiming History: Arthur Schomburg," *Archives and Manuscripts* 46, no. 3 (2018): 269–88. Also, for a series of compelling essays on the themes and thinking that animate Black archival praxis specifically, see the 2022 special double issue of *The Black Scholar* on Black Archival Practice (especially see Tonia Sutherland and Zakiya Collier, "Introduction: The Promise and Possibility of Black Archival Practice," *The Black Scholar* 52, no. 2, (2022): 1–5, https://doi.org/10.1080/00064246.2022.2043722; and Tonia Sutherland and Zakiya Collier, "The Revolutionary and Radical in Black Archival Practice," *The Black Scholar* 52, no. 4, (2022): 1–4, https://doi.org/10.1080/00064246.2022.2111647).

29. Katherine Dunham, *Journey to Accompong* (New York: Holt, 1946), 33 (emphasis added).

CONCLUSION

Epigraph: Hartman made this statement at an event celebrating the publication of Christina Sharpe's book *In the Wake: On Blackness and Being* (Durham, NC: Duke University Press, 2016), which was held on February 2, 2017, at Barnard College. See Christina Sharpe, Hazel Carby, Kaiama Glover, Saidiya Hartman, Arthur Jafa, and Alex Weheliye, "In the Wake: A Salon in Honor of Christina Sharpe," https://vimeo.com/203012536.

1. For more on how Black life disappears in the archives, see Vincent Brown, *The Reaper's Garden: Death and Power in the World of Atlantic Slavery* (Cambridge, MA: Harvard University Press, 2008); and Tonia Sutherland, "Archival Amnesty: In Search of Black American Transitional and Restorative Justice," *Journal of Critical Library and Information Studies* 2 (2017), https://journals.litwinbooks.com/index.php/jclis/article/view/42.

2. Carlos Fuentes, "Remember the Future," *Salmagundi* no. 68/69 (1985): 333–52, www.jstor.org/stable/40547836.

3. As quoted in Thora Siemsen, "On Working with Archives: An Interview with Saidiya Hartman," *The Independent*, February 3, 2021 (originally published April 18, 2018), https://thecreativeindependent.com/people/saidiya-hartman-on-working-with-archives/.

4. Sharpe, *In the Wake*, 14.

5. Sutherland and Collier, "Introduction: The Promise and Possibility of Black Archival Practice."

6. Zakiya Collier et al., "Call to Action: Archiving State-Sanctioned Violence against Black People," *Medium*, June 6, 2020, https://medium.com/community-archives/call-to-action-archiving-state-sanctioned-violence-against-black-people-d629c956689a.

7. I am thinking here of intentional projects such as the Murkutu content management system, which allows for community-informed appropriate access to archival materials. See, for example, the Plateau People's Web Portal (https://plateauportal.libraries.wsu.edu/) and Murkutu CMS (https://mukurtu.org/).

8. Art of Collective Care and Responsibility, "Art of Collective Care and Responsibility," https://web.archive.org/web/20220330080406/www.artofcollectivecare.com/.

9. La Tanya Autry, "Beholding and Curating with Care," *Hyperallergic*, January 19, 2022, https://hyperallergic.com/706626/beholding-and-curating-with-care/.

10. See Karen G. Gervais, *Redefining Death* (New Haven, CT: Yale Uni-

versity Press, 1986), 159; and Clive Seale, *Constructing Death: The Sociology of Dying and Bereavement* (Cambridge, UK: Cambridge University Press, 1998), 34.

11. John S. Mbiti, *African Religions and Philosophy* (London: Doubleday, 1970), 108.

12. I am grateful to my colleague Dr. Vanessa Irvin for sharing both this practice and this resource with me. For more, see Sanya Ojo, "Making Markets with the Dead: Residential Burial among the Yoruba," *Journal of Consumer Behaviour* 16, no. 6 (2017): 591–604.

13. North American enslavers were correct to worry about such rebellions and uprisings, as funerals in the Caribbean had proved to be opportunities to plan exactly these forms of resistance and moves toward liberation. For a discussion of some of these acts of resistance, see, for example, Tonia Sutherland, Paulette Kerr, and Linda Sturtz, *Resistance in/and the Pre-Emancipation Archives* (New York: Routledge, 2022).

14. Hartman, *Lose Your Mother*, 2.

15. keondra bills freemyn, "Expanding the Black Archival Imagination: Digital Content Creators and the Movement to Liberate Black Narratives from Institutional Violence," in Shauntee Burns-Simpson, Nichelle M. Hayes, Ana Ndumu, Shaundra Walker, and Carla Diane Hayden, eds., *The Black Librarian in America: Reflections, Resistance, and Reawakening* (Lanham, MD: Rowman and Littlefield, 2021), 252.

16. US Department of Justice Civil Rights Division, "Investigation of the Ferguson Police Department," March 4, 2015, www.justice.gov/sites/default/files/opa/press-releases/attachments/2015/03/04/ferguson_police_department_report.pdf.

17. For more on sousveillance, see M. Fischer and K. Mohrman, "Black Deaths Matter? Sousveillance and the Invisibility of Black Life," *Ada: A Journal of Gender, New Media, and Technology*, no. 10 (2016), DOI:10.7264/N3F47MDV.

18. See Zakiya Collier and Tonia Sutherland, "Witnessing, Testimony, and Transformation as Genres of Black Archival Practice," *The Black Scholar* 52, no. 2 (2022): 6–14, https://doi.org/10.1080/00064246.2022.2042666; and Browne, *Dark Matters*.

19. In just one striking example from the Department of Justice Civil Rights Division's "Investigation of the Ferguson Police Department," in June 2014—just two months before the killing of Michael Brown—a Black couple who had taken their children to play at the park allowed their small children to urinate in the bushes next to their parked car. An officer stopped them,

threatened to cite them for allowing the children to "expose themselves," and checked the father for warrants. When the mother asked if it was really necessary for the officer to detain a father in front of the children, the officer turned to the father and said, "You're going to jail because your wife keeps running her mouth." The mother began recording the officer on her cell phone. The Ferguson Police Department officer, now irate, declared: "You don't videotape me!" As the officer drove away with the father in custody for "parental neglect," the mother drove after them, continuing to record. The officer pulled over and arrested her for traffic violations. When the father asked the officer to show mercy, he responded, "no more mercy, since she wanted to videotape," and declared "nobody videotapes me." The officer took the phone, which the couple's daughter was holding. After posting bond, the couple found that the sousveillance video had been deleted (US Department of Justice Civil Rights Division, "Investigation of the Ferguson Police Department," 27).

20. Johnetta Elzie, "If I'm arrested today please know I'm not suicidal. I have plenty to live for. I did not resist, I'm just black." Twitter, August 10, 2015, 8:15 a.m., https://twitter.com/Nettaaaaaaaa/status/630804684744212480.

21. Bergis Jules, Ed Summers, and Vernon Mitchell Jr., "Ethical Considerations for Archiving Social Media Content Generated by Contemporary Social Movements: Challenges, Opportunities, and Recommendations," April 2018, www.docnow.io/docs/docnow-whitepaper-2018.pdf.

22. Twitter also was the dominant platform for sharing information about subsequent high-profile police shootings of unarmed African Americans and the protests that followed those incidents, including the deaths of Sandra Bland, Eric Garner, Freddie Gray, Philando Castile, Ahmaud Arbery, Breonna Taylor, George Floyd, and so many others.

23. Jules, Summer, and Mitchell, "Ethical Considerations for Archiving Social Media."

24. Sharpe et al., "In the Wake: A Salon in Honor of Christina Sharpe."

Bibliography

Acker, Amelia, and Jed R. Brubaker. "Death, Memorialization, and Social Media: A Platform Perspective for Personal Archives." *Archivaria* 77 (2014): 1–23. http://archivaria.ca/index.php/archivaria/article/view/13469.

AdAge Staff. "How Brands and Agencies Responded to Racial Injustice in the First Month Following George Floyd's Death." *AdAge*. July 7, 2020. https://adage.com/article/cmo-strategy/how-brands-and-agencies-responded-racial-injustice-first-month-following-george-floyds-death/2265626.

Agostinho, Daniela. "Archival Encounters: Rethinking Access and Care in Digital Colonial Archives." *Archival Science: International Journal on Recorded Information* 19 (2019):141–65. https://doi.org/10.1007/s10502-019-09312-0.

Anson, Robert Sam. "To Die Like a Gangster." *Vanity Fair*. March 1997. www.vanityfair.com/culture/1997/03/tupac-shakur-rap-death#.

Apel, Dora, and Shawn Michelle Smith. *Lynching Photographs*. Berkeley: University of California Press, 2007.

Art of Collective Care and Responsibility. https://web.archive.org/web/20220330080406/www.artofcollectivecare.com/ (accessed March 30, 2022).

Aschenbrenner Joyce. *Katherine Dunham: Dancing a Life*. Urbana: University of Illinois Press, 2002.

——. "Katherine Dunham: Reflections on the Social and Political Contexts of Afro-American Dance." With notations of the Dunham Method and Technique by Lavinia Williams Yarborough. *Dance Research Annual*, 12. New York: Congress on Research in Dance, Inc., 1981.

Autry, La Tanya. "Beholding and Curating with Care." *Hyperallergic*. January 19, 2022. https://hyperallergic.com/706626/beholding-and-curating-with-care/.

Bardhan, Ashley. "Men Are Creating AI Girlfriends and Then Verbally Abusing Them." *Futurism*. January 18, 2022. https://futurism.com/chatbot-abuse.

Beauchamp, Tom L., and James F. Childress. *Principles of Biomedical Ethics*. New York: Oxford University Press, 1979.

Benchetrit, Jenna. "Dead Celebrities Are Being Digitally Resurrected—And the Ethics Are Murky." *CBS News* (Canada). August 8, 2021. www.cbc.ca/news/entertainment/dead-celebrities-digital-resurrection-1.6132738.

Benjamin, Ruha. "Informed Refusal: Toward a Justice-based Bioethics." *Science, Technology, and Human Values* 4, no. 6 (2017): 967–90.

—— (@ruha9). "Note to selves: remember to imagine and craft the worlds you cannot live without, just as you dismantle the ones you cannot live within." Twitter. November 22, 2017. https://twitter.com/ruha9/status/926180439827591168.

Berg, Madeleine. "The Highest-Paid Dead Celebrities of 2020." *Forbes*. November 13, 2020. www.forbes.com/sites/maddieberg/2020/11/13/the-highest-paid-dead-celebrities-of-2020/?sh=49f016013b4b.

Bollmer, Grant David. "Millions Now Living Will Never Die: Cultural Anxieties about the Afterlife of Information." *The Information Society* 29, no. 3 (2013): 142–51. DOI: 10.1080/01972243.2013.777297.

Brock, André L. *Distributed Blackness: African American Cybercultures*. New York: New York University Press, 2020.

Brown, Vincent. *The Reaper's Garden: Death and Power in the World of Atlantic Slavery*. Cambridge, MA: Harvard University Press, 2008.

Brown, William Wells. "Narrative of William W. Brown, A Fugitive Slave, Written by Himself, 1849." In *Slave Auctions: Selections from 19th-Century Narratives of Formerly Enslaved African Americans*. National Humanities Center Resource Toolbox. *The Making of African Ameri-*

can Identity: Volume 1, 1500–1865. http://nationalhumanitiescenter.org/pds/maai/enslavement/text2/slaveauctions.pdf.
Browne, Simone. *Dark Matters: On the Surveillance of Blackness.* Durham, NC: Duke University Press, 2015.
Buchanan, Larry, Quoctrung Bui, and Jugal K. Patel. "Black Lives Matter May Be the Largest Movement in U.S. History." *New York Times.* July 3, 2020.
Campt, Tina. "Black Visuality and the Practice of Refusal." *Women and Performance.* February 25, 2019. www.womenandperformance.org/ampersand/29-1/campt.
———. *Listening To Images.* Durham, NC: Duke University Press, 2017.
Canetti, Elias. *Crowds and Power.* London: Phoenix Press, 1962.
Carlisle, Oliva. "Trends in the Runaway Slave Advertisements." North Carolina Digital Library on Slavery's North Carolina Slave Advertisements Database. http://libcdm1.uncg.edu/cdm/trends/collection/RAS (accessed March 3, 2023).
Caswell, Michelle. *Archiving the Unspeakable.* Madison: University of Wisconsin Press, 2014.
Caswell, Michelle, and Marika Cifor. "From Human Rights to Feminist Ethics: Radical Empathy in the Archives." *Archivaria* 81 (2016): 23–44.
Christen, Kimberly. "Opening Archives: Respectful Repatriation." *American Archivist* 74 (2011): 185–210.
Cifor, Marika, Patricia Garcia, T. L. Cowan, Jas Rault, Tonia Sutherland, Anita Say Chan, Jennifer Rode, Anna Lauren Hoffmann, Niloufar Salehi, and Lisa Nakamura. *Feminist Data Manifest-No.* 2019. www.manifestno.com/ (accessed March 3, 2023).
Clark, Vévé. "Performing the Memory of Difference in Afro-Caribbean Dance: Katherine Dunham's Choreography, 1938–1987." In *History and Memory in African-American Culture,* edited by Genevieve E. Fabre and Robert G. O'Meally, 188–201. New York: Oxford University Press, 1994.
Clark, William A., and Dorothy H. Geary. "The Story of the American Type Culture Collection—Its History and Development (1899–1973)." *Advances in Applied Microbiology* 17 (1974): 295–309.
Collier, Zakiya, and Tonia Sutherland. "Witnessing, Testimony, and Transformation as Genres of Black Archival Practice." *The Black Scholar* 52, no. 2, (2022): 6–14. https://doi.org/10.1080/00064246.2022.2042666.

Collier, Zakiya, et al. "Call to Action: Archiving State-Sanctioned Violence against Black People." *Medium*. June 6, 2020. https://medium.com/community-archives/call-to-action-archiving-state-sanctioned-violence-against-black-people-d629c956689a.

Davidson, Bill. "Probing the Secret of Life." *Colliers* (May 14, 1954): 78–83.

Debord, Guy. *Society of the Spectacle*. Detroit, MI: Black and Red Press, 1970.

Douglass, Frederick. "The Civil Rights Case." Civil Rights Mass Meeting. Washington, DC. October 22, 1883.

Drake, Jarrett Martin. "Blood at the Root." *Journal of Contemporary Archival Studies* 8, no. 6 (2021). https://elischolar.library.yale.edu/jcas/vol8/iss1/6.

Duarte, Marisa Elena, and Miranda Belarde-Lewis. "Imagining: Creating Spaces for Indigenous Ontologies." *Cataloging & Classification Quarterly* 53, no. 5–6 (2015): 677–702. DOI: 10.1080/01639374.2015.1018396.

Dunham, Katherine. "Form and Function in Primitive Dance." *Educational Dance* 4, no. 10 (October 1941): 2–4.

———. *Journey to Accompong*. New York: Holt, 1946.

———. Program: *Southland* in Santiago, Chile, World Premiere, January 1951. In *Kaiso! Katherine Dunham: An Anthology of Writings*, edited by Vévé Clark and Margaret B. Wilkerson. Berkeley: Institute for the Study of Social Change, 1978.

Edwards, Elizabeth. *Raw Histories: Photographs, Anthropology, Museums*. Oxford, UK: Berg, 2001.

Elzie, Johnetta. "If I'm arrested today please know I'm not suicidal. I have plenty to live for. I did not resist, I'm just black." Twitter. August 10, 2015. 8:15 a.m. https://twitter.com/Nettaaaaaaaa/status/630804684744212480.

Estate of Henrietta Lacks (plaintiff) v. Thermo Fischer Scientific, Inc. (defendant). US District Court of Maryland. Filed October 4, 2021. www.courthousenews.com/wp-content/uploads/2021/10/henrietta-lacks-thermo-fisher.pdf.

Facebook. "Memories of Friends Departed Endure on Facebook." October 26, 2009. www.facebook.com/notes/10160196742716729/.

Fagone, Jason. "The Jessica Simulation: Love and Loss in the Age of A.I." *San Francisco Chronicle*. July 23, 2021. www.sfchronicle.com/projects/2021/jessica-simulation-artificial-intelligence/.

Fanon, Frantz, and Richard Philcox. 1952. *Black Skin / White Masks*. New York: Grove Press.

Fischer, Mia, and K. Mohrman. "Black Deaths Matter? Sousveillance and the Invisibility of Black Life." *Ada: A Journal of Gender, New Media, and Technology*, no. 10 (2016). DOI:10.7264/N3F47MDV.

Fitch, Asa. "Could AI Keep People 'Alive' after Death?" *Wall Street Journal*. July 3, 2021. www.wsj.com/articles/could-ai-keep-people-alive-after-death-11625317200.

Fox-Amato, Matthew. "How Activists Used Photography To Help End Slavery." *Washington Post*. April 24, 2019. www.washingtonpost.com/outlook/2019/04/24/how-activists-used-photography-help-end-slavery/.

Francis, Megan Ming. *Civil Rights and the Making of the Modern American State*. New York: Cambridge University Press, 2014.

Frazier, Darnella. Testimony of Darnella Frazier. "Trial of Derek Chauvin, Charged with Killing George Floyd, Day 2, Direct Feed." *PBS News Hour*. Livestreamed on March 30, 2021. www.youtube.com/watch?v=1zOyVPmAJns&t=6826s.

———. "They killed him right in front of cup foods over south on 38th and Chicago!! No type of sympathy 💔💔 #POLICEBRUTALITY." Facebook. May 25, 2020. www.facebook.com/darnellareallprettymarie/videos/1425398217661280/.

Freedom on the Move. "Freedom on the Move." Yale University. https://freedomonthemove.org/ (accessed December 6, 2022).

Freelon Deen, Michael Bossetta, Chris Wells et al. "Black Trolls Matter: Racial and Ideological Asymmetries in Social Media Disinformation." *Social Science Computer Review* (April 2020). DOI:10.1177/0894439320914853.

Freeman, Elisabeth. "The Waco Lynching." Report, 1916. Anti-Lynching File. NAACP Papers, Manuscript Division, Library of Congress, Washington, DC.

freemyn, keondra bills. "Expanding the Black Archival Imagination: Digital Content Creators and the Movement to Liberate Black Narratives from Institutional Violence." In *The Black Librarian in America: Reflections, Resistance, and Reawakening*, edited by Shauntee Burns-Simpson, Nichelle M. Hayes, Ana Ndumu, Shaundra Walker, and Carla Diane Hayden, 251–61. Lanham, MD: Rowman and Littlefield, 2022.

Fuentes, Carlos. "Remember the Future." *Salmagundi* no. 68/69 (1985): 333–52. www.jstor.org/stable/40547836.

Garcia, Patricia, Niloufar Salehi, Tonia Sutherland et al. "No! On Refusal and the Feminist Data Manifest-No." *Conference Companion from the 25th ACM Conference on Computer-Supported Cooperative Work and Social Computing.* Spring 2022. https://doi.org/10.1145/3557997.

Gates, Henry Louis. "Frederick Douglass's Camera Obscura: Representing the Antislave 'Clothed and in Their Own Form.'" *Critical Inquiry* 42 (2015): 31–60.

Gervais, Karen G. *Redefining Death.* New Haven, CT: Yale University Press, 1986.

Guerin, Frances, and Roger Hallas. *The Image and the Witness: Trauma, Memory, and Visual Culture.* London: Wallflower Press, 2007.

Hale, Grace Elizabeth. *Making Whiteness: The Culture of Segregation in the South, 1890–1940.* New York: Vintage Books, 2002.

Harris, Aisha. "Picture Me LOLin'." *Slate.* June 16, 2017. https://slate.com/culture/2017/06/all-eyez-on-me-the-new-tupac-biopic-reviewed.html.

Hartman, Saidiya V. *Lose Your Mother: A Journey along the Atlantic Slave Route.* New York: Farrar, Straus, and Giroux, 2008.

———. *Scenes of Subjection: Terror, Slavery, and Self-Making in Nineteenth-Century America.* New York: Oxford University Press, 2010.

———. "Venus in Two Acts." *Small Axe: A Journal of Criticism*, no. 26 (2008): 1–14.

Hartocollis, Anemona. "Who Should Own Photos of Slaves? The Descendants, Not Harvard, a Lawsuit Says." *New York Times.* March 20, 2019. www.nytimes.com/2019/03/20/us/slave-photographs-harvard.html.

"Henrietta Lacks: Science Must Right a Historical Wrong." *Nature.* September 1, 2020. www.nature.com/articles/d41586-020-02494-z.

"Henry Watson, Narrative of Henry Watson, A Fugitive Slave, 1848." In *Slave Auctions: Selections from 19th-Century Narratives of Formerly Enslaved African Americans.* National Humanities Center Resource Toolbox. *The Making of African American Identity: Vol. 1, 1500–1865.* http://nationalhumanitiescenter.org/pds/maai/enslavement/text2/slaveauctions.pdf.

Hensen, Stephen, and the Society of American Archivists. *Describing Archives: A Content Standard*, second edition. Chicago: Society of American Archivists, 2013. www2.archivists.org/groups/technical-subcommittee-on-describing-archives-a-content-standard-dacs/dacs.

Hudson, Kathy L., and Francis S. Collins. "Biospecimen Policy: Family Matters." *Nature* 500, no. 7461 (2013): 141–42. DOI:10.1038/500141a.

Imani, Zellie (@zellieimani). "You shouldn't have to see footage of murdered Black people to be convinced of their humanity." Twitter. June 13, 2020. https://twitter.com/zellieimani/status/1271788340967280643.

Infobase and Home Box Office, dirs. *The Immortal Life of Henrietta Lacks*. Home Box Office, 2019.

Institute of Medicine (US) Committee on Resource Sharing in Biomedical Research, K. I. Berns, E. C. Bond, and F. J. Manning, editors. *Resource Sharing in Biomedical Research*. Washington, DC: National Academies Press, 1996. 2, *The American Type Culture Collection*. www.ncbi.nlm.nih.gov/books/NBK209072/.

Ishmael, Hannah J. M. "Reclaiming History: Arthur Schomburg." *Archives and Manuscripts* 46, no. 3 (2018): 269–88. DOI:10.1080/01576895.2018.1559741.

Jackson, Lauren Michele. "Shudu Gram Is a White Man's Digital Projection of Real-Life Black Womanhood." *The New Yorker*. May 4, 2018. www.newyorker.com/culture/culture-desk/shudu-gram-is-a-white-mans-digital-projection-of-real-life-black-womanhood.

Jimerson, Randall C. *Archives Power: Memory, Accountability, and Social Justice*. Chicago: Society of American Archivists, 2010.

Johns Hopkins Medicine. "The Legacy of Henrietta Lacks: The Importance of HeLa Cells." www.hopkinsmedicine.org/henriettalacks/importance-of-hela-cells.html (accessed March 2, 2023).

Johnson, Jessica Marie. "Markup Bodies: Black [Life] Studies and Slavery [Death] Studies at the Digital Crossroads." *Social Text* 36, no. 4 (2018): 57–79.

Johnson, Sara E. "Introduction: Diamonds on the Toes of Her Feet." In *Kaiso! Writings by and about Katherine Dunham*, edited by Katherine Dunham, Vévé Clark, and Sara E. Johnson, 3–18. Madison: University of Wisconsin Press, 2005.

Jones, Howard W. "Record of the First Physician to See Henrietta Lacks at the Johns Hopkins Hospital: History of the Beginning of the HeLa Cell Line." *American Journal of Obstetrics and Gynecology* 176, no. 6 (1997): s227–s228. https://doi.org/10.1016/S0002-9378(97)70379-X.

Jones, Howard W., Victor A McKusick, Peter S. Harper, and Kuang-Dong Wuu. "George Otto Gey (1899–1970): The HeLa Cell and a Reappraisal of its Origin." *American Journal of Obstetrics and Gynecology* 38, no. 6 (1971): 945–49.

Jones III, James Thomas. "All Eyez on Me: A Missed Opportunity to Politicize Young Black America." *Manhood, Race, and Cul-*

ture. www.manhoodraceculture.com/2017/06/17/all-eyez-on-me-a-missed-opportunity-to-politicize-young-black-america/ (available at https://web.archive.org/web/20170906172128/http://www.manhoodraceculture.com/2017/06/17/all-eyez-on-me-a-missed-opportunity-to-politicize-young-black-america/).

Jules, Bergis, Ed Summers, and Vernon Mitchell Jr. "Ethical Considerations for Archiving Social Media Content Generated by Contemporary Social Movements: Challenges, Opportunities, and Recommendations." April 2018. www.docnow.io/docs/docnow-whitepaper-2018.pdf.

Kaine, Tim. "Darnella Frazier, the teenager who filmed the video of George Floyd's murder, should win a Pulitzer Prize for photojournalism. She is a stellar example of how everyday people can be powerful in documenting injustice and creating momentum for accountability." Twitter. April 21, 2021. https://twitter.com/timkaine/status/1384854910836031488.

Kelley, Robin D. G. "Why Black Marxism, Why Now?" *Boston Review*. February 1, 2021. https://bostonreview.net/articles/robin-d-g-kelley-tk-2/.

Kim, Linda. "A Law of Unintended Consequences: United States Postal Censorship of Lynching Photographs." *Visual Resources* 28, no. 2 (2012): 171–93. DOI:10.1080/01973762.2012.678812.

Kreps, Daniel. "Whitney Houston's Hologram Is Coming to Las Vegas." *Rolling Stone*. July 22, 2021. www.rollingstone.com/music/music-news/whitney-houston-hologram-concert-las-vegas-residency-1201006/.

Landecker, Hannah. *Culturing Life: How Cells Became Technologies.* Cambridge, MA: Harvard University Press, 2007.

Library of Congress. "Katherine Dunham on Her Anthropological Films." Video recording. 2002. http://lcweb2.loc.gov/diglib/ihas/loc.natlib.ihas.200003841/default.html.

———. "Katherine Dunham on Need for Dunham Technique." Video recording, 2002. http://lcweb2.loc.gov/diglib/ihas/loc.natlib.ihas.200003845/default.html.

Linfield, Susie. *The Cruel Radiance: Photography and Political Violence.* Chicago: University of Chicago Press, 2010.

Lorenzi, Lucia (@empathywarrior). "I once asked Dionne Brand about how to deal with the violence and pain of the archive of Black history. She told me to look for the red ribbon. A detail, she notes, from the newspaper description of an enslaved girl who had escaped - last seen

with a red ribbon in her hair." Twitter. April 19, 2020. https://twitter
.com/empathywarrior/status/1252095554852548609.
Lucey, Brendan P., Walter A. Nelson-Rees, and Grover M. Hutchins.
"Henrietta Lacks, HeLa Cells, and Cell Culture Contamination."
Archives of Pathology and Laboratory Medicine 133, no. 9 (September
2009): 1463–67. https://doi.org/10.5858/133.9.1463.
Magloire, Marina. "An Ethics of Discomfort: Katherine Dunham's Vodou
Belonging." *Small Axe: A Caribbean Journal of Criticism* 23, no. 3
(2019): 1–17.
Manfuso, Jamie, and Stephanie Desmon. "Honoring the Henrietta Lacks
Legacy at Hopkins." May 20, 2011. www.hopkinsmedicine.org/news
/publications/hopkins_medicine_magazine/archives/springsummer
_2011/web_extra_honoring_the_henrietta_lacks_legacy_at
_hopkins.
Maryland State Archives. MSA SC 3520-16887. https://web.archive.org
/web/20210314234454/https://msa.maryland.gov/msa/educ/exhibits
/womenshall/html/lacks.html (accessed April 1, 2023).
Mbiti, John S. *African Religions and Philosophy*. London: Doubleday,
1970.
McCormick, Thomas R. "Principles of Bioethics." University of Washington Department of Bioethics and Humanities. https://depts
.washington.edu/bhdept/ethics-medicine/bioethics-topics/articles
/principles-bioethics (accessed March 2, 2023).
McGranahan, Carole. "Theorizing Refusal: An Introduction." *Cultural
Anthropology* 31, no. 3 (2016): 319–25.
McKittrick, Katherine. "'Who Do You Talk To, When a Body's in
Trouble?': M. Nourbese Philip's (Un)Silencing of Black Bodies in the
Diaspora." *Social & Cultural Geography* 1, no. 2 (2000): 223–36.
McPherson and Oliver, photographer. Escaped slave Gordon, also known
as "Whipped Peter," showing his scarred back at a medical examination, Baton Rouge, Louisiana. United States Baton Rouge Louisiana,
1863. Publisher not identified, April 2. www.loc.gov/item/2018648117/.
Minneapolis Police Department. "Man Dies after Medical Incident
During Police Interaction." May 25, 2020. www.insidempd.com/2020
/05/26/man-dies-after-medical-incident-during-police-interaction/.
Minnesota v. Derek Chauvin. "Complaint and Order of Detention
(Amended)." 27-CR-20-12646: *State vs. Derek Chauvin*. Filed June 3,
2020. www.mncourts.gov/media/StateofMinnesotavDerekChauvin
.aspx.

Mitchell, W.J.T. *What Do Pictures Want?: The Lives and Loves of Images.* Chicago: University of Chicago Press, 2005.

Morrison, Toni. "Introduction: Friday on the Potomac." In *Race-ing Justice, En-Gendering Power: Essays on Anita Hill, Clarence Thomas, and the Social Construction of Reality*, edited by Toni Morrison, vii–xxx. New York: Pantheon, 1992.

Moten, Fred. *In the Break: The Aesthetics of the Black Radical Tradition.* Minneapolis: University of Minnesota Press, 2003.

Muhammad, Khalil Gibran. *The Condemnation of Blackness: Race, Crime, and the Making of Modern Urban America.* Cambridge, MA: Harvard University Press, 2010.

Mull, Amanda. "Brands Have Nothing Real to Say about Racism." *The Atlantic.* June 3, 2020. www.theatlantic.com/health/archive/2020/06/brands-racism-protests-amazon-nfl-nike/612613/.

Murphy, Elizabeth. "Inside 23andMe Founder Anne Wojcicki's $99 DNA Revolution." *Fast Company.* October 14, 2013. www.fastcompany.com/3018598/for-99-this-ceo-can-tell-you-what-might-kill-you-inside-23andme-founder-anne-wojcickis-dna-r.

MyHeritage. "Deep Nostalgia." www.myheritage.com/deep-nostalgia (accessed March 2, 2023).

NAACP. "The Waco Horror." *The Crisis* 12, no. 3 (supplement) (July 1916). NAACP Papers, Manuscript Division, Library of Congress, Washington, DC.

NAACP Board of Directors. Minutes, June 12, 1916. NAACP Papers, Manuscript Division, Library of Congress, Washington, DC.

———. Minutes, July 10, 1916. NAACP Papers, Manuscript Division, Library of Congress, Washington, DC.

———. Minutes, November 13, 1916. NAACP Papers, Manuscript Division, Library of Congress, Washington, DC.

Nash, Jennifer C. *The Black Body in Ecstasy: Reading Race, Reading Pornography.* Durham, NC: Duke University Press, 2014.

Nash, Roy. "Waco Horror Stirs to Action." Letter, 1916. Anti-Lynching File. NAACP Papers, Manuscript Division, Library of Congress, Washington, DC.

National Archives. Photograph 165-JT-230; Overseer Artayou Carrier whipped me. I was two months in bed sore from the whipping; 4/2/1863. Photographic Prints in John Taylor Album, ca. 1861–ca. 1865. Records of the War Department General and Special Staffs, Record

Group 165. National Archives at College Park, MD. www.docsteach.org/documents/document/peter.

Nelson, Alondra. *Body and Soul: The Black Panther Party and the Fight against Medical Discrimination.* Minneapolis: University of Minnesota Press, 2011.

Newton, Casey. "Speak, Memory." *The Verge.* www.theverge.com/a/luka-artificial-intelligence-memorial-roman-mazurenko-bot (accessed March 2, 2023).

Noble, Safiya Umoja. "Teaching Trayvon: Race, Media, and the Politics of Spectacle." *The Black Scholar* 44, no. 1 (2014): 12–29. DOI:10.1080/00064246.2014.11641209.

Nora, Pierre. "Between Memory and History: Les Lieux de Mémoire." *Representations* 1, no. 26 (April 1989): 7–24. https://doi.org/10.2307/2928520.

Northup, Solomon. *Twelve Years a Slave.* New York: Miller, Orton & Mulligan, 1855.

Oakes, James. *Slavery and Freedom: An Interpretation of the Old South.* New York: Knopf, 1990.

Obasogie, Osagie K. "High-Tech, High-Risk Forensics." *New York Times.* July 25, 2013. www.nytimes.com/2013/07/25/opinion/high-tech-high-risk-forensics.html.

Odumosu, Temi. "The Crying Child : On Colonial Archives, Digitization, and Ethics of Care in the Cultural Commons." *Current Anthropology* 61 (2020): 289–302. https://doi.org/10.1086/710062

Ojo, Sanya. "Making Markets with the Dead: Residential Burial among the Yoruba." *Journal of Consumer Behaviour* 16, no. 6 (2017): 591–604.

Padover, Arielle. "Legal Protection of a Digital Resurrection." *Cornell Journal of Law and Public Policy: The Issue Spotter.* March 8, 2017. http://jlpp.org/blogzine/legal-protection-of-a-digital-resurrection/.

Parker, Laura. "How to Become Virtually Immortal." *The New Yorker.* April 4, 2014. www.newyorker.com/tech/annals-of-technology/how-to-become-virtually-immortal.

Pasquale, Frank. "From Territorial to Functional Sovereignty: The Case of Amazon." Law and Political Economy Project. December 6, 2017. https://lpeproject.org/blog/from-territorial-to-functional-sovereignty-the-case-of-amazon/.

PBS Newshour. "Trial of Derek Chauvin, Charged with Killing George Floyd, Resumes in Minneapolis." March 30, 2021. www.pbs.org

/newshour/nation/watch-live-trial-of-derek-chauvin-charged-with-killing-george-floyd-resumes-in-minneapolis.

"The 'Peculiar Institution' Illustrated." *The Liberator* (Boston). June 12, 1863, p. 2.

Philip, Marlene Nourbese. *A Genealogy of Resistance: And Other Essays.* Toronto: Mercury Press, 1997.

Pilgrim, David. *Understanding Jim Crow: Using Racist Memorabilia to Teach Tolerance and Promote Social Justice.* Oakland, CA: PM Press, 2015.

Pilkington, Ed. "Juror Says Video of George Floyd's Death Was Like Attending a Funeral Every Day." *The Guardian.* April 28, 2021. www.theguardian.com/us-news/2021/apr/28/juror-derek-chauvin-george-floyd-brandon-mitchell.

Pinn, Anthony B. *Terror and Triumph: The Nature of Black Religion.* Minneapolis, MN: Fortress Press, 2003.

Poole, Lynn, George O. Gey, Anthony Farrar, and Joel Chaseman. "Cancer Will Be Conquered." Originally broadcast as a segment of the television program *Johns Hopkins Science Review* on April 10, 1951, from the studios of WAAM in Baltimore, MD.

Roberts, Dorothy. *Killing the Black Body: Race, Reproduction, and the Meaning of Liberty.* New York: Vintage, 1998.

Robinson, Cedric J. *Black Marxism: The Making of the Black Radical Tradition.* Chapel Hill: University of North Carolina Press, 2000.

Rogers, Michael. "The Double-Edged Helix." *Rolling Stone* 209 (March 25, 1976): 48–51.

Rose, Albirda. *Dunham Technique: A Way of Life.* Dubuque, IA: Kendall/Hunt Publishing Company, 1990.

Rosenstein, Jenna. "People Can't Tell If This Fenty Model Is Real or Fake." *Harper's Bazaar.* February 9, 2018. www.harpersbazaar.com/beauty/makeup/a16810663/shudu-gram-fenty-model-fake/.

"The Scourged Slave's Back." *The Liberator* (Boston). September 4, 1863, p. 3.

Seale, Clive. *Constructing Death: The Sociology of Dying and Bereavement.* Cambridge, UK: Cambridge University Press, 1998.

Shakur, Tupac (2Pac). "Only Fear of Death." *R U Still Down? (Remember Me).* Amaru Entertainment. Released November 25, 1997.

Sharpe, Christina Elizabeth. *In the Wake: On Blackness and Being.* Durham, NC: Duke University Press, 2016.

Sharpe, Christina, Hazel Carby, Kaiama Glover, Saidiya Hartman, Arthur

Jafa, and Alex Weheliy. "In the Wake: A Salon in Honor of Christina Sharpe." Event recorded on February 2, 2017, at Barnard College. https://vimeo.com/203012536.

Sherlock, Alexandra. "Larger Than Life: Digital Resurrection and the Re-Enchantment of Society." *The Information Society* 29, no. 3 (2013): 164–76. DOI:10.1080/01972243.2013.777302.

Siemsen, Thora. "On Working with Archives: An Interview with Saidiya Hartman." *The Independent*. February 3, 2021 (originally published April 18, 2018). https://thecreativeindependent.com/people/saidiya-hartman-on-working-with-archives/.

Simpson, Audra. "On Ethnographic Refusal: Indigeneity, 'Voice' and Colonial Citizenship." *Junctures: The Journal for Thematic Dialogue* 9 (December 2007). https://junctures.org/index.php/junctures/article/view/66/60.

Skinner Auctioneers. "Carte-de-Visite of Enslaved Man with Whipping Scars, Escaped Slave Known as Gordon or Peter (2015)." www.skinnerinc.com/auctions/2865B/lots/11 (accessed December 5, 2022).

Skloot, Rebecca. *The Immortal Life of Henrietta Lacks*. New York: Crown, 2011.

Smith, Zadie. "Generation Why?" *New York Review of Books*. November 25, 2010. www.nybooks.com/articles/2010/11/25/generation-why/.

Sobande, Francesca. "Woke-Washing: 'Intersectional' Femvertising and Branding 'Woke' Bravery." *European Journal of Marketing* (2019): 2723–45. https://doi.org/10.1108/EJM-02-2019-0134.

"Social Media's Impact on Trayvon Martin Case." *CBS Local Miami*. April 28, 2013. https://miami.cbslocal.com/2013/04/28/social-medias-impact-on-trayvon-martin-case/.

Society of American Archivists. "A Guide to Deeds of Gift." www2.archivists.org/publications/brochures/deeds-of-gift (accessed March 2, 2023).

———. "What Are Archives." Updated September 12, 2016. www2.archivists.org/about-archives.

SPARC. "About SPARC." https://sparcopen.org/ (accessed March 2, 2023).

Square, Jonathan. "Is Instagram's Newest Sensation Just Another Example of Cultural Appropriation?" *Fashionista*. March 27, 2018. https://fashionista.com/2018/03/computer-generated-models-cultural-appropriation.

Stadler, Gustavus. "Never Heard Such a Thing: Lynching and Phonographic Modernity." *Social Text* 28, no. 1 (March 2010): 87–105.

Stauffer John, Zoe Trodd, Celeste-Marie Bernier, Henry Louis Gates, and Kenneth B Morris. *Picturing Frederick Douglass: An Illustrated Biography of the Nineteenth Century's Most Photographed American.* Revised edition. New York: Liveright Publishing Corporation, a Division of W. W. Norton & Company, 2018.

Stupp, Jason. "Slavery and the Theatre of History: Ritual Performance on the Auction Block." *Theatre Journal* 63, no. 1 (March 2011): 61–84.

Sutherland, Tonia. "Archival Amnesty: In Search of Black American Transitional and Restorative Justice." *Journal of Critical Library and Information Studies* 2 (2017): 1–23.

———. "The Carceral Archive: Documentary Records, Narrative Construction, and Predictive Risk Assessment." *Journal of Cultural Analytics* (2019).

Sutherland, Tonia, and Zakiya Collier. "Introduction: The Promise and Possibility of Black Archival Practice." *The Black Scholar* 52, no. 2 (2022): 1–5. https://doi.org/10.1080/00064246.2022.2043722.

———. "Introduction: The Revolutionary and Radical in Black Archival Practice." *The Black Scholar* 52, no. 4 (2022): 1–4. https://doi.org/10.1080/00064246.2022.2111647.

Svalastog, Anna Lydia, and Lucia Martinelli. "Representing Life as Opposed to Being: The Bio-objectification Process of the HeLa Cells and Its Relation to Personalized Medicine." *Croatian Medical Journal* 54, no. 4 (2013): 397–402. DOI:10.3325/cmj.2013.54.397.

Tamara Lanier v. President and Fellows of Harvard College, Harvard Board of Overseers, Harvard Corporation, Peabody Museum of Archaeology and Ethnology and Harvard University. Filed April 25, 2019. Case number: 1:2019cv10978. US District Court for the District of Massachusetts. https://dockets.justia.com/docket/massachusetts/madce/1:2019cv10978/209402.

"A Typical Negro." *Harper's Weekly.* July 4, 1863, p. 429.

US Department of Health and Human Services. "The Belmont Report." April 18, 1979. www.hhs.gov/ohrp/regulations-and-policy/belmont-report/read-the-belmont-report/index.html.

US Department of Justice Civil Rights Division. "Investigation of the Ferguson Police Department." March 4, 2015. www.justice.gov/sites/default/files/opa/press-releases/attachments/2015/03/04/ferguson_police_department_report.pdf.

Vansina, Jan. *Kingdoms of the Savanna.* Madison: University of Wisconsin Press, 1966.

von Gleich, Paula. "Afro-pessimism, Fugitivity, and the Border to Social Death." In *Critical Epistemologies of Global Politics*, edited by Woons Marc and Sebastian Weier. Bristol, UK: E-International Relations, 2017. https://www.e-ir.info/2017/06/27/afro-pessimism-fugitivity-and-the-border-to-social-death/.

Vrselja, Z., S. G. Daniele, J. Silbereis et al. "Restoration of Brain Circulation and Cellular Functions Hours Post-mortem." *Nature* 568 (2019): 336–43. https://doi.org/10.1038/s41586-019-1099-1.

Wernimont, Jacqueline. *Numbered Lives: Life and Death in Quantum Media*. Cambridge, MA: MIT Press, 2019.

Whorley, Tywanna. "The Tuskegee Syphilis Study: Access and Control over Controversial Records." PhD Dissertation, University of Pittsburgh, 2006.

"The Will-to-Lynch." *New Republic* 8, no. 102 (October 14, 1916): 261–62.

Winn, Samantha R. "Ethics of Access in Displaced Archives." *Provenance: Journal of the Society of Georgia Archivists* 33, no. 1 (2015). http://hdl.handle.net/10919/64319.

Yeo, Geoffrey. "Concepts of Record (1): Evidence, Information, and Persistent Representation." *American Archivist* 70 (2007): 315–43.

Young, Harvey. "The Black Body as Souvenir in American Lynching." *Theatre Journal* 57 (2005): 639–57.

———. *Embodying Black Experience: Stillness, Critical Memory, and the Black Body*. Ann Arbor: University of Michigan Press, 2010.

Index

Note: page numbers followed by *n* refer to notes, with note number.

Act Prohibiting Importation of Slaves of 1807, 92
African diasporic spiritual traditions: and ancestral knowledge available in transcendent state, 132. *See also* Dunham, Katherine; mourning and deathcare practices, Black
Agassiz, Louis, 21, 172n22
Agostinho, Daniela, 33–34
AI. *See* artificial intelligence
All Eyez on Me (2017 film), 87
American Society for Microbiology, 61
American Type Culture Collection (ATCC): Catalogue of Cultures published by, 63; as commercial enterprise, 63; establishment of, 61; HeLa cells sold by, 63; standardization and distribution of cell cultures, 61–63
Ancestry.com, 118–19
Apel, Dora, 47
Arbery, Ahmaud, 130–31

archival access: definition of, 137; as expanded issue in digital age, 137–38; and interests of archive vs. those of creators of materials, 143; stipulations of deeds of gift and, 143–44
archival access, appropriate: as alternative to open access, 143; cultural appropriateness as necessary standard, 145; respect for indigenous epistemologies and, 143
archival access, appropriate, for archives documenting Black lives: and Black memory technologies in defiance of anti-Black social order, 145; Black memory workers as final arbiters of, 145, 181n28; and items to be withheld from white gaze, 145; as necessary standard, 143
archival access, open: complex norms and practices inhibiting, 142; and cultural imperialism, 28–29; origin in Western higher education, 141

archival access, open online: ethics of, for materials from donors unaware of possibility, 144; need for revision of standards to accommodate, 13, 141–42. *See also* Dunham's documentation of her work, online open access to

archival amnesty, 147

archives: Black memory work in, 147–48, 149; fixed vs. mutable, 99; idea of Black death in, 153; institutionalization of memory in, 137; as memory type, vs. Dunham Technique, 130–31; preservation of records as mission of, 24; process of creating cultural meaning in, 25; and radical empathy, 117; and uniquely Black archival practices, development of, 181n28; values of imperialism and colonialism reflected in, 135–36. *See also* Blackness in archives

archives, description of records in, 25–26; as political act, 26; racial and other stereotypes in, 62; violence and Othering in, 26

archives of Atlantic slavery: artifacts in, as white creations, 22, 26–27; exploitation by white institutions, as parallel to slavery, 30–31; feeding of slavery's afterlife by, 9–10, 24; immense size of, 165n15; importance of considering impacts on present, 27–28; importance of focus on slaves as human beings, 27; reinforcement of white-created categories of exploitation in classification systems, 24, 26–27. *See also* Danish West-Indies: Sources of History site; digitized archives of Atlantic slavery; Freedom on the Move database

Archives Power (Jimerson), 99

artificial intelligence (AI): and animations of photographs, 121–23; and deep fake images, 122; and digital afterlife tools, 107, 113–14, 116–17; and digital blackface, 107

"Art of Collective Care and Responsibility" virtual teach-in (2020), 150–51

ATCC. *See* American Type Culture Collection

The Atlantic, 53–54

Autry, LaTanya S., 151

Bacteriological Collection and Bureau for the Distribution of Bacterial Cultures, 61. *See also* American Type Culture Collection (ATCC)

Barbeau, Joshua, 113–14

Beauchamp, Tom, 74

Belarde-Lewis, Miranda, 26

Belmont Report, 74

Benjamin, Ruha, 13, 14, 108, 125, 126, 154

Biden, Joe, 41–42

biodefectors, 125

biological citizenship, and biodefectors, 125

Black body: commodification in digital afterlife practices, 107–8; and narrative of racial progress, 55, 89, 95; objectifying of, in "Scourged Back" photograph, 20–21; ongoing state-sanctioned violence against, 132; and racism in health care, 170n8; as site of pleasure, 101; as target for abuse in America, 132; white pleasure in punishing, for deviance from white norm, 101

Black Body imaginary: and commodification of Black people, 3–4; danger to real Black people created by, 55; harmful mythologies formed around, 4; perpetuation of, in online images of dead Black people, 55–56; projection onto material bodies of Black people, 3, 55; and separation of idea from lived experience, 4–5, 55, 89. *See also* Black digital afterlives

The Black Body in Ecstasy (Nash), 55

Black "brute": protection of white women from, as rationalization for lynch mobs and slave patrols, 76–77; purported characteristics of, 76; as white construct, 76

Black care: as antidote to violence, 159; "Art of Collective Care and Responsibility" on, 150–51; as focus of Black memory work, 149, 156–57, 159

Black digital afterlives: control over, as issue, 5; families' lack of control over, 6, 7. *See also* right to be forgotten

INDEX 203

Black epistemology: alternate, in Black memory work, 14, 137–46; Black memory work's focus on, 14, 148, 150; and roots of Black revolt, Robinson on, 131. *See also* critical refusal
blackface, digital. *See* digital blackface
blackface minstrelsy, psychological basis of, 107
Black liberation: reclaiming ancestral way of escape from limitations of body as key to, 132; spiritual freedom as essential to theorization of, 130–32
Black liberation epistemologies. *See* critical refusal
Black lives: making visible in positive way, as goal, 14; precarity and disposability of, 5; violence and harm in white remembrance of, 130, 137
Black Lives Matter: companies' support of, as profit-driven, 53–54; founding of, 50
Black Marxism (Robinson), 130–31
Black memory technologies in defiance of anti-Black social order: as alternative to harm in white remembrance of Black lives, 130, 137; as both bound to body and spiritually free, 130; Dunham Technique as, 13–14, 145–46; limiting white access to archives documenting Black lives, 145; and right to remember, 145. *See also* Dunham Technique
Black memory work: abuse intervention questions for, 151; alternate epistemologies of, 14, 137–46; "Art of Collective Care and Responsibility" on, 150–51; and Black feminist tradition, 149; and Black liberation as goal, 150; burden of, 160; "Call to Action" following death of George Floyd, 149, 150; as collective effort, 150; consensus on goals of, 159; as corrective work of healing, 154; and critical refusal, 149–50; and digital records, 154; Dunham Technique as, 130, 135, 136–37; effort to end past patterns of abuse in white supremacist histories, 141; focus on beauty of Black life, 148, 149; focus on Black experience and epistemologies, 14, 148, 150; focus on care, 149, 156–57, 159; forgetting as part of, 154; HoloPac (Tupac Shakur hologram) and, 159; and honoring Black people's right to be remembered, 151; as invocation, 148; long history of, 158; multiple modalities and epistemologies of, 150; as not always safe, 156–57; online records and, 154–55; permission as importance concept in, 140–41; as reparative framework centering Black lives, 148; and reshaping of narrative, 156; and restriction of white access, 149; and rewriting of history, 149; social media and, 154–55; as wake work, 148; vs. Western archival memory, 6, 135–36; what is remembered and who has right to remember as issues in, 146. *See also* Documenting the Now (DocNow); *sousveillance*
Black Memory Workers Group, 181n28
Black memory work in archives, 147–48, 149; and anti-Blackness of traditional archives, 148; and care for Black archival lives in digital age, 154–55; and development of uniquely Black archival practices, 181n28; recovery of Blackness in archives through, 147–48; tensions with Western archival practices, 149, 154
Black Mirror "Black Museum" episode, 100–101
Blackness: legal right to fear, 49–50; link to criminality, as manufactured, 49–50
Blackness in archives: archives' blotting out of Black suffering, 154; and entanglement of right to be remembered and right to be forgotten, 153; intentional exclusion of (archival amnesty), 147; recovery through Black memory work, 147–48; white treatment as property of whiteness, 149
Black people: and digital sovereignty, 13, 124–25; and right to be forgotten, 124
Black people as property: Black Body imaginary and, 3–4; in digital afterlife practices, 93–95, 99–100, 107–8, 159; and enduring legacy of slavery in

Black people as property *(continued)* commodification of Black bodies, 23; and enslaved people's legibility as commodities, 34; history of concept, 161n1; Hurricane Katrina media coverage and, 2–3. *See also entries under* slavery

"Black Visuality and the Practice of Refusal" (Campt), 124

Black women: existence in interstices of (white) womanhood and (male) Blackness, 78–79; fetishization of, 106–7; inability to craft their own narratives, 77; in-betweenness of identities, 77; lack of white women's protections from risk, 77; mythologizing as embodiment of risk and danger, 77

Black women's bodies: as caught in critical discourses between feminism and antiracism, 78; as contradiction itself in America, 70, 73; in-betweenness of identities, 78–79

bodies as data: Henrietta Lacks and, 77–78; and resurrection of dead from cellular data, 78. *See also entries under* DNA

Bollmer, Grant, 110

Brand, Dionne, 36–37, 167n41

Brock, André, 50

Brown, Michael, death of, 5; family's lack of control over images of, 7; protests in response to, 156; *sousveillance* project in response to, 155, 156; and valorization of Black suffering, 3

Brown, William Wells, 94

Browne, Simone, 32, 156

Bryant, Kobe, 98

businesses: claimed ownership of data gathered online, 177–78n28; long-time support of racism, 54; profit as motive for supporting Black Lives Matter, 53–54

California: Celebrities Rights Act of 1985, 97–98; laws prohibiting photographs of dead celebrities, 98

"Call to Action: Archiving State-Sanctioned Violence against Black People," 149, 150

Campt, Tina, 124, 126

Canetti, Elias, 100

Carlisle, Olivia, 31–32

Caswell, Michelle, 117

Celebrities Rights Act of 1985 (California), 97–98

cell cultures: ATCC standardization and distribution of, 61–63; as lucrative commodity, 69; medical uses of, 170n6; sources for, 170n6; unique properties of HeLa cell line and, 66–67. *See also* HeLa cell line

cells: cloning and freezing of, 80; as data for reconstruction of bodies, 77–78, 82; information recorded in, 80–81

cellular resurrection: and questions about nature of life and meaning of death, 80; technology for, 80, 172–73n33

Census data, and genealogical research, 118–19

Center for Media Engagement, 120

CGI. *See* computer generated imagery

Chauvin, Derek, 39, 40

Childress, James, 74

Christen, Kimberly, 143

Chung, Patrick, 120

Cifor, Marika, 117

Civil Rights and the Making of the Modern American State (Francis), 46

Coachella Valley Music and Arts Festival, 86–87. *See also* HoloPac performance at Coachella Festival

Coates, Ta-Nehisi, 21–22

collecting institutions, three types of, 99

Collins, Francis S., 75

commodity fetishism, and digital resurrection of Black performers, 95

compositing, in digital resurrection, 90

computer generated imagery (CGI), and digital resurrection, 90–91

computer graphics (CG) aided resurrections, 90–91

The Condemnation of Blackness (Muhammad), 49

cookies, and corporations' claimed ownership of data gathered online, 177–78n28

Court of Justice of the European Union, on right to be forgotten, 109

The Crisis article on Jesse Washington lynching, 45–47
critical refusal: Black liberation approaches to, 124–26; Black memory work and, 149–50; and challenging of harmful data practices, 126; and digital sovereignty, 108, 125–26; informed refusal, 108; and space for alternative narratives, 125
Crowds and Power (Canetti), 100
Crump, Ben, 81
"The Crying Child" (photograph), and decontextualization of images, 29–30
Culturing Life (Landecker), 69, 72

Danish West-Indies: Sources of History site, 33–34
Data Protection Directive of 1995 (EU), 109
death practices: in Ancient Egypt, 152; in Yoruba tradition, 151–52. *See also* mourning and deathcare practices, Black
deaths of Black people, archives' view of, 153. *See also* online images of dead Black people
Debord, Guy, 95
deep fakes, AI-generated images and, 122
Deep Nostalgia AI-generated animations of photographs, 121–23
Describing Archives (Society of American Archivists), 25
Dickerson, Ernest R., 86
D-ID, 121–22
digital afterlife: AI in creation of, 107, 113–14, 116–17; and commodification of Black bodies, 107–8; definition of, 7; and questions about nature of life and meaning of death, 79; vs. right to be forgotten, 110. *See also* Black digital afterlives; digital clones; digital immortality practices; digital resurrection
digital blackface: definition of, 107; digital clones and, 115; rise in, 13, 107; Shudu Gram and, 106–7
digital clones: creation of imagined person for gendered or racialized abuse, 115–16; and digital blackface, 115; sale of data provided by customers as real interest of companies offering, 120–21
digital clones of dead people, 113–14; as beyond control of cloned person, 114; need for analysis and intervention in, 108; potential impact on memory of deceased, 117–18; and social afterlife, 116–17
digital clones of living people, 114–16
digital culture, definition of, 6
Digital Domain, 96–97
digital images of Black people: and separation of Black Body imaginary from lived experience, 4–5. *See also* Black digital afterlives; online images of dead Black people
digital immortality practices: and Black rights to privacy and control of self, 108; and collapsed distinction between life and digital afterlife, 112–13; and devaluation of human life, 112; Google and Microsoft and, 116; need for analysis and intervention, 108; problems with, 111–12; as shaped by white supremacy, 108, 111; and social afterlife, 116–17; on social media, 111–12; and white supremacist compulsion to own Black bodies, 12–13. *See also* digital afterlife; digital clones; digital resurrection
digital remains: definition of, 114; uses of, as threat to personal identity, 114
digital resurrection, 79–80; basic form of, 90; critiques of, 97; full, 91; issues raised by, 88; laws regulating, 97–98; legal and ethical questions in, 12, 97; technologies used in, 12, 87–88, 89–91; uncanniness of, 88–89, 90, 91; unrealistic aspects of appearance, 90; uses of, 89–90. *See also* digital clones
digital resurrection of Black performers: and Black body as souvenir, 88, 100; and commodity fetishism, 95; and harmful myths of Blackness projected onto celebrity, 98; issues raised by, 88; of Michael Jackson, 12, 88, 96, 99; parallels to slave auctions, 88, 92; as prison- or slavery-like containment of Black body, 98–100; profit motive of,

digital resurrection of Black performers *(continued)* 88; as spectacle for white gaze, 88, 92, 94–95, 98–100, 101; white supremacy in narratives attached to, 89; and white supremacy's need to possess and control Black bodies, 99–100. *See also* HoloPac (Tupac Shakur hologram)

digital resurrection of celebrities: and afterlife agents, 96; benefits for family and promoters, 95–96; celebrities' creation of legal documents about, 7, 97, 98; as growing industry, 95, 96–97; of Marilyn Monroe, 96; of Whitney Houston, 97

digital sovereignty (data sovereignty): and Black critical refusal, 125–26; Black people and, 13, 124–25; call for Black assertion of, 108; corporations' refusal to recognize, 177–78n28; data on criminal behavior as most-deleted, 110; definition of, 108–9; and DNA testing services, 120–21; and individuals' inability to know about or control data about themselves, 123; laws on, 109–10; and power relations implicit in contemporary data practices, 125–26; U.S. legal environment and, 110, 176n9

digital sphere, as real, 6

Digital Underground, 85

digitization of archives: benefits of, 28; and public access to records, 28; and social justice, 33

digitized archives of Atlantic slavery: classification system's reinforcement of white-created categories of exploitation, 9, 31–33, 34–36; and cultural imperialism, 28–29; and datafying and quantifying of dead, 34; and decontexualization of images, 9, 29–30; distancing of viewer from lived experience of those in records, 29–30; and historical subjects' inability to construct their representations in present, 30; human lives rendered invisible in, 31–32; ongoing imperiling and devaluing of Black Lives by, 9, 24, 36–37; ownership of records as issue, 30; potential impact on historical understanding, 34, 36; and privacy denied to non-white subjects, 30; reconstructing to emphasize Black lives, potential for, 36–37; resistance to trauma narrative, 36–37; and slaves' legibility as commodities, 34; white exploitation of, as parallel to slavery, 31

"Dis Place—The Space Between" (Philip), 70

DNA: and right to privacy, 75–76; use by insurance companies, 76

DNA genealogical databases: as tool to control Black people's bodies, 121; use by police to trace criminals, 75, 121

DNA testing services, and lost control of personal data, 120–21

Documenting the Now (DocNow), 157–59; documentation of social media content after Brown's death in Ferguson, 157–58; issues addressed in, 158; as model for Black memory work in digital environments, 157; recommendations about Black memory work, 158–59

Douglass, Frederick: on abolitionist photography, 19–20; AI animation of photograph of, 122; as critical theorist of photography, 46; and importance of images, 164n6

Duarte, Marisa, 26

Du Bois, W.E.B.: and lynching of Jesse Washington, 45–47; on power of photographs, 46

Dunham, Katherine: and alternatives to Western view of body, 6; belief in value of collective, 146; Black memory work as focus of, 145–46; on Black peoples' right to remember stolen past, 128; on consequences of broken rhythm in individual or society, 133; and dance as cultural exchange, 179n3; and dance as reparative memory work, 128–29; fieldwork on dances of African diaspora, 127; and participant observation method, 128; reluctant embrace of Western modes of knowledge, 137; research-to-performance method of, 134, 135; on rhythm as connective tissue in African diaspora community, 133–34; on shift from tribal to folk culture in enslaved Africans, 128; *Southland Ballet*, 133–34, 140; as trained vodou practitioner, 132; use of dance to reawaken cultural memory in African diaspora youth, 128–29

Dunham's documentation of her work, 138–39; and effort to end past patterns of abuses in white supremacist histories, 140–41; ethics of open online access to, for donor unaware of possibility, 144; films of her teaching techniques, 139; films of restricted-access Caribbean dances, 138–39; online open access to, 139–40; online open access to, without permission of those filmed, 140–41, 154; records in Library of Congress, 139–40; various archives holding, 139

Dunham Technique: as antidote to Western archivy, 138; as artform, 129; as Black memory technology, 13–14, 130, 136–37, 145–46; and Black memory technology as defiance of racist, anti-Black social order, 145; as challenge to acquire literacy about Black culture, 134; as collective memory technology, 146; and creation of space for holding black memories, 138; dynamic pedagogy in, 137; as epistemological framework, 130; as means of restoring cultural bonds broken by slavery, 134; recognition of body-spirit connection, 131–32; and rhythm as embodied technology of remembering, 132–33, 134–35; sources of dances in, 133; three theoretical models underlying, 179n6; use of body to transmit cultural knowledge/memory, 129; vs. Western archival memory, 130–31; what is remembered and who has right to remember as issues in, 146

Egypt, Ancient, death practices in, 152
Elzie, Johnetta, 156
EMBL. *See* European Molecular Biology Laboratory
Epps, Omar, 86

Eterni.me, 116, 117
EU. *See* European Union
eugenics, 24
European Molecular Biology Laboratory (EMBL), 75
European Union (EU): laws on data sovereignty, 109–10; and right of erasure, 109; and right to be forgotten, 109
An Evening with Whitney (hologram show), 97
"Expanding the Black Archival Imagination" (freemyn), 154–55

Facebook: advertising-driven profits of, 52–53; digital immortality practices on, 111–12; as functional sovereignty, 123; number of users, 52; profits from Trayvon Martin's death, 52; support of racism, 54; and Trayvon Martin's digital afterlife, 110
facial recognition software, technology to defeat, 121–22
Feed the Children campaign, 162–63n3
Feminist Data Manifest-No, 125–26
Ferguson, Missouri: Justice Department's investigation of police department in, 183–84n19; police harassment of *sousveillance* efforts, 156, 183–84n19; police use of *sousveillance* videos to identify protesters, 157, 158; racist overpolicing in, 155, 183–84n19; *sousveillance* in, after death of Michael Brown, 155, 156. *See also* Brown, Michael, death of
fetishization of Black women, 106–7
film industry, and digital resurrection, 89–90, 96, 97
Fisher, Carrie, 7, 96
Floyd, George, 38–42; and Black memory work, 150; family's lack of control over images of, 7; murder of, companies' response as profit-driven, 53–54; and right to be forgotten, 110, 111; and separation of Black Body imaginary from lived experience, 5
Floyd's murder: as example of anti-Black police violence, 40; and scientists' reckoning with past injustice, 81; trial and conviction of police officer for, 40–41

Floyd's murder, protests in response to, 40, 167n3; as mass protest against racial capitalism, 131; and revival of *Black Marxism*, 130–31

Floyd's murder, videos of, 38–40, 41, 42; and Black *sousveillance*, 157; and social media companies' profit, 53; viral spread of, 39–40

Francis, Megan Ming, 46

Frazier, Darnella, 38–40, 41, 42, 53, 157

Freedom on the Move database: classification system's reinforcement of white-created categories of exploitation, 35–36; and girl with the red ribbon, 37

Freeman, Elizabeth, 42–43, 45, 47

freemyn, keondra bills, 154–55

Fuentes, Carlos, 147

Gartler, Stanley, 71–73

GDRP. *See* General Data Protection Regulation (GDRP) of 2016 (EU)

genealogical databases: as tool to control Black people's bodies, 121; use by police to trace criminals, 75, 121

genealogical research: as difficult for Black Americans, 118; through DNA matching, and lost control of personal data, 120–21

genealogical websites, 118; and AI-generated animations of photographs, 121–23; and charges for accessing public data, 118–20; popularity with Black Americans, 118

General Data Protection Regulation (GDRP) of 2016 (EU), 109–10

Gey, George Otto: acquisition of HeLa cell line, 65; announcement of HeLa cell line, 59–60, 61, 67–68; cancer research by, 65; death of, 71; distribution of HeLa cells, 69; hiding of HeLa origins, 67; hope for curing cancer, 59–60, 71; tissue culture research by, 66

Gey, Margaret, 65, 66

ghost slavery, digital resurrection of performers as, 97

Gildersleeve, Fred "Gildy": NAACP publication of lynching photographs, 45–47; photographs of Jesse Washington lynching, 44–45; sale of lynching photographs, 45

girl with the red ribbon, and search for hope in slavery archives, 36–37

Google: and digital immortality practices, 116; profits made from images of dead Black people, 51–52

Google Spain v. AEPD and Mario Costeja González (2014), 109

Gordon [aka Peter] (subject of "Scourged Back" photograph): account of his ordeal, 18; historians' focus on what was done to him, rather than his lived experience, 27; published versions of his story, 19; self-emancipation of, 18–19. *See also* "Scourged Back" photograph

Gram, Shudu (Black internet model): exposure as digital creation, 105–6; popularity, 105; as white man's digital blackface, 106–7

Hale, Grace Elizabeth, 48

Harris, Aisha, 87

Hartman, Saidiya, 6, 24, 33, 147–48, 154, 159

Harvard University. *See* portraits of Renty and Delia Taylor

HeLa cell line: aggressive growth of, 63–64, 71; announcement of discovery of, 59–60, 61, 67–68; and appropriation of Black Body for benefit of white male scientists, 70; and biological specimen repositories, 81; calls for ending use of, 81; and cell production industry, 69–70; conflation of identity with Lacks herself, 71; contamination of other cell cultures by, 63–64, 71–72; harvesting of, 64–65; and HPV (human papilloma virus), 63; medical and political importance of, 78; medical breakthroughs using, 68, 69; origins of, hidden for decades, 67; and ownership issue, parallels to slave-era womb laws, 67; profits made from, 69–70; racialization of, 72–73; sale by ATCC, 63; and stigmatization of Lacks, 64; unique properties of,

65–67. *See also* Lacks, Henrietta; Lacks family
Hill, Anita, 73
HoloPac (Tupac Shakur hologram): as carceral fantasy, 98–100, 101; commodification of, as horrifying, 159; as directly opposed to Tupac's wishes, 102; dress and appearance of, 91; motives of Snoop Dogg and Dr. Dre in creating, 159; relegation to Shakur estate's archives, 159; unrealistic aspects of appearance, 90, 91; and white supremacy's need to possess and control Black bodies, 99–100
HoloPac performance at Coachella Festival: approval by Tupac's mother, 91; bump in album sales from, 96; crowd's response to, 91–92; parallels to slave auction, 92, 93–95; predominately white audience for, 91; Snoop Dogg and Dr. Dre's participation in, 87, 91; as spectacle for white gaze, 94–95; and white enjoyment of anti-Black violence, 101
homegoing rituals in Black communities: as celebrating of soul's return to creator, 152, 153; as celebration of life, 153; components of, 153; and death as well-earned rest, 152, 153; intermingling of life and death in, 153; and invocation of right to be remembered, 153; mix of Christian and African traditions in, 152–53; spirit of the dead as living speaking entity in, 153
Houston, Whitney, digital resurrection of, 97
HPV. *See* human papilloma virus
Hudson, Kathy L., 75
Huffman, Steve, 54
human papilloma virus (HPV), and HeLa cell line, 63
Hurricane Katrina: author's painful experience of, 1–3, 5; and objectification of Black bodies, 2–3
Hutson, Ronald, 136

Imani, Zellie, 4–5
The Immortal Life of Henrietta Lacks (Skloot), 10, 60, 172n32

informed refusal, 108
injustices of past, new willingness to address, 81
Instagram. *See* Gram, Shudu (Black internet model)
Institute for Durham Certification, 137
insurance companies: anti-Black racism in calculation of risk, 76–77; use of DNA to evaluate risk, 76
internet: companies' profits from images of dead Black people, 51–53; deceased users' accounts, lack of standard practice for, 12; demands for social justice on, in authentically Black way, 124–26; individuals' inability to know about or control data about them, 123; permanence of data and images on, 8, 54–55. *See also* social media; *entries under* online
Ishmael, Hannah, 181n28

Jackson, Michael, digital resurrection of, 12, 88; earnings from, 96; parallels to slavery, 88, 99; as spectacle for white gaze, 94–95
Jimerson, Randall C., 99
Johns Hopkins Hospital: profit and prestige from HeLa cell line, 69, 70; and treatment of Lacks's cancer, 10, 64–65; willingness to take Black patients, 64. *See also* Gey, George Otto
Johnson, Jessica Marie, 32
Johnson, Wanda, 150–51
Jones, Howard W., Jr., 64–65
Jones, James Thomas III, 86
Juice (1992 film), 86

Kaine, Tim, 42, 168n6
Killing the Black Body (Roberts), 162n5
Kim, Linda, 45, 168n7
Knight, Marion "Suge," 84
Kral Collection, Vienna, 61
Kuyda, Eugenia, 113, 114, 123

Lacks, Henrietta: and Black women's inability to craft their own narratives, 77; and bodies as data, 77–78; conflation of identity with HeLa cell line, 71; dehumanizing of, in use of HeLa cells,

Lacks, Henrietta *(continued)* 70; erasure, stigmatization, and resurrection of, 79; genome published online without permission, 11, 75–76; and informed consent laws, 74–75; life, illness, and death of, 64–65; and misogynoir, 73–74, 81; paradoxical life-in-death of, 11, 60, 71, 78; publication of medical records without consent, 74–75; and questions about nature of life and meaning of death, 79; and reduction of Black bodies to data, 11; resurrection through data stored in HeLa cells, 11, 78, 82; stigmatization of, 64, 72–74; story of, as irrationality in the flesh, 79; turn of public attention to, 60, 68. *See also* HeLa cell line

Lacks family: anger at secret use of HeLa cells, 70; discovery of HeLa cell line uses, 68–69, 70; efforts to gain public recognition for Lacks, 81, 82; lack of compensation for HeLa cell line, 67–69; lawsuits to recover profits from HeLa cell line, 81–82

Lacks-Whye, Jeri, 82

Landecker, Hannah, 60, 69, 72

Lanier, Tamara, 30–31

Liljenquist Family Collection of Civil War Photographs (Library of Congress), 17, 20

Lorenzi, Lucia, 36–37

Lott, Eric, 107

Luka, 113, 114, 116

lynching: Black "brute" construct as justification for, 76–77; and body parts as souvenirs, 43, 100–101; Dunham's *Southland Ballet* on, 133–34; as means of social control, 48; scholarship on, 168n10. *See also* Washington, Jesse

lynching photographs: AI-animation of, 122–23; images of Jesse Washington lynching, 44–45; and legitimization of violence against Black bodies, 47–48; NAACP publication of Washington lynching photographs, 45–47; as postcards and collectors' items, 45, 47; scholarship on, 168n7; technologies allowing dissemination of, 47–48

Lynching Photographs (Apel and Smith), 47

Martin, Trayvon: criminalization of digital body of, 49, 50, 51–52; digital afterlife of, 110; dual response to death of, 50; and legal right to fear Blackness, 49–50; protests against death of, 49; and right to be forgotten, 111; shooting by white man, 48; shooting of, and launch of Black Lives Matter, 50

Martin's body, images circulated online, 48–49; as means of power and control, 50; as profitable for internet companies, 51–53; as reinscribing of hate, 51; and role of technology, 50–51; similarity to circulated lynching images, 50–51

Mazurenko, Roman, 113

McKittrick, Katherine, 70, 77, 78–79

medical ethics, and informed consent laws, 74–75

memorialization of dead, vs. right to be forgotten, 110

memory: modern, and technological dependence, 129–30; Western, institutionalization in documents, 137. *See also* right to be remembered

Mercer, J. W., 17

methodology of this book, 6–7

Microbiological Associates, 69–70

Microsoft, and digital immortality practices, 116

Minnesota v. Derek Chauvin (2020), 41

misogynoir: digital clones and, 115; Henrietta Lacks and, 73–74, 81

Mobley, Mamie Till, 4

Monroe, Marilyn, digital resurrection of, 96

Mori, Masahiro, 89

Morrison, Toni, 73

mourning, digital immortality practices and, 112

mourning and deathcare practices, Black, 151–54; and closeness of dead, 152–53; roots in African practice, 151–52; roots in slave beliefs about homegoing, 152; under slavery, 153, 183n13; as unique to African diaspora populations, 151. *See also* homegoing rituals in Black communities

Muhammad, Khalil Gibran, 49

Mull, Amanda, 53–54

museum descriptive practices, racial and other stereotypes in, 62

musical necrophilia, digital resurrection of performers as, 97

music festivals: and Black spectacle, 92; mainly white audiences at, 92. *See also* HoloPac performance at Coachella Festival

MyHeritage website, and AI-generated animations of photographs, 121–23

Nash, Jennifer C., 55, 89

Nasreddin, Semhal, 105–6

National Association for the Advancement of Colored People (NAACP) response to lynching of Jesse Washington, 43, 45–47

New Republic, 46

Noble, Safiya, 49, 51–52

Nora, Pierre, 129–30

North Carolina Runaway Slave Advertisements Database, 31–32, 35

Northup, Solomon, 94

Oakes, James, 93

Odumosu, Temi, 6, 28–29

"one drop" rule: as pseudoscience, 172n22; and stigmatization of HeLa cell line, 72–73

online data: and Black memory work, 154–55; co-opting by whiteness for anti-Black purposes, 155; current treatment as separate from person referenced by data, 110–11, 114; individual's right to control, 109. *See also entries under* digital

online images of dead Black people: "Art of Collective Care and Responsibility" on, 150–51; and Black Body imaginary, perpetuation of, 55–56; intervention needed to remove, 56; as means of social control, 55; permanence of, 54–56; profits made from, 52–53; as reinscribing of hate, 51; and separation of Black Body imaginary from lived experience, 55–56; as traumatic for Black people, 56, 150

"Opening Archives" (Christen), 143

Pasquale, Frank, 123

Pepper, John Henry, 87

Pepper's Ghost technology, 87–88, 89–91

Perry, Katy, 92

Philip, M. Nourbese, 70

photographs: AI animations of, 121–22; of dead celebrities, California law prohibiting, 98; early types of, 163n1. *See also* lynching photographs; online images of dead Black people

photographs of enslaved people: and camera's dehumanizing gaze, 19–20; as mostly taken by slaveholders, 22; as taken without consent or compensation, 22. *See also* portraits of Renty and Delia Taylor; proslavery photographs of Black Bodies; "Scourged Back" photograph

polio vaccine: HeLa cells and, 68; initial restriction to whites only, 171n12

portraits of Renty and Delia Taylor: described, 21–22; digitized version of, and distancing of viewer from lived experience, 29; Harvard's exploitation of, as parallel to slavery, 22, 23, 30–31; issues of archival classification raised by, 26; ownership of images as issue, 30–31; as white supremacist propaganda, 22

Principles of Biomedical Ethics (Beauchamp and Childress), 74

principlism, 74

prison industrial complex in America, as transparent extension of chattel slavery, 98–99

privacy. *See* right to privacy

proslavery photographs of Black Bodies, 21. *See also* portraits of Renty and Delia Taylor

records: definitions of, 24–25; process of creating cultural meaning in, 25

records of deceased Black people: and changing of past lives through reinterpretation, 6; maintenance by white

records of deceased Black people (*continued*)
  people, 5. *See also* Black digital afterlives; Black memory work; digitized archives of Atlantic slavery; photographs of enslaved people; right to be forgotten
Reddit's support of racism, 54
Replika digital clones, 113, 114–16; coercive extraction of data by, 123; monetizing of data collected by, 123–24
resurrection, in mythology and religion, 79–80. *See also* cellular resurrection; digital resurrection
Reynolds, Simon, 97
Rice, Samaria, 150–51
right of erasure, EU law on, 109
rights: definitions of, 163n8; as multivalent concept, 163n8, 176n7
right to be forgotten: Black people and, 124; as data protection right, 109; digital afterlife and, 110; digital records of deceased Black people and, 6; EU law and, 109; George Floyd and, 110; as linked to whiteness, 111; vs. memorialization of dead, 110; vs. right to be remembered, in Black memory work, 153, 157; vs. right to privacy, 176n9
right to be remembered: honoring of, in Black memory work, 151; vs. right to be forgotten, in Black memory work, 153, 157
right to privacy: denial to non-white subjects in digitized archives of slavery, 30; digital immortality practices and, 108; DNA and, 75–76; vs. right to be forgotten, 176n9
Roberts, Dorothy, 162n5
Robinson, Cedric, 27, 130–31, 132
Rose, Albirda, 134–35, 137
Rosenstein, Jenna, 106
rotoscoping, in digital resurrection, 90

Salk, Jonas, 68
Scholarly Publishing and Academic Resources Coalition (SPARC), 142
"Scourged Back" photograph, 17–21; circumstances of photograph, 19; digitized, and distancing of viewer from lived experience of Gordon, 29; issues of archival classification raised by, 26; in Liljenquist Collection, note on verso of, 17, 20; as objectified Black Body, 20–21; photography's dehumanizing gaze and, 19–20; public access to digital version of, 28; sold by Skinner Auctioneers, note on verso of, 18, 20; use in Union anti-slavery propaganda, 19, 20–21; white gaze determining interpretation of, 20; whites' dehumanizing descriptions of, 20. *See also* Gordon [aka Peter] (subject of "Scourged Back" photograph)
Selection from the Katherine Dunham Collection (Library of Congress), 140
Shakur, Afeni, 85, 91, 173n1
Shakur, Tupac: as embodiment of Black-male myth, 86; family and early life, 84–85; in *Juice* (1992 film), 86; mother's involvement with Black Panthers, 85; murder of, 84; music career, 85–86; origin of name, 173n1. *See also* HoloPac (Tupac Shakur hologram)
Sharpe, Christina, 6, 148, 150–51
Shoard, Catherine, 97
Simpson, Audra, 125
Skloot, Rebecca, 10, 60, 172n32
slave auctions: as common and lucrative, 93; parallels to HoloPac performance at Coachella Festival, 93–95; as spectacle for white gaze, 93, 94; theatricality of, 93, 94
slave patrols: as origin of modern-day law enforcement, 76, 121; protection of white women from Black "brutes" as purpose of, 76–77
slavery: Black mourning and deathcare practices under, 153; as capitalist enterprise, 22, 23; digitized records of, and Black memory work, 154; enduring legacy in commodification of Black bodies, 23; justifications for, 24; prison industrial complex in America as transparent extension of, 98–99; as racialized enterprise, 22; womb laws, HeLa cell line and, 67. *See also* digitized archives of Atlantic slavery
slavery, afterlife of: and challenges of

Black memory work, 147–48; feeding of, by archives of Atlantic slavery, 9–10, 24; ongoing imperiling and devaluing of Black Lives by, 9, 24, 36–37
slave trade: and Act Prohibiting Importation of Slaves of 1807, 92; history of, 22–23; increased demand for slaves in Industrial Revolution, 92
Smith, Shawn Michelle, 47
Smith, Zadie, 112
social justice: digitization of archives and, 33; on internet, demand for, in authentically Black way, 124–26; and radical empathy in archival work, 117
social media: and Black memory work, 154–55; Black people's lack of awareness about uses of data on, 158; digital immortality practices on, 111–12; and Documenting the Now project, 157–58; images of dead Black men on, as reinscribing of hate, 51; individuals' inability to know about or control data about them, 123; and lack of distinction between living and dead persons, 110; profits made from images of dead Black men, 52–53; sovereignty of social media companies, 123
Social Security Death Index, 119
Society of American Archivists, 25, 137
Society of American Bacteriologists, 61
The Society of the Spectacle (Debord), 95
sousveillance: as Black memory work, 156; dangers of, 156–57; definition of, 156; in Ferguson, after death of Michael Brown, 155, 156; police harassment of *sousveillance* efforts, 156, 183–84n19
Southland Ballet (Dunham), 133–34, 140
SPARC. *See* Scholarly Publishing and Academic Resources Coalition
spectacle for white gaze: archives of slave records as, 36; death of George Floyd and, 40; digital resurrection of Black performers as, 88, 92, 94–95, 98–100, 101; internet and, 51; and narrative of racial progress, 55, 95; slave auctions as, 93, 94; and subjugation of Black people, 55, 56. *See also* lynching

Stewart, Kristen, 92

Taylor, Breonna, 130–31, 150
Taylor, Renty and Delia. *See* portraits of Renty and Delia Taylor
Thermo Fisher Scientific, Inc., 81–82
Thomas, Clarence, 73
Till, Emmett: online information about, 52, 110; open casket funeral of, 4; and right to be forgotten, 111
tissue cultures, Geys' research on, 66
transcendent state in African diasporic spiritual traditions: availability of ancestral knowledge in, 132; bodily rhythm as door to, 132
Tuskegee Syphilis Experiment, 74
Twelve Years a Slave (Northup), 94
23andMe, 120–21
Twitter: and Documenting the Now project, 157–58; as functional sovereignty, 123; profits made form Trayvon Martin's death, 52; support of racism, 54
Tyson-Seldon heavyweight fight (1996), 83–84

uncanny valley, digital resurrection images and, 89, 90, 91
Ursache, Marius, 117

valorization of Black suffering: Michael Brown's death and, 3; and monetization of white savior complex, 3, 162–63n3
Vansina, Jan, 23
violence against Black people: in archive's descriptions of records, 26; Black care as antidote to, 159; companies' response to, as profit-driven, 53–54; ongoing state-sanctioned violence, 132. *See also* lynching; online images of dead Black people
visual media documenting anti-Black violence: lynching photographs as origin of, 42; as means of white social control, 42; modern forms of, 48. *See also* lynching photographs; online images of dead Black people
visual records of Black body, questions raised by, 8–9

vodou, and escape from limitations of body, 132

Washington, Jesse: and banality of white evil in America, 46; conviction for rape and murder, 42–43; crowd of spectators at lynching of, 43, 44, 46; lynching of, 43; NAACP publication of lynching photographs, 45–47; photographs of lynching, as collectors' items, 44–45
Wells, Ida B., 168n10
Wernimont, Jacqueline, 32
Whalley, Tom, 86
"Whipped Peter." *See* "Scourged Back" photograph
white body, as site of reverence and desire, 101
white gaze: Black archival items to be withheld from, 145; interpretation of historical record through, 20–21. *See also* spectacle for white gaze
white savior complex, monetization of, 3, 162–63n3

white supremacist view of Black lives: as justification for slavery, 24; as sources of entertainment and profit, 14
white supremacy: Black memory work's effort to end patterns of abuse in, 141; desire to control what is imaginable by those it oppresses, 36; digital immortality practices and, 12–13, 89, 99–100, 108, 111; Dunham's efforts to end patterns of abuses in, 140–41; shaping of digital immortality practices, 108, 111
"Who Do You Talk To, When a Body's in Trouble?" (McKittrick), 70, 77
Wilson, Darren, 3, 156
Winn, Sam, 142

Yoruba tradition, death practices in, 151–52
Young, Harvey, 3, 6, 89, 98

Zimmerman, George, 48–50, 169n21